ALSO BY JEANNETTE FERRARY
AND LOUISE FISZER

Season to Taste:
Herbs and Spices in American Cooking

The California-American Cookbook:
Innovations on American Regional Dishes

Sweet Onions and Sour Cherries

A Cookbook for Market Day

JEANNETTE FERRARY
and
LOUISE FISZER

SIMON & SCHUSTER
New York   London   Toronto   Sydney   Tokyo   Singapore

SIMON & SCHUSTER
Simon & Schuster Building
Rockefeller Center
1230 Avenue of the Americas
New York, New York 10020

Designed by Deirdre C. Amthor

Illustrations by Lauren Jarrett
Manufactured in the United States of America

10   9   8   7   6   5   4   3   2   1

Library of Congress Cataloging in Publication Data
Ferrary, Jeannette, 1941–
   Sweet onions and sour cherries: a cookbook for market
day/Jeannette Ferrary, Louise Fiszer.
      p.   cm.
   Includes bibliographical references and index.
   1. Cookery (Vegetables)   2. Cookery (Fruit)   I. Fiszer,
Louise.   II. Title.
TX801.F47   1992
641.6′5—dc20   92-424
                                                      CIP
                ISBN 0-671-70084-7

Acknowledgments

We are once again grateful to Peter and Max for being the way you have to be when your mate serves you, at one sitting, six different kinds of squash and asks you how you like them, on a scale of one to six. For eating with a sense of humor, for not flinching, for listening, for laughing on the outside, for the third book in a row, thanks, guys.

We also thank our editors, Carole Lalli, Kerri Conan, and Toula Polygalaktos, who have supported this project from beginning to end with their concern. This is our third book with Simon & Schuster and, although some of the people have come and gone over the years, we are grateful to the publisher for the extra care and subtle serendipities that accrue only from such long-term relationships.

We also thank the friends who helped and encouraged us, especially Elizabeth Schneider, whose authoritative *Uncommon Fruits and Vegetables* is a classic in its field. Her counsel was invaluable in helping us give shape to our investigations.

Of course we feel tremendous appreciation and admiration for the farmers and growers who are providing us all with such exciting varieties of fresh fruits and vegetables. In addition, the people who work to bring the benefits of farmers' markets into our communities and neighborhoods deserve a special measure of commendation for their often thankless offstage efforts.

As for our agent and friend, Fred Hill, who makes all the phone calls, reads all the fine print, and even makes the recipes, we are ever grateful.

Contents

Introduction

A certain camaraderie has developed around produce counters these days as people point quizzically to various mysterious-looking roots and leaves. From the farmers' market to the corner grocery store, perfect strangers are likely to strike up impromptu conversations about produce: "What *is* that, do you think?" "How do you cook it, or do you even cook it at all?" "Can this possibly taste any good?" "Are there recipes for these things?"

Since we are so involved in teaching and writing about food, we found, to our embarrassment, that people expected us to have instant answers to these puzzlements. And so we started asking our own questions, partly to save ourselves any further humiliation, but also because we were fascinated by the almost infinite variety of produce we were seeing. We gathered information here, there, and wherever we could find it; but what we learned, essentially, was that available, practical data about today's fresh produce was scattered and incomplete. What's more, the popularity of local farmers' markets has meant that small producers can grow and sell varieties of fruits and vegetables that are not commercially feasible. We might find one grower who could tell us everything about his own baby Chioggia beets (the ones with the pink and white rings) but had nothing to say about his neighbor's zebra-stripe tomatoes. It was a rare produce department that could explain the differences among Vidalia onions, Walla Wallas, and regular old onions. Or among O'Henry peaches, white Babcocks, and yellow clings; or tell us if Crane melons were any different from Israeli Ogens or Persians. And as for salad, although green ingredients proliferate as never before, few people could tell us which leaves and lettuces would be taste-provoking panoplies of flavor and which would be bitter disasters. Cookbooks were even more frustrating, yielding neither specific information, serving suggestions, nor recipes for these newcomers.

We also went exploring. We would walk a mile for a purple asparagus or drive hours into the wine country for an otherwise unavailable melon. From our long and pleasant hours spent with growers, seed people, chefs, and home cooks, we began to appreciate the peculiarities of each type and variety of produce we investigated; we catalogued information and experts' recommendations. And through it all, we tasted everything—raw, cooked, every which way. (We had to, it was our job.) With such abundance, we concentrated on using fruits and vegetables as the bases of meals, with meats, fish, poultry, and cheeses serving as condiments and accents. We did a lot of grilling; devised sauces, dressings, and salsas of mixed-vegetable/herb purees; and created entire meals using uncooked fresh produce. We kept things simple and honest, making use of fresh herbs and aromatics to enhance and accentuate flavors. The richness of the resulting recipes comes from within, from the intrinsic flavors of the ingredients. These ingredient-based fruit and vegetable dishes, which include all courses, from appetizers through desserts, are part of today's health-conscious lifestyle.

The focus of this book is not on the exotic and rare but on the extraordinary varieties of the ordinary: potatoes that might be blue or red as well as white, corn that is silver-white, tiny tomatoes shaped like teardrops. Our purpose is not to overwhelm the reader with encylopedic quantities of minute distinctions, nor to list every variation of every fruit and vegetable likely (or unlikely) to show up in the supermarket. The book simply provides the home cook with confidence and information for selecting, storing, and cooking some of these intriguing unknowns. Our hope is to encourage exploration and experimentation. And when you have shopped with too much exuberance—when the cherries were too beautiful and you couldn't resist the gloriously multicolored peppers—take a peek in these pages. This book is meant for just those moments of enthusiasm.

WHO'S WHO IN THE MARKETPLACE

A funny thing happens when you start thinking too much about broccoli. You start to realize something beyond the botanical and agricultural and gastronomical. Suddenly, you understand not just *what* broccoli is but *who* broccoli is. It can be frightening.

You can see broccoli as a bushy-headed, green-armed rascal, an underappreciated overachiever—you know the type—with so much going for it that it puts people off. Before you know it, you recognize personality types all over the produce department: the Shameless Flirt (persimmon); the Sourpuss (cranberry); the Independent Spirit (pear). You walk through a farmers' market or past a produce stand and, instead of an anonymous collection of fruits and vegetables, you're surrounded by a cast of characters.

The whole idea sounds crazy. Anybody would think so.

But you soon discover that, whether they admit it or not, most people have strong visceral feelings about food in general, and about fruits and vegetables in particular.

Mention okra and watch your listener's face.

Mention parsnips. Rhubarb.

Where do they come from, these reactions, these winces and smiles and licked lips?

They come from the close kinship between food and feelings; from passions born some place we believe in but can't remember.

Broccoli, strawberries, mangoes: they are experience, relationships, intuition, even prejudice. Serve some strawberries and see what happens. They don't sit idly on the plate. They immediately begin interacting with everyone at the table. With your brother, for example, visiting from the coast (any coast), who tidies his napkin as these strawberries become, in his mind, the shortcakes at your aunt's, the one who did things "proper," with full manners. The same strawberries, for your neighbor who makes everything into a project, are jam, cauldrons of it to be brewed up for gifts the following day, which is why when you serve her, she looks at you generously, as if she has just decided what she's giving you for your birthday.

For your part, these flats of strawberries, bought this morning direct from the farmer who grew them, are the Earth Mother herself. You wouldn't dream of transforming her life and ripeness into jam or gussying them up into shortcakes. You and your strawberries understand each other. That's how it is with vegetables and fruits, broccoli to strawberries, sweet onions to sour cherries. As they appear in this book, some of them may have different personalities from the ones you know. But that's only natural, when you think about it.

How to Use This Book

The book consists of two parts—Vegetables and Fruits; chapters are arranged alphabetically within each part. Each chapter begins with a general profile of the vegetable or fruit, some fables and facts about it, and information about some of the more interesting varieties and how they are prepared and eaten in different parts of the world. The Consumer and Cooking Guide provides an at-a-glance reference to selection, availability, storage, flavor enhancers, nutritional values, and any special handling or cooking notes, including suggested cooking times according to the Basic Cooking Method described below. When a recipe calls for a specific variety of a given vegetable or fruit, this is noted in the list of ingredients. Most, however, do not. Our goal was to provide workable, versatile recipes that would yield delicious results regardless of which varieties or types were available to you in your area. In the chapter "Categorically Cooking," recipes are listed under four easy-to-consult headings of most interest to today's health-conscious, time-crunched home cook: Quick Fixes—dishes that can be prepared in about thirty minutes; Crowd Pleasers—meals suitable for entertaining a crowd; Low-Lows—dishes low in fat and cholesterol; and Great on the Grill. The "Basic Recipes" and "Methods" chapters explain terms and techniques mentioned throughout the book.

BASIC COOKING METHODS

Unless otherwise indicated, cook vegetables, uncovered, in boiling water. To minimize nutrient loss, use only enough water to cover the vegetables. To steam vegetables (and retain nutrients), place them in a steamer, over boiling water, and cover the vessel. Recommended cooking times, included in the individual Consumer and Cooking Guides, are for sliced or diced vegetables. Either method will yield tender-crisp results. *Blanching* means briefly boiling vegetables and fruits (for 1 to 2 minutes) to loosen their skins (e. g., tomatoes, peaches) or to prepare them for further cooking. Directions for all other cooking methods—such as sautéing, braising, baking, or grilling—are included in the recipes themselves.

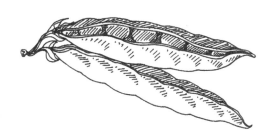

VEGETABLES

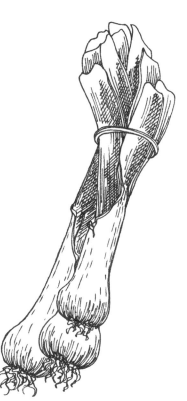

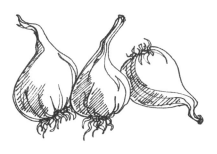

ARTICHOKES

U NTIL RECENTLY, artichokes were merely funny-looking green things that were hard to eat. Thanks to the introduction of some new varieties, however, some artichokes are now funny-looking purple things that are hard to eat. This achievement generated more enthusiasm than it would seem to warrant. But people liked the novelty of the apple-shaped, purple plant, which was touted to have more leaves, fewer thorns, and a bigger heart than the traditional green species. Some artichoke connoisseurs claim to detect a distinctive almond taste, but perhaps the best news is that this lavender newcomer behaves and tastes exactly like its loden-green cousin.

In Italy, they also have a purple artichoke. That artichoke, however, is traditionally sliced in thin slivers, piled on a plate, splashed with olive oil, and eaten as is, no cooking required. It is truly an artichoke of a different color.

Completing the spectrum is the white artichoke from France, grown by the blanching method. The growing plant is not exposed to light and thus develops little color and a less assertive taste. France also specializes in the spindle-shaped *Provençal*, a lavender artichoke variety, and the prized *verts de Florence*, originally of Italian origin—both totally edible raw.

But in American markets, the artichoke of choice is the old reliable globe, complete with thorns and the usual dullish-green leaves. The worst-looking ones might be the best, in fact; artichokes that have been through a frost, which some claim improves the flavor, often have rusty or bronze-tinged leaves. With their individual thorns, the leaves constitute a sort of fibrous suit of armor surrounding the choke—yet another impediment to the real goal, the heart. Delayed gratification is not the only reward for the pleasurable task of eating through all these barriers. Artichokes also provide that rare opportunity to play with one's food in a socially acceptable manner and the even rarer chance to make a big mess. As writer Richard Armour says, "The artichoke is the only vegetable . . . of which there is more after it has been eaten."

The first people to see the flowering plant with its fine spray of thin purple needles must have been struck by its beauty, especially in contrast to the dry, pallid surroundings in which it grows. We can only imagine how they figured out what to do with this Mediterranean giant thistle to make it edible or how they knew instinctively to dip the leaves in mayonnaise. People such as the first-century Roman encyclopedist Pliny were mystified by the artichoke's popularity. In an uncharitable burst of categorization, he called them "monstrous productions of the earth" and pointed out that "four-footed beasts instinctively refuse to touch them." There is always the possibility, given the inherent confusion in such matters, that Pliny was actually referring to the cardoon, a close cousin. Nevertheless, by the second century, artichokes were the costliest garden vegetable in the Roman marketplace.

In the mid-1500s, Catherine de Médicis selected the artichoke as one of the items in the seemingly bottomless Italian larder she transported into French gastronomy, via the court of Henry II. In fact, a hint of scandal surrounded her strong devotion to artichokes: rumor has it she was practically addicted to artichoke-heart fritters because of their presumed aphrodisiac properties. For whatever reason, the vegetable's popularity spread through France, Italy, and Spain, but when it landed in the New World, probably with that same unexpurgated reputation, it was generally rejected. According to some eighteenth-century records, however, artichokes were eaten by wealthy

Virginia planters, and one version of *Martha Washington's Booke of Cookery* contains a recipe "To Make Hartichoak Pie."

These days, artichoke recipes abound. They include everything from creamy satin mousses and artichoke bread to an Alfredo-type sauce for fettuccine. The French have endless ideas on the subject, including a recipe for raw artichokes with a pinch of salt, called *artichauts à la croque-au-sel*. Braised with mushrooms and ham, they are called *à la barigoule;* with peas and lettuce, they become *à la Clamart;* thick-sliced and fried they're called *Baron-Brisse*. There are even recipes for the stalk alone (called *moelle d'artichaut; moelle* means "marrow"), which can be curried or served *en fritot* (fried in batter).

Italian dishes have slightly more intriguing names, such as *carciofi a l'inferno* —sautéed, filled with garlic, bread crumbs, and capers; and *carciofi alla giudia* ("Jewish-style," so called because medieval ghetto Jews made them in this fashion)—whole young artichokes deep-fried until they turn black and the leaves open, giving them the appearance of beautiful black flowers. The latter remain a specialty of the restaurants located in Rome's former ghetto section.

California continues to be virtually the only artichoke producer in the United States. Most of the crop still comes from Castroville, whose main street is draped with a banner that reads: WELCOME TO CASTROVILLE, THE ARTICHOKE CAPITAL OF THE WORLD.

A few years ago, San Francisco columnist and local institution Herb Caen wrote lovingly about artichokes and how luscious he finds them in almost every preparation. His one exception was a liqueur made from the plant— which, whatever its taste, must certainly be the fastest way to an artichoke's heart.

Market Selection: The globe-type artichoke is the most commonly found variety, in varying shades of green and purple. The small ones (about 1½ inches in diameter), sometimes called *artichoke hearts,* are the young vegetable. They need much less trimming as almost the entire artichoke is edible. Select tight, compact heads. Dark or bronze-tipped leaves do not affect flavor.

Availability: Year-round; peak—March to May

Storage: Refrigerate in a plastic bag for up to 1 week.

Flavor Enhancers: Dill, mustard, citrus-flavored sauces.

Equivalents: 1 artichoke (or 4 baby artichokes) = 1 serving

Nutritional Value: Good source of potassium and vitamins A and C

       1 medium = 35 calories

Cooking and Handling Notes:

WHOLE: With a sharp stainless-steel knife, cut off the stem. Remove and discard the coarse outer leaves. Cut off the top quarter of the artichoke. Snip off the thorny tips of the remaining leaves with kitchen scissors. Cook immediately in boiling acidulated water. Artichokes are done when the leaves can be gently pulled off.

HEARTS: Remove and discard the outer leaves until a central core of pale green leaves is reached. Cut off the stem and thorny tip of the artichoke heart. Cut in half lengthwise and remove fuzzy center (choke). Proceed with the recipe directions.

BOTTOMS: Cut off the stem and the top third of the artichoke. Using a paring knife, cut away the leaves at the base of the stem. Sever the leaves from the base of the artichoke, leaving a disk-shaped bottom. Clean any remaining fuzzy choke from the bottom. Rub the bottom with lemon juice and proceed with the recipe.

Basic Cooking Methods: Cook, covered, in a large amount of acidulated, salted boiling water for about 25 minutes, or until a leaf pulls out easily (see page 347).

    Steam for 30 minutes.

Artichokes with Honey-Mustard Dipping Sauce

SAUCE

¾ cup plain yogurt (low-fat
  or nonfat)
½ teaspoon fresh lemon juice
¼ cup hot-sweet mustard
2 tablespoons chopped fresh
  chives

6 cooked whole artichokes at
  room temperature or
  chilled

MAKES 1 CUP

Combine the sauce ingredients until smooth. (The sauce may be prepared ahead of time and stored in the refrigerator, tightly covered, until ready to use.) Serve as a dip alongside the artichokes.

Artichoke Soup with Lemon and Tarragon

4 cups chicken broth or stock
  (page 343)
1½ pounds fresh artichoke
  hearts, trimmed and
  halved, or two 12-ounce
  packages frozen artichokes,
  thawed
1 bunch green onions,
  chopped
1 medium baking potato,
  peeled and diced
¼ cup fresh lemon juice
1 tablespoon fresh tarragon
  Salt and pepper

SERVES 4

In a medium saucepan, bring the broth to a boil. Add the artichoke hearts, onion, and potato and cook, covered, for 20 minutes.

In a food processor or blender, puree the mixture with a little of the cooking liquid until smooth. Return to the pot to heat. Stir in the lemon juice and tarragon. Season with salt and pepper and serve.

Braised Artichoke Bottoms with Mustard and Dill

2 tablespoons butter or oil
1 medium shallot, chopped
3 tablespoons dry white
  wine
6 large artichoke bottoms,
  trimmed and cut into
  sixths
  About 1½ cups chicken
  stock (page 343)
  Salt and pepper
¾ cup heavy cream
1 tablespoon Dijon mustard
2 tablespoons chopped fresh
  dill

SERVES 4 AS A SIDE DISH
OR APPETIZER

THIS DISH may be served alone or used as a sauce over rice or pasta.

In a medium skillet, heat the butter. Add the shallot and cook until soft. Add the wine, stirring until bubbly, and then add the artichokes. Add enough stock to half cover the artichokes and bring to a boil. Cover, reduce the heat, and simmer for about 30 minutes.

Remove the artichokes with a slotted spoon and keep them warm. Boil the liquid remaining in the pan until only about 3 tablespoons remain. Stir in the cream and bring to a boil for a few minutes. Stir in the mustard and dill until smooth; return the artichokes to the skillet. Heat gently, basting the artichokes with the sauce.

Sautéed Chicken with Artichoke Hearts and Black Olives

6 skinless, boneless chicken-
  breast halves
  Salt and pepper
4 tablespoons oil or butter
1 small onion, chopped
1½ pounds fresh artichoke
  hearts, trimmed and
  quartered, or two 12-
  ounce packages frozen
  artichoke hearts, thawed
¾ cup dry white wine
¼ cup heavy cream
½ cup Greek olives, pitted
  and coarsely chopped
1 tablespoon fresh lemon
  juice
½ cup chopped fresh parsley

SERVES 6

Pound the chicken breasts to flatten them slightly and sprinkle them with salt and pepper. In a large skillet, heat the butter. Sauté the chicken breasts for 3 minutes per side over medium-high heat. Remove the chicken from the skillet and keep it warm.

Add the onion to the skillet and cook until soft. Add the artichoke hearts and wine; bring to a boil, lower the heat, simmer, covered, for about 10 minutes, or until the artichoke hearts are tender.

Uncover and turn the heat up; reduce the liquid until it is syrupy. Stir in the cream, olives, and lemon juice, and cook for 2 minutes.

To serve, top the chicken breasts with the artichoke mixture and sprinkle with parsley.

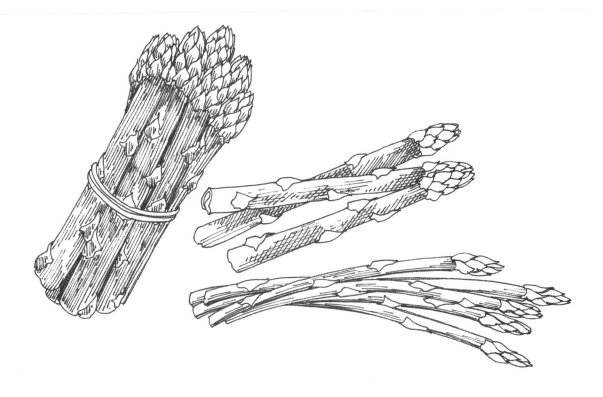

ASPARAGUS

Even people who don't believe in aphrodisiacs believe in the come-hither quality of asparagus. There's something sultry and beckoning about this shapely member of the lily family. You don't serve it any old time to just anybody who comes along. Asparagus often involves ulterior motives, whether admitted or not. Sir Richard Burton, the English adventurer, translated a book on the subject of aphrodisiacs called *The Perfumed Garden for the Soul's Delectation,* by Shaykh Nafzawi. "He who boils asparagus," Sir Richard tells us, "and then fries them in fat, and then pours upon them the yolks of eggs with pounded condiments, and eats every day of this dish, will . . . find in it a stimulant for his amorous desires."

Nonetheless, some people don't like to share their asparagus no matter what the consequences might be. Bernard de Fontenelle, the eighteenth-century French encylopedist, was once moved to despair by the arrival of a surprise dinner guest because it meant he had to give up part of his asparagus. As it turned out, de Fontenelle lived to be a few weeks short of age one hundred, an achievement he credited to his passion for asparagus *à la flamande* (accompanied by melted butter and hard-boiled eggs); he undoubtedly considered asparagus deprivation a matter of life or death.

Asparagus, derived from the Persian word for "sprout," has been cultivated since ancient times. It was a favorite of the Emperor Augustus, who reputedly was fond of saying "Quicker than you can cook asparagus" whenever he wanted some fast action. In the middle of the second century A.D., explorers in Africa reported seeing asparagus twelve feet high. And in the famous early Roman gardens of Ravenna, individual stalks are said to have reached a weight of three pounds. Louis XIV devised a way to enjoy asparagus year-round: he promised his gardener, Quintinie, a title and some parcels of land for coming up with perennial asparagus.

Spring brings asparagus lovers to Malines, Belgium, for the prized plump white variety; to Switzerland and Germany for giant white *Spargel;* to Navarre, Spain, for tender, almost translucent stalks; to Ravenna for some lavender-tipped whites, and to Tuscany for the luscious greens. The French have an asparagus society, an asparagus museum (at Argenteuil), and a national passion for debating the relative merits of different varieties. Probably very few fellow countrymen agree with the opinion of French chef Jean Troisgros, that American asparagus is the best in the world.

Asparagus festivals are held everywhere, from Limburg, Holland, to Stockton, California. Calling itself the Asparagus Capital of the World, Stockton hosts an annual two-day festival during the last weekend in April. California produces more than 70 percent of this country's 200 million pounds of fresh asparagus per annum, most of it in the San Joaquin/Sacramento delta area. Asparagus is also produced in Michigan and in the Mid-Atlantic and New England states, where locals claim that their thin, delicate shoots are most delicious when eaten raw.

Thin or thick, white, green, or lavender, warm, cold, or hot, asparagus generates much discussion. When it comes to cooking it, the world's experts vigorously disagree: James Beard advised: "Place asparagus in a skillet. Pour in enough cold water to cover and add salt. Bring to a boil." André Simon countered: "Never put asparagus in cold water and bring the water to the boil." Recipes range from the advice of Richard Olney (*Simple French Food),* who insists that asparagus needs no saucing whatever, to an early Fanny

Farmer asparagus salad, sauced with catsup; and from the intriguingly named Asparagus in Ambush (the spears are nestled in a roll under sauce) to Escoffier's hard-to-believe Asparagus Ice Cream. The Spanish expression "Go fry asparagus" is not a recipe at all but the Iberian equivalent of "Go fly a kite."

Some people also like to worry about what to drink with asparagus, especially since the vegetable's sulphur content causes wine to taste sweet. Wine experts usually recommend dry whites, anything from a California Gewürztraminer to a medium-dry French Colombard.

In the face of all these countervailing recommendations, we dare to add our own bit of asparagus advice: whenever possible, eat it with your fingers.

CONSUMER AND COOKING GUIDE: Asparagus

Market Selection: Green asparagus is the most common variety, with the costly imported white and the newly developed red varieties making occasional appearances on the produce scene. All types should have firm stalks with tightly closed tips. Stalk thickness is a matter of personal preference.
Availability: March through June, although imported asparagus may be found year-round.
Storage: Refrigerate, upright, in a container of water. If space is a problem, wrap the bottom of the stalks ends in a damp towel and seal in a plastic bag in the refrigerator. Do not store for more than 4 days.
Flavor Enhancers: Flavored butters, citrus, grated cheese
Equivalents: 1 pound = about 15 stalks
      1 pound, trimmed and peeled = 3 cups
      1 serving = ½ pound
Nutritional Value: Good source of vitamins A and C
      35 calories per cup
Cooking and Handling Notes: Asparagus stalks have an outer fibrous membrane that should be removed with a vegetable peeler before cooking. Cutting off approximately 1½ inches from the bottoms of the stalks should leave a succulent remainder. "Snapping" off the bottoms can be too wasteful, in our opinion.
Basic Cooking Methods: Cook in salted boiling water for 3 to 4 minutes.
   Steam for 5 to 6 minutes.

Asparagus Spears with Two Dipping Sauces

3 pounds asparagus spears,
   peeled, cooked just until
   tender, and cooled

SWEET-AND-HOT RED-PEPPER SAUCE

3 ounces roasted red bell
   peppers (see page 348),
   drained
1 jalapeño pepper, seeded
   and deveined
1 tablespoon honey
½ cup mayonnaise
½ cup plain yogurt or sour
   cream
1 tablespoon chopped fresh
   cilantro leaves
Salt and pepper

Puree the sauce ingredients in a food processor until smooth. Season with salt and pepper.

SESAME GINGER SAUCE

2 tablespoons fresh lemon
   juice
2 tablespoons white-wine
   vinegar
1 slice fresh ginger, peeled
1 tablespoon brown sugar
1 clove garlic
1 tablespoon prepared
   mustard
2 tablespoons sesame oil
½ cup vegetable or peanut oil

Process all of the ingredients except the vegetable oil in a food processor until smooth. With the motor running, slowly pour in the vegetable oil until the mixture is thick.

   To serve: Place the asparagus in a spokelike pattern on a serving platter. Pour the sauces into bowls and place them in the center.

SERVES 8 AS AN
HORS D'OEUVRE

Warm Asparagus and Parmesan Salad

2 pounds asparagus, peeled
  and cut into 1-inch pieces
2 teaspoons fresh lemon
  juice
3 tablespoons extra-virgin
  olive oil
Freshly ground pepper
One ¼-pound piece Italian
  Parmesan
Butter lettuce leaves

SERVES 6

Bring a large pot of salted water to a boil. Add the asparagus and cook for 1½ minutes from the time the water returns to a boil. Drain the asparagus and rinse them briefly under cold water to set their color. (They will still be warm.)

Toss the asparagus with the lemon juice, olive oil, and freshly ground pepper to taste. With a vegetable peeler, shave thin slices of Parmesan on top. Mound on lettuce leaves and serve immediately.

Asparagus-Prosciutto Ragoût with Penne

3 tablespoons oil or butter
¼ pound prosciutto, diced or
  chopped
1 medium leek, white part
  only, thinly sliced
¼ cup white wine
¾ cup chicken stock
  (page 343)
2 tablespoons heavy cream
2 pounds asparagus, cut
  into 1-inch pieces, cooked
  just until tender
¼ cup chopped fresh chives
1 pound freshly cooked
  penne
2 ounces grated Gruyère
  cheese

SERVES 6 TO 8 AS A FIRST
COURSE OR 4 AS A MAIN
COURSE

In a large skillet, heat the oil. Sauté the prosciutto and leek for about 5 minutes. Add the wine and stock and boil, stirring every so often, for about 8 minutes. The sauce should be slightly syrupy and reduced at this point.

Stir in the cream and cook for another minute. Add the asparagus and chives and heat through. Toss with freshly cooked pasta and sprinkle with cheese.

Grilled Salmon with Asparagus Puree

PUREE

1½ pounds asparagus, peeled
   and cooked until very
   tender
2 tablespoons butter, at
   room temperature
¼ cup whole-milk ricotta
   cheese
¼ cup chicken stock
   (page 343)
1 tablespoon fresh lemon
   juice
1 teaspoon mild prepared
   mustard
1 tablespoon chopped fresh
   dill
   Salt and pepper

6 salmon steaks
   Salt and pepper
2 tablespoons olive oil
   Additional asparagus tips,
   blanched, for garnish
   (optional)

SERVES 6

Preheat the grill.

Combine the puree ingredients in a food processor or blender and process until very smooth.

Sprinkle the salmon with salt and pepper and brush with oil. Grill for about 4 minutes per side. Meanwhile, heat the puree gently.

To serve: Ladle some puree on each plate and place a grilled salmon steak over it. Garnish with additional asparagus tips if desired.

BEETS

ANYONE WHO HAS EVER thumbed through a children's alphabet book realizes the importance of beets. More often than not, beets are the *B* word. Nothing could be more appropriate, according to Lucius Junius Moderatus Columella, one of the world's first food writers. Columella, who discoursed elegantly, even poetically, on agricultural matters during the first century A.D., claims that the beet got its original name, *beta, because* of its resemblance to the second letter of the alphabet.

Beets continue to make luscious illustrations because of their varying shapes, from squat to ovoid to long and turnip-shaped. Today's beets also come in an array of colors: red, golden-yellow, white. One variety, the

Chioggia, has a cherry-red exterior that, when cut, reveals its true stripes, which are alternating red and white. Mixed together in a bowl, an assortment of many-colored beets makes an intriguing salad, especially since all beets taste just about the same. They must be cooked separately, however, because the red dye, *betacyanin*, leaches into the cooking water. Some say that a dash of vinegar or lemon juice added to the cooking water reduces leaching.

In Columella's time, and before, beets were more monochromatically described as either "black" or "pale," but they were still eaten everywhere from Britain to India. Perhaps it was instinct that motivated their widespread consumption, since beets are, from the bottoms of their swollen hypocotyls to the tips of their leafy greens, exceptionally high in nutrients as well as fiber. And yet, so learned an expert as John Gerard wrote in his 1597 *Herball* that the beet "eaten when it is boyled, . . . nourishes little or nothing, and is not so wholesome as Lettuce." On the other hand, he admits that it "will make many and diverse dishes, both faire and good."

Indeed, there seems no end to diversity: the roots may be roasted, boiled, or steamed, served hot or cold, pickled, and made into hot soup, cold borscht, or an unusual (and, to some, unimaginable) wine. One recipe for the latter suggests that rhubarb be used as the acid. Beet greens are prepared like any other greens and have even more nutrients than the vegetable's lower extremities. In fact, the greens were originally the only parts of the vegetable considered edible. In this country the beet has become regionally compartmentalized: Greens are most popular in the South, the roots appeal to New Englanders for use in both red flannel hash and sweet-and-sour Harvard beets (or Yale beets, depending on preferences more psychological than culinary). The Pennsylvania Dutch classic, pickled beets and red eggs, is crimson testimony to the vegetable's painterly talents. Beet dye was, in fact, used in colonial times to add a rosy aspect to icing for cakes and to the colonial favorite, pink pancakes.

Perhaps the most fascinating member of beetdom is the beet we don't eat directly at all—the white, tapered sugar beet, which is 8 percent sugar by weight. In the late eighteenth century, François Achard, a Berliner of French origin, introduced the process of producing sugar from these beets. Ultimately, this resulted in the ability to satisfy, on a worldwide basis, the basic human craving for sugar. According to *Foodbook* author James Trager, "In terms of botany, the development of the sugar beet surpasses any other achievement of human ingenuity in food creation."

Market Selection: red; golden; white; candy-stripe; baby beets. All types should be firm, with smooth skins and deep green, unwilted leaves.

Availability: Year-round; peak—June through October

Storage: Remove the tops (leaves and most of stem). Refrigerate, unwashed, in a plastic bag for up to 1 week. Greens may be used in salads or for cooking.

Flavor Enhancers: Dill, cumin, parsley, garlic

Equivalents: Five 2½-inch beets = 1 pound

　　　　1 pound = 2½ cups, cooked

Nutritional Value: Good source of potassium, and vitamins C and A

　　　　55 calories per cup

Cooking and Handling Notes: Cook trimmed, unpeeled beets in a large pot of boiling water for 45 minutes for medium to large beets, 30 minutes for baby beets. When cool enough to handle, slip the skins off.

　　Trimmed, unpeeled beets may be baked at 300 degrees in a covered pan until tender (1 hour for baby beets, 1½ hours for large beets).

Buttermilk, Beet, and Cucumber Soup

5 medium beets, cooked
    until tender
3 cups chicken stock
    (page 343)
1 cup buttermilk
1 tablespoon fresh lemon
    juice
1 cucumber, peeled, seeded,
    and diced
    Salt and pepper

SERVES 4 TO 6

When the beets are cool enough to handle, slip the skins off. Slice the beets and puree them in a food processor with the chicken stock. Stir in the buttermilk, lemon juice, and cucumber. Season with salt and pepper. Serve chilled.

Beet and Bean Salad with Garlic-Dill Vinaigrette

4 beets, cooked until tender,
    peeled and cut into ½-inch
    cubes
1 pound green beans, cooked
    until tender and cut into
    1-inch pieces
1½ cups cooked white beans
1 small red onion, diced
2 tablespoons capers, rinsed
    and drained

DRESSING

¼ cup fresh dill
2 cloves garlic
3 tablespoons red-wine
    vinegar
⅓ cup olive oil
    Salt and pepper

SERVES 4

Combine the beets, both beans, onion, and capers in a salad bowl.

To make the dressing: Place the dill, garlic, and vinegar in the bowl of a food processor; process until smooth. Add the oil slowly, until the dressing is emulsified. Season with salt and pepper and pour over beet mixture. Toss well to combine.

DRIED BEAN COOKING NOTE: Soak beans in water to cover overnight. Drain. In a large pot of boiling, unsalted water add 1 cup of dried beans, 1 small peeled onion, a bay leaf, and 1 teaspoon ground black pepper. Simmer, partially covered, about 45 minutes or until beans are tender. Drain and discard the onion and bay leaf.

Beet Green and Mushroom Gratin

2 pounds beet greens,
    washed
4 tablespoons oil
2 tablespoons butter
1 clove garlic, minced
1 pound mushrooms, sliced
    Salt and pepper
½ cup ricotta cheese
¼ cup grated Parmesan
2 eggs, beaten
½ cup dry bread crumbs

SERVES 6

Preheat the oven to 375°F.

Steam the beet greens for 2 minutes; squeeze them dry and chop finely. In a skillet, heat 2 tablespoons of the oil and the butter. Sauté the garlic and mushrooms for about 3 minutes. Add the beet greens and stir well to combine.

Remove the pan from the heat and season to taste with salt and pepper. Stir in the cheeses and eggs. Pour the mixture into a greased shallow 9-inch baking dish. Sprinkle with the bread crumbs and the remaining 2 tablespoons oil and bake for about 35 minutes, or until golden-brown.

Beet and Apple Sauté

6 medium beets, scrubbed
    and cooked until tender
3 tablespoons butter
3 shallots, minced
2 tart green apples, peeled,
    cored, and thinly sliced
1 tablespoon sugar
    Salt and pepper
⅓ cup apple-cider vinegar
½ cup toasted walnuts (see
    page 349), coarsely
    chopped

SERVES 6

When the beets are cool enough to handle, slip the skins off and slice the beets about ¼ inch thick. In a skillet, heat the butter. Add the shallot and cook for about 2 minutes. Add the apple, sugar, salt and pepper, and vinegar; simmer, uncovered, for about 10 minutes, or until the apples are tender. Add the beets and cook for another 3 minutes. Sprinkle with walnuts and serve.

Broccoli and Cauliflower

Broccoli

Horror is what broccoli lovers feel when they see their favorite vegetable, with florets green as a forest, and stems crunchy as walnuts, thrown into boiling water and left there even a moment too long. It doesn't seem fair, defenders of broccoli contend, that a vegetable which tastes so good raw should be ruined by cooking, especially since anybody can serve a delicious broccoli dish simply by doing nothing.

For some reason, however, many people feel compelled to change broccoli, as if it's not quite all there the way it comes naturally. Or they want to disguise broccoli, make us think we're eating something else. Sensitive-nosed dissenters complain of its cabbagey qualities, which, according to some, can be diminished by throwing a piece of bread into the cooking water.

Broccoli is a pleasant enough tidbit, neither bland nor particularly assertive. Like the rest of us, broccoli did not choose its relatives, which come from the cabbage family and range from the lowlife cabbage itself to the highbrow cauliflower. Broccoli, however, is neither peasant nor poet. It's sort of a good guy in the middle, with more to offer, nutritionally, than just about any other vegetable commonly consumed in this country. Broccoli is crammed with vitamins and minerals; its often-discarded leaves have more of them than its buds.

Then again, if people were attracted to what is good for them, movie theaters would sell cartons of hot buttered broccoli, and ball field gourmets would gorge on broccoli in a bun with mustard and relish.

Varieties of broccoli include those with purple, white, chartreuse, or dark green buds. Sprouting broccoli is a leafy, less compact, and pretty variation with many small white or purple florets. The white broccoli found in England is a form of winter cabbage. Broccoli rabe—actually a type of turnip —looks like clusters of leaves on a stem and has small buds and flowers. It can be prepared like broccoli, though generally it is not eaten raw. By contrast, Chinese broccoli, or *gai lon,* which sports dull green, narrow leaves and white flowers, is excellent raw with dips or in any broccoli recipe. Broccoli itself works well in any recipe for cauliflower or asparagus.

Chefs have long appreciated broccoli's many attributes. They use the bristle-brush florets as a vehicle for colorful dips and sauces. They julienne and chop the stems, scattering them like celery-green confetti into salads and vegetable dishes. Even in Roman times, chefs like Apicius flavored broccoli with strong spices, like cumin and coriander. Chinese cooks have traditionally kept it crisp, applying a quick stir-fry to tiny clustered florets and grated stalks. Sixteenth-century French chefs knew nothing of broccoli and probably cared less. But those who cooked for Catherine de Médicis, who introduced the vegetable to France upon her marriage to Henry II in 1533, soon learned to prepare it in a multitude of ways fit to please a queen. Italian chefs, who are perhaps most adept with broccoli, also prepare the vegetable in myriad ways; in one recipe, the vegetable and seasonings are smothered in red wine and cooked for a shockingly long time. Instead of emerging limp and colorless, however, it is delicious, the flavors intermingling like a congenial stew, the textures melting and rich.

Broccoli's associations with Italy include its very name, which is derived from *brocco,* meaning "branch." Because broccoli is the diminutive plural, it is grammatically correct to say things like "Broccoli are good for you." Which, of course, it are.

CONSUMER AND COOKING GUIDE: Broccoli

Market Selection: Green-budded broccoli is the most common variety, but today one can also find broccoli with purple and white heads. Broccoli rabe, actually the flower shoots of a turnip, has tiny yellow buds and a slightly acrid flavor. Chinese broccoli, *gai lon,* is leafy, with white flowers. All types should be crisp-looking, with good color and nonwoody stems.
Availability: Year-round
Storage: Refrigerate in a plastic bag for up to 5 days.
Flavor Enhancers: Garlic, oregano, thyme, cheese
Equivalents: 1 large head = 1½ pounds
      1 large head = 4 cups, cut up
Nutritional Value: Excellent source of vitamins A and C. High in calcium, potassium, and iron
      40 calories per cup
Cooking and Handling Notes: Broccoli stems are the sweetest part of the vegetable if properly prepared. With a sharp knife or vegetable peeler, peel the tough outer membrane from the stems before cooking. This not only enhances the taste and texture of broccoli but also allows it to cook more evenly. (Florets and stems will be tender at the same time.)
Basic Cooking Methods: Cook stems in boiling salted water for 4 to 6 minutes, florets 3 to 4, or until tender-crisp.

Steam for 6 to 8 minutes.

Broccoli and Tomato Soup with Garbanzos

3 tablespoons olive oil
1 large onion, chopped
2 cloves garlic, minced
¼ teaspoon crushed red-
   pepper flakes
¼ cup chopped fresh parsley
One 28-ounce can whole
   tomatoes, chopped
4 cups chicken broth
   (page 343)
1 bunch broccoli, stems
   peeled and sliced and
   florets cut into small
   pieces
One 16-ounce can
   garbanzo beans, drained
Salt and pepper

In a large saucepan, heat the oil. Cook the onion, garlic, pepper flakes, and parsley for about 6 minutes. Stir in the tomatoes and cook for 10 minutes.

Add the broth; bring to a boil, lower the heat, and simmer for 15 minutes. Add the broccoli and garbanzo beans and cook for 10 minutes. Season with salt and pepper and serve.

SERVES 6 TO 8

Warm Broccoli, Bacon, and Black Olive Salad

1 bunch broccoli, stems and
   florets cut into bite-size
   pieces and cooked just
   until tender
1 head Belgian endive, sliced
½ pound bacon, diced
2 cloves garlic, minced
3 tablespoons balsamic
   vinegar
3 tablespoons golden raisins
1 cup imported black olives,
   pitted and halved
Salt and pepper

In a large bowl, toss the broccoli with the endive. Cook the bacon in a medium skillet until crisp. Remove with a slotted spoon, leaving about ⅓ cup rendered fat in the skillet. Cook the garlic in the bacon fat until aromatic. Stir in the vinegar and raisins and simmer for about 1 minute.

Pour over the broccoli mixture and sprinkle with the reserved bacon and olives. Toss well and season with salt and pepper.

SERVES 6

Cold Broccoli with Red-Hot Peanut Sauce

1 bunch broccoli, lower
stems removed and
reserved for other use

SAUCE

1 tablespoon peanut or
vegetable oil
1 teaspoon chili paste
2 tablespoons tomato paste
2 cloves garlic, minced
½ cup chicken stock
(page 343)
½ teaspoon sugar
1 tablespoon peanut butter
¼ cup hoisin sauce
¼ cup unsalted peanuts,
ground
1 red chili pepper, seeded
and minced

SERVES 6 AS AN
HORS D'OEUVRE

Cook the broccoli just until tender; drain it under cold water. Break it into stalks; arrange the stalks around the outer edge of a serving plate. Cover and chill.

To make the sauce: In a small saucepan, heat the oil. Add the chili paste, tomato paste, and garlic. Cook until fragrant, about 30 seconds. Whisk in the chicken stock, sugar, peanut butter, and hoisin sauce. Bring to a boil; lower the heat and simmer, stirring constantly, for about 3 minutes. Add the peanuts and chili pepper. Let cool and pour into a small bowl, to be set in the center of the broccoli plate.

Broccoli, Carrots, and Prawns with Oriental Noodles

2 tablespoons vegetable or
    peanut oil
½ pound medium prawns,
    shelled
1 tablespoon minced fresh
    ginger
2 cloves garlic, minced
2 carrots, peeled and thinly
    sliced on the diagonal
½ cup chicken broth (page 343)
3 tablespoons soy sauce
1 bunch broccoli, cut into
    bite-size pieces
1 tablespoon sesame oil
3 green onions, thinly sliced
½ pound Oriental noodles
    (soft, Japanese style),
    cooked and drained
½ cup chopped fresh cilantro

SERVES 4

In a skillet or wok, heat the oil. Cook the prawns until they turn pink, about 2 minutes. Remove and keep warm.

Add the ginger and garlic to the pan and stir-fry over medium heat for 20 seconds. Add the carrots and cook, stirring occasionally, for about 4 minutes. Add the broth and soy sauce; bring to a boil and add the broccoli. Cook for 4 minutes. Stir in the sesame oil, green onion, and reserved prawns. Cook for 1 minute to heat through.

Pour over noodles and toss well to combine. Garnish with cilantro and serve.

Rabe and Rice

3 tablespoons oil
2 cloves garlic, minced
1 shallot, minced
1 small bunch broccoli rabe,
    roots discarded and stems
    and leaves coarsely
    chopped
1 cup raw rice
¼ cup white wine
2 cups chicken stock (page 343)
½ cup grated Fontina cheese
    Salt and pepper

SERVES 4

In a medium sauté pan, heat the oil. Cook the garlic and shallot for about 2 minutes; add the broccoli rabe. Cook until wilted, about 2 minutes.

Stir in the rice and cook, stirring, until translucent. Add the wine and cook until it has almost evaporated.

Add the stock; bring to a boil, cover, lower heat, and simmer for 15 minutes. Stir in the cheese and season with salt and pepper.

Rigatoni with Broccoli and Hot Sausage

3 pounds hot Italian
   sausage, cooked and sliced
2 onions, chopped
2 carrots, diced
2 cloves garlic, minced
   Two 28-ounce cans
   imported Italian tomatoes,
   drained and chopped
½ cup dry red wine
½ cup beef stock (page 344)
½ teaspoon each, dried
   oregano and thyme
½ cup chopped fresh parsley
2 pounds rigatoni, cooked
   and drained
2 bunches broccoli, cut up
   and cooked just until
   tender
2 pounds mozzarella cheese,
   diced
1 cup grated Parmesan

SERVES 12

In a large skillet, heat the sausage until some of the fat is rendered. Add the onion, carrot, and garlic and cook until soft, about 10 minutes. Stir in the tomato, wine, stock, and herbs. Bring to a boil, lower the heat, and simmer for 20 minutes.

Preheat the oven to 350°F.

In a large bowl, toss the rigatoni with the sausage mixture, broccoli, and mozzarella. Transfer to a large baking dish and sprinkle with the Parmesan. Bake for about 40 minutes or until bubbly and golden-brown.

NOTE: The ingredients can be halved to make 6 servings.

Cauliflower

A ROSE IS A ROSE and may even be a rose, but a cauliflower is a different story. The cauliflowers of Paris, for example, are quite distinct from their Provençal siblings, which, in turn, differ significantly from the giant cauliflowers of Napoli. Italy also grows purple and green varieties, determined gardeners have searched out some bronze-headed species, and eclectic botanists have developed a hybrid of cauliflower and broccoli that combines the finest qualities of both vegetables. To complicate attempts at color coding even further, purple cauliflower turns green when cooked.

Yet, when most people think of cauliflower, they think white. Piles of snow, clumps of clouds, mounds of whipped cream: that's cauliflower. And yet, this showy, bright member of the cabbage family would not exist at all if it hadn't been, in a sense, invented.

Cultivated for its flowering structures, the original cabbagelike plant eventually developed into the now-familiar solid-headed clusters of florets. To this day, cauliflower demands special attention from seed to harvest. As the plant grows, its leaves must be tied around its head, which protects the white florets—or curds—from the sun, preventing the development of chlorophyll. Judging from its continuous popularity dating back to the ancient Orient, cauliflower has been accorded this kind of special attention for quite some time.

In the twelfth century, the Arabs introduced it to Spain, and from there it went on to charm every country in Europe. In eighteenth-century France, it became the subject of a cheese-sauced, fried cauliflower dish created in honor of Louis XV's mistress, Madame du Barry. Its life-style was more predictably domestic in this country, where it was first planted in Setauket, Long Island, by a seventeenth-century Dutch family.

Cauliflower shines in all courses and cuisines: Indian curries and masalas; French gratins; Greek salads; Pennsylvania Dutch chow chows. It is used for purees, relishes, tarts, sautés, fritters, and stir-fries. Its thick stalks can be used for soups; its hide-and-seek leaves taste like the most tender of cabbage leaves.

Among the vegetable's unique properties are high iron and calcium content, making it attractive to anyone allergic to milk products. A high folic-acid content has won cauliflower the incongruous nickname of ''vegetable liver," which, though nutritionally flattering, lacks a certain sprightliness of phrase. More regal and certainly more appealing is another age-old designation, Queen of Cabbages.

CONSUMER AND COOKING GUIDE: Cauliflower

Market Selection: Until recently only snowy-white heads of cauliflower were available in this country. Commercial growers have produced a purplish-green type that is actually a cross between broccoli and cauliflower and is sometimes referred to as *choux fleur.* All vestiges of purple disappear when it is cooked. White heads should be unblemished, with no traces of yellowing, and purple heads should be bright in color. Both types should have heavy, compact heads with crisp green leaves.

Availability: Year-round

Storage: Refrigerate in plastic wrap for up to 2 weeks.

Flavor Enhancers: Curry, cumin, cayenne, chives

Equivalents: 1 medium head = 2 pounds

       1 head, cut up = 4 cups

Nutritional Value: Good source of vitamin C and potassium

       30 calories per cup

Basic Cooking Methods: Cook in boiling salted water for 6 minutes.

  Steam for 9 minutes.

Cream of Cauliflower and Green Pea Soup

3 tablespoons oil
1 small onion, chopped
1 celery rib, chopped
1 tablespoon curry powder
½ teaspoon ground cumin
½ teaspoon ground coriander
  Florets from 1 large head
  cauliflower
5 cups chicken stock
  (page 343)
1 cup heavy cream
  Salt and pepper
  One 10-ounce package
  frozen peas

In a large saucepan, heat the oil. Cook the onion and celery until wilted, about 6 minutes. Stir in the spices and cook for another minute. Add the florets and stir to coat with the onion mixture. Add the stock; bring to a boil, lower the heat, and simmer, partially covered, for 25 minutes.

Puree the mixture and return it to the pan with the cream. Season with salt and pepper and add the peas. Cook over low heat for 10 minutes.

SERVES 6

Cauliflower, Mushroom, and Red Pepper Sauté

3 tablespoons oil
1 shallot, minced
½ pound mushrooms, sliced
½ teaspoon dried tarragon
1 red bell pepper, halved,
  seeded, and thinly sliced
1 medium head cauliflower,
  trimmed and cut into
  small florets
½ cup chicken stock
  (page 343)
1 cup toasted bread crumbs
3 tablespoons grated dry
  Monterey Jack cheese
  Salt and pepper

In a large skillet, heat the oil. Sauté the shallot, mushrooms, tarragon, and red pepper for about 6 minutes, or until soft. Stir in the cauliflower and add the chicken stock. Cover and cook for 3 minutes; remove the cover and cook for another 2 minutes. Toss with the bread crumbs and cheese and cook for another minute. Season with salt and pepper.

SERVES 8

Cauliflower Salad with Sweet Sausage and Three-Mustard Dressing

Florets from 2 heads
cauliflower, cooked just
until tender
½ pound sweet Italian
sausage, cooked and sliced
1 bunch green onions, thinly
sliced

THIS RECIPE may be easily halved or doubled.

Combine the cauliflower, sausage, and green onion in a large bowl. In a small bowl, combine the dressing ingredients, stirring until smooth. Fold the dressing into the cauliflower mixture and season with salt and pepper. Refrigerate if not serving immediately.

DRESSING

1 cup mayonnaise
1 tablespoon fresh lemon
juice
2 tablespoons whole-grain
mustard
1 tablespoon hot-sweet
mustard
1 tablespoon Dijon mustard

Salt and pepper

SERVES 12

Cauliflower Puree du Barry

1 medium head cauliflower,
trimmed and chopped
1 potato, peeled and chopped
1 large carrot, peeled and
chopped
2 tablespoons butter
4 tablespoons heavy cream
2 tablespoons fresh dill
1 teaspoon fresh lemon juice
Salt and pepper

Cook the vegetables in boiling water until soft, about 10 minutes. Drain well. Puree them through a food mill or in a food processor until smooth. Add the butter, cream, dill, and lemon juice and mix until smooth. Season with salt and pepper.

SERVES 6

Cauliflower and Gorgonzola Tart

1 recipe Pâte Brisée
   (page 344)
2 cups cauliflower florets,
   coarsely chopped and
   cooked just until tender
4 ounces young Gorgonzola
   cheese, crumbled
3 eggs
½ cup cream or half-and-half
¼ cup milk
½ cup chopped fresh chives

SERVES 8

Preheat the oven to 400°F. Roll out the pastry to fit a 10-inch tart pan with a removable bottom. Fit the pastry into the pan. Line with parchment or foil and fill with weights. Bake for 10 minutes; remove the paper and weights and bake for another 5 minutes, or until the crust is lightly colored and looks dry. Remove from the oven and let cool. Lower the heat to 375°F.

Place the florets on the bottom of the tart shell and sprinkle with the cheese. Beat the eggs with the cream and milk until well combined and pour over the cauliflower-cheese mixture. Sprinkle with the chives and bake for about 35 minutes, or until the top is golden-brown. Let rest for 15 minutes before serving.

Cauliflower and Zucchini Pancakes

4 cups cauliflower florets,
   cooked until soft
2 eggs
½ cup flour
1 teaspoon baking powder
¼ teaspoon cayenne
½ teaspoon oregano
1 teaspoon salt
½ teaspoon pepper
1 medium zucchini, finely
   shredded
2 tablespoons butter
2 tablespoons oil

MAKES ABOUT 15 PANCAKES

In a food processor, puree the cooked cauliflower with the egg, flour, baking powder, cayenne, oregano, salt, and pepper. Stir in the zucchini by hand.

In a large skillet, heat the butter and oil. Ladle the batter into the pan in 4-tablespoon batches and cook the pancakes for about 2 minutes per side. Use more oil and butter as needed. Serve immediately.

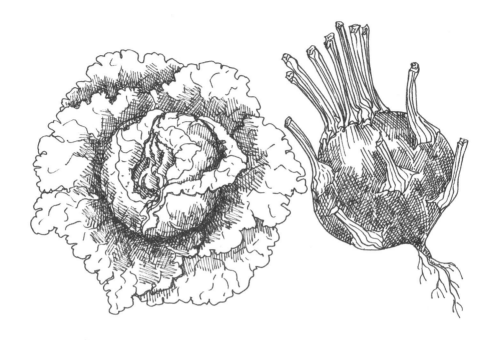

CABBAGE AND KOHLRABI

ENTERPRISING PRODUCE DEPARTMENTS have begun planting what look like designer labels amidst the spiffy rows of fruits and vegetables. Their purpose is to identify each specific variety of produce and suggest how best to take advantage of it. For a really well-stocked cabbage department, this could become a daunting task.

Green and purple cabbages, which need no introduction, are only the beginning. Even the ruffled Savoys, or the compact Danishes or Hollanders, are reasonably familiar. But the proliferation of Asian cabbages, with their special uses and subtle differences, is sure to exasperate any label maker, let alone consumer.

Under the category Chinese cabbages, we find—for starters—the slightly crinkled Nappa (or Napa), the tall Michihli (also called celery cabbage), the flat cabbage, the flowering white cabbage, Pe-tsai, Tai-sai, Lei-choi, and Pak-choi, also known as bok choy. In Chinese, the word for "vegetable" is *choi*, which is the same word for cabbage, so we get some idea of the enormity of the category.

Kohlrabi (also known as cabbage turnip and stem cabbage) is a member of the same species. Its tender leaves—delicious stir-fried or raw in salads—are usually missing by the time the vegetable reaches the market, but the swollen stem has a natural sweetness that is excellent raw as well as lightly steamed. Usually white or ivory-colored, kohlrabi also comes in pink to lavender varieties, with graceful names like Purple Danube and Early Vienna.

Altogether, these cabbages provide a vast culinary resource. With an infinite number of cabbages, we could always make superlative coleslaw (try a Savoy), pickled cabbage (use one of the reds or purples) or a fragrant stir-fry (look for baby bok choy). The cabbage has a place in almost every cuisine from Korean *kim chee,* German sauerkraut, and Irish colcannon, to New England corned beef and cabbage. Kohlrabi is popular in Austrian, German, and Eastern European soups and stews; in Chinese dishes, where it often substitutes for the similar-tasting Chinese broccoli; and in the American South, where it joins any gathering of mixed boiled greens. Mrs. Rorer's *Philadelphia Cook Book* (1886) advised cooking it in any recipe for turnips or serving it uncooked and sliced, like radishes. In the first cookbook written by an American (1796), Amelia Simmons addressed the subject with a certain helplessness: "Cabbage requires a page, they are so multifarious." They are also not her favorite multifarious vegetable, as we may surmise from her next comment: "If grown in an old town and in old gardens, they have a rankness, which at times, may be perceived by a fresh air traveller."

This rankness, as she calls it, was no discovery of hers. For centuries, the highly odoriferous quality of cabbage has kept it from gracing polite dinner tables, especially if the tables are located anywhere near the kitchen. A boiling cabbage head is no secret to any nearby nose. The fact that modern science has explained such antisocial emissions as simply a release of hydrogen sulfide fails to render them any the more fragrant. In fact, the longer cabbage is cooked, the greater the amount of hydrogen sulfide produced. This is not exactly news, as we can tell from the ancient Greek saying: "Cabbage twice cooked is death."

Naturally, the clever cook has always known what cabbage needs. According to the 1803 *Almanach des Gourmands*, when cooking cabbage, "Everything depends on the seasoning. It is thus that the most vulgar phrases are ennobled by the pen of a great poet." Closer to home, Mrs. Rorer advised boiling young cabbage for one hour, older cabbage for two, always with a piece of chili pepper "to diminish the unpleasant odor."

Despite these olfactory drawbacks, cabbage has been quite popular for the last 2,500 years. La Varenne, chef to Henry IV and France's first important gastronomic writer, included five recipes for cabbage in his seminal work, *Le Cuisinier Français* (1651). The Romans cultivated it and some of them, like Cato, ate it before and after meals, a practice he advised to his countrymen: "It will make you feel as if you had not eaten," he assured them, "and you can drink as much as you like."

Because of its more delicate nature, kohlrabi has escaped much of this controversy. It has also escaped the notice of a fair number of cooks. Richard Gehman's *The Haphazard Gourmet* designated it "most underrated vegetable" —a dubious honor we hereby hope to rectify.

CONSUMER AND COOKING GUIDE: Cabbage and Kohlrabi

Market Selection: Cabbage varieties include green, red, Savoy, and Napa. Kohlrabi is generally green, but newer varieties of red kohlrabi are available. The outer leaves of cabbage should be blemish-free and have good color for the variety. Cabbages should feel heavy and compact. Kohlrabi should have smallish firm bulbs with fresh-looking leaves.
Availability: Cabbage—year-round; kohlrabi—June through November
Storage: Both may be refrigerated in plastic bags for up to 1 week.
Flavor Enhancers: Apples, pears, raisins, curry, caraway, dill
Equivalents: One 1½-pound cabbage = 8 cups, shredded
Nutritional Value: Good source of vitamin C and potassium
      20 calories per cup—cabbage
      40 calories per cup—kohlrabi
Basic Cooking Methods: Cook, cut into wedges, in boiling salted water for about 10 minutes.

Steam for 12 minutes.

Caramelized Cabbage with Farfalle

3 tablespoons butter
3 tablespoons oil
1 large sweet onion, thinly
   sliced
2 cloves garlic, minced
1 head Savoy or green
   cabbage, cored and
   shredded
2 tablespoons sugar
1 teaspoon freshly ground
   black pepper
2 tablespoons poppy seed
½ pound farfalle noodles,
   freshly cooked and drained

SERVES 4 TO 6 AS A FIRST
COURSE OR 2 AS A MAIN
COURSE

In a large skillet, heat the butter and oil. Cook the onion until very soft, about 10 minutes. Add the garlic and cabbage and cook until limp, about 5 minutes. Stir in the sugar and continue cooking until the cabbage turns golden-brown, about 20 minutes. Stir in the pepper and poppy seed and toss with the farfalle.

Kohlrabi–Mushroom Soup

3 tablespoons oil
1 medium onion, chopped
1 clove garlic, minced
½ pound mushrooms, sliced
2 medium tomatoes, seeded
   and coarsely chopped
4 cups chicken stock
   (page 343)
4 small kohlrabi, peeled and
   sliced
   Salt and pepper
2 teaspoons fresh dill

SERVES 4

In a medium saucepan, heat the oil. Cook the onion, garlic, and mushroom over medium-high heat until the mushroom begins to color. Stir in the tomato and cook for another 3 minutes. Add the stock, bring to a boil, and add the kohlrabi. Lower the heat and simmer for 15 minutes. Season with salt and pepper and stir in the dill.

Napa Cabbage and Carrot Slaw with Toasted Sesame Seed

3 carrots, shredded
1 small head Napa cabbage,
   shredded
1 bunch green onions, thinly
   sliced
¼ cup coarsely chopped fresh
   cilantro leaves
2 tablespoons fresh lemon
   juice
1 tablespoon white-wine
   vinegar
1 teaspoon sugar
1 tablespoon sesame oil
½ teaspoon Tabasco
¼ cup vegetable oil
¼ cup toasted sesame seed

In a large bowl, combine the carrot, cabbage, onion, and cilantro. Combine the remaining ingredients, except the sesame seed, until blended and toss with the cabbage mixture. Sprinkle with sesame seed.

SERVES 6

Marinated Kohlrabi and Carrots

6 small kohlrabi, peeled and
   cut into matchsticks
3 medium carrots, peeled
   and cut into matchsticks
½ cup olive oil
2 tablespoons fresh lemon
   juice
2 tablespoons sherry vinegar
1 teaspoon sugar
1 tablespoon capers, rinsed
   and drained
½ teaspoon dried thyme
   Salt and pepper

Cook the kohlrabi and carrot in boiling water for 2 minutes. Drain well and place in a jar or bowl. Whisk together the remaining ingredients. Pour over the vegetables and cover. Refrigerate for 48 hours, stirring the vegetables occasionally.

Drain some of the marinade before serving. Serve as part of an antipasto platter or as a salad.

SERVES 6 TO 8

Caraway Cabbage with Potatoes and Sausage

4 tablespoons (½ stick)
   butter or oil
1 medium onion, thinly
   sliced
1 medium head Savoy or
   green cabbage, coarsely
   shredded
4 medium red potatoes,
   scrubbed and sliced
2 tablespoons caraway seed
½ cup beef or chicken stock
   (pages 344 and 343)
2 tablespoons red-wine
   vinegar
1 pound Polish sausage,
   sliced
2 tablespoons hot-sweet
   mustard
   Salt and pepper

In a large skillet, heat the butter. Add the onion and cabbage and cook until wilted. Add the potato, caraway, stock, and vinegar. Bring to a boil; cover, reduce heat, and simmer for 12 minutes. Add the sausage and cook, uncovered, for another 6 minutes. Stir in the mustard and season with salt and pepper.

SERVES 8

Red Cabbage, Green Apples, and Crisp Bacon

½ pound bacon strips, halved
1 large head red cabbage,
   cored and shredded
2 large green apples, cored
   and sliced
1 large onion, chopped
2 tablespoons honey
2 tablespoons fresh lemon
   juice
½ cup red wine
   Salt and pepper

Cook the bacon strips until crisp. Remove and reserve. Remove all but 4 tablespoons of the bacon fat from the pan and add the cabbage. Cook over medium heat for about 10 minutes.

Stir in the remaining ingredients and simmer, covered, for about 1 hour. Season to taste with salt and pepper. Just before serving, sprinkle with the reserved bacon.

SERVES 8

CARROTS

W E CAN ONLY WONDER about those husky-looking, clublike, faded orange roots that pass for carrots in the produce sections of many supermarkets. Dry and woody, they seem more suitable for the carpenter's whittling knife than for any of the cook's utensils. But actually, these large, chunky specimens have their place in the vegetable realm. Known as "keepers," they are intended for the long haul. They can be stored for extended periods, like turnips, potatoes, and other root vegetables associated with winter. But now that restaurants and sensitive grocers and farmers' markets have introduced us to more tender and smaller versions of the clunkier carrots of yore, we are willing to consider two-level carrot shopping:

one for eating today or tomorrow—the "carrot du jour"—and one for storing virtually indefinitely.

The "carrots du jour" don't necessarily have to be "baby carrots," which often have no taste either, if they are merely younger versions of regular carrots. But breeders are developing special small varieties intended for eating out of hand; they are exceptionally sweet, tender, and ephemeral.

There are two nonmysterious things that everybody knows about carrots. They are orange, and they help prevent night blindness because they are chock-full of vitamin A. Both of these "facts" are technically incorrect. Carrots were formerly every color but orange: red, black, yellow, white, and especially purple. First cultivated in Afghanistan in the seventh century, carrots originally had purple exteriors and yellow flesh. Not until the Middle Ages did the Dutch develop the bright orange carrot we now know as the proud bearer of carotene. Once in contact with the human intestine, carotene is converted to vitamin A.

As often happens, events have come full circle, and some markets occasionally feature carrots of a different color: yellow, purple, scarlet, and white, the last having the strongest flavor. Green areas on the crown indicate a slight case of sunburn and do not adversely affect a carrot's taste.

Because of the vegetable's inherent sweetness (only beets have more sugar than carrots), it has been used for desserts and candies since long before the invention of the all-too-ubiquitous carrot cake. German cooks boast a long tradition of carrot-nut bread. The Irish and English make carrot pudding and the French a lovely-sounding *charlotte aux cheveux d'ange*, a cake-lined mold filled with threads of candied carrot ("angel hair") folded in cream. *Gajar halva* is a Hindu celebration confection; *tzimmes* the traditional sweetened carrots served on the Jewish New Year and other holidays. Early New Englanders gave carrot cookies as Christmas gifts. In the colonial kitchen, carrots were also popular in the form of pickles, relishes, and preserves. Even the green tops of carrots are used as a cooked vegetable or dried for herbs.

Although it is difficult to imagine the common carrot as a status symbol, there was a time when proper English ladies adorned their best *chapeaux* with garlands of carrot greens. On hatless occasions, they fastened the frilly green bouquets to the sleeves of their gowns.

Two billion pounds of carrots are grown annually in this country alone, mainly in Texas, Wisconsin, and Minnesota. Quite a few also emanate from Holtville, California, which dubs itself the "Carrot Capital of the World." Carrot juice makes a delicious drink and is also used as a coloring for cheese.

Recently, modern technology has struck again, providing machinery that quickly harvests carrots at their peak. However, as is so often the case with these great advancements of agribusiness, the machines unfortunately destroy the most tender and succulent of the species. So, unless we grow and/or pick our own, the only carrots we taste will be the survivors—not the best, but the fittest.

CONSUMER AND COOKING GUIDE: Carrots

Market Selection: Long and short best describes the types of carrots available. They should have a bright orange-gold color and be well shaped. If the tops are attached, the leaves should be bright and fresh-looking.
Availability: Year-round
Storage: Carrots will keep in the refrigerator in a plastic bag for up to 2 weeks.
Flavor Enhancers: Dill, coriander, chervil
Equivalents: 1 medium bunch = approximately 1 pound
     1 large carrot = approximately ¼ pound
     1 large carrot = 1 cup, shredded
Nutritional Value: Good source of vitamin A
     35 calories per cup
Basic Cooking Methods: Cook in boiling salted water for 5 minutes.
  Steam for about 7 minutes.

Chilled Curried Carrot Soup

2 cups chicken stock
  (page 343)
1 strip orange zest
1 pound carrots, peeled and
  sliced
1 bunch green onions,
  chopped
1 tablespoon fresh orange
  juice
1 to 2 teaspoons curry
  powder
  Salt and pepper
½ cup half-and-half or plain
  yogurt
  Mint sprigs for garnish

SERVES 4

In a medium saucepan, bring the stock and orange zest to a boil. Add the carrot and green onion, cover, reduce heat, and simmer for 15 minutes. Stir in the orange juice and curry powder and cook for another minute. Season with salt and pepper.

Puree in a blender or food processor with the half-and-half. Chill and serve, garnished with mint.

Pickled Carrots with Ginger

1 pound baby carrots, peeled
1 cup mild white vinegar
  (rice vinegar is good)
½ cup granulated sugar
½ teaspoon salt
2 slices fresh ginger
4 sprigs fresh cilantro

SERVES 4

Place the carrots in a mixing bowl. In a medium saucepan, bring the vinegar, sugar, salt, ginger, and cilantro to a boil and cook until the sugar has dissolved, stirring occasionally. Pour over the carrots and let cool completely.

Pack the entire mixture in an airtight container and refrigerate overnight. Serve as part of an antipasto tray or as an hors d'oeuvre.

Green Pasta with Spicy Carrots

3 tablespoons olive oil

1 clove garlic, minced

1 jalapeño pepper, seeded
and minced

1 slice fresh ginger, minced

1 teaspoon ground cumin

¼ teaspoon cayenne

3 carrots, peeled, cut into
matchsticks, and cooked
just until tender

½ cup chicken stock
(page 343)

¼ cup sour cream

½ cup fresh cilantro leaves
Salt and pepper

1 pound freshly cooked
spinach fettuccine

SERVES 4 AS A MAIN
COURSE OR 6 AS A FIRST
COURSE

In a large skillet, heat the oil. Cook the garlic, jalapeño, ginger, cumin, and cayenne for about 3 minutes. Stir in the carrots and toss well to coat. Cook for about 2 minutes; add the stock. Bring to a boil, reduce heat, and simmer for 3 minutes.

Meanwhile, puree the sour cream and cilantro. Add to the carrot sauce and heat through. Season with salt and pepper. Add the pasta to the skillet and toss well with sauce. Serve immediately.

Sautéed Chicken with Carrots and Currants

3 tablespoons oil
Salt and pepper
Flour for dredging
3 whole skinless, boneless
   chicken breasts, split
1 clove garlic, minced
1 jalapeño pepper, seeded
   and minced
½ onion, chopped
4 large carrots, peeled and
   coarsely grated
½ cup white wine
½ cup chicken stock (page 343)
1 teaspoon ground cumin
½ cup currants
Fresh parsley or cilantro
   for garnish

SERVES 6

In a skillet, heat the oil. Salt and pepper the chicken pieces and dredge them in flour. Cook them for about 3 minutes on each side, or until golden-brown. Remove and reserve.

In the same pan, cook the garlic, jalapeño, onion, and carrot until tender, about 3 minutes. Stir in the wine and stock, scraping up any bits on the bottom of the pan, and bring to a boil. Add the cumin and currants; lower the heat, cover, and cook for about 3 minutes.

Return the chicken to the pan and cook over low heat for about 5 minutes. Serve each chicken-breast half topped with the carrot mixture and garnished with parsley.

Flourless Carrot Torte

1½ cups ground almonds or
   walnuts
6 eggs, separated
1 tablespoon fresh lemon
   juice
1 cup sugar
¼ cup unsweetened cocoa
½ teaspoon ground ginger
2 cups finely grated carrot
½ teaspoon salt
Confectioners' sugar
   (optional)

SERVES 10

Preheat the oven to 375°F. Grease a 9-inch springform pan and dust it with about 2 tablespoons of the ground nuts.

Beat the egg yolks with the lemon juice and ½ cup of the sugar until pale and thick. Stir in the remaining ground nuts, cocoa, ginger, and carrot.

In a separate bowl, beat the egg whites until foamy. Add the salt and beat until thick. Add the remaining ½ cup sugar a little at a time and continue to beat until stiff and shiny. Fold the whites into the carrot mixture and pour into the prepared pan.

Bake for about 45 minutes, or until a tester inserted in the center comes out dry. Allow to cool ½ hour before unmolding. Dust with confectioners' sugar if desired.

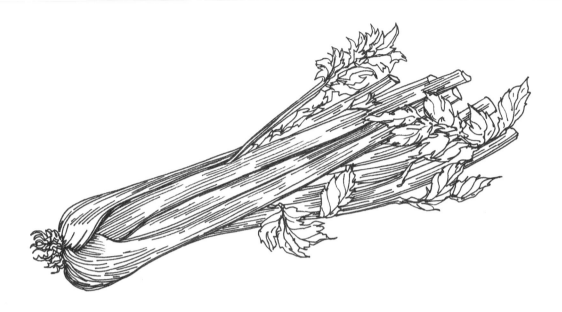

CELERY

No ONE KNOWS if it's true, as the Dutch gynecologist Van de Velde says in his book, *Ideal Marriage*, that celery is an effective aphrodisiac. Nor does anyone know if celery offers protection from hangovers, as the Romans contended. It may be possible, or so thought many medieval magicians, that a few celery seeds placed in the shoes can help a person fly. True or not, rumors of celery power have been convincing enough to win the vegetable a prominent place on the crowns and crests of royalty.

An innocent-looking vegetable, celery has always been extremely popular. The Greeks used it as a seasoning, the ancient Romans made a dessert from it(!), and sixteenth-century Europeans employed it, seeds, leaves, and all, as a food and flavoring and as a medicine. The seventeenth-century gardener, author, and member of England's Royal Society, John Evelyn, once praised celery as "the grace of the whole board."

In this country, our ancestors ate so much of this vegetable that a French observer noted Americans in the 1800s "incessantly nibble [celery] from the beginning to the end of their repasts." In that same era, many people owned pressed-glass holders designed specifically to display the long, elegant stalks. The Cajuns of Louisiana have long cherished celery as one of what they call the "holy trinity" of their cookery. (Onion and bell pepper are the other two.)

In Denmark, where it is called *Blad-selleri*, the vegetable is used as the base of a rich blue-cheese soup. The famous Waldorf salad is essentially celery and apples in equal parts. Just about any salad profits from the vibrant crunch of celery, and soup stocks develop instant personality with the inclusion of its frilly leaves.

The French started cultivating celery, or *Apium graveolens*, in the 1600s, and by the beginning of this century at least thirty kinds had been developed. An incredible 1.7 billion pounds of celery is sold annually in this country, of which California and Florida produce 80 percent. Celery's current rise in popularity might be due to the basic nutritious nature of this member of the carrot family or simply to the fact that it takes more calories to consume than it provides. The celery we most commonly see in markets is the thinnish, light-green-stemmed Pascal celery, but there are also white celeries, and a chartreuse variety called Golden Yellow. Most unusual by far are the red celeries with provocative names like Giant Pink, Carter's Incomparable Crimson, and the purple-tinged Violet de Tours. These are most dramatic when served raw because cooking by any method draws out some color.

Despite a bland exterior, celery is rich with potential. Because of its year-round availability, it is always easy to serve as a side-dish vegetable, salad, or aromatic, and its presence is always more than subtle. It may not be the kind of food that you dream of or rhapsodize about; rather, it's the stuff of long-term relationships—more like a pal than a paramour.

CONSUMER AND COOKING GUIDE: Celery

Market Selection: The most common variety is Pascal. A newcomer to the greengrocer's shelf is a red celery called Violet de Tours (which turns green in cooking). Stalks should be rigidly crisp and leaves fresh-looking.
Availability: Year-round
Storage: Refrigerate in plastic bag or wrap, unwashed, for up to 2 weeks.
Flavor Enhancers: Oregano, thyme, bay leaf, parsley, capers
Equivalents: 1 stalk = 1 cup, sliced or chopped
Nutritional Value: Good source of vitamins A, B, C, and E
  8 calories per cup

Pickled Celery and Carrots

½ cup olive oil
5 tablespoons fresh lemon
    juice
2 tablespoons chopped fresh
    dill
½ teaspoon dried thyme
2 sprigs parsley
1 bay leaf
½ teaspoon salt
½ teaspoon freshly ground
    black pepper
4 ribs celery, trimmed and
    cut into 2-inch pieces
4 medium carrots, scraped,
    quartered lengthwise, and
    cut into 2-inch pieces

SERVES 6

In a large saucepan, combine the oil, lemon juice, herbs, salt, and pepper. Bring to a boil and add the celery and carrot. Add enough water to almost cover (vegetables should not be completely submerged); lower the heat and simmer, covered, for about 15 minutes. The vegetables should be tender but crisp. Remove the pan from the heat and let the vegetables cool in the marinade.

Store the vegetables and marinade in a covered glass jar in the refrigerator for 24 hours before using. Use as part of an antipasto platter or as a garnish for a sandwich plate.

Baked Barley with Red Onions and Celery

4 tablespoons oil or butter
1 large red onion, diced
2 stalks celery, diced
2 cups pearl barley
½ teaspoon dried thyme
3½ cups chicken stock
    (page 343)
½ cup white wine
    Salt and pepper
½ cup chopped fresh chives

SERVES 8

Preheat the oven to 350°F.

In a flameproof oven casserole, heat the oil. Cook the onion and celery until soft, about 6 minutes. Stir in the barley and cook for about 3 minutes. Add the thyme, stock, and wine and bring to a boil.

Cover the casserole and place it in the oven. Bake for about 45 minutes, or until all of the liquid has been absorbed. Season with salt and pepper and stir in the chives.

Celery, Apple, and Blue-Cheese Cream Soup

2 tablespoons butter
2 tablespoons vegetable oil
1 bunch green onions,
   trimmed and chopped
6 ribs celery with leaves,
   chopped
1 large pippin or Granny
   Smith apple, cored and
   diced
1 small white potato, diced
4 cups chicken stock
   (page 343)
3 ounces blue cheese
1 cup heavy cream or
   half-and-half
Salt and pepper
Celery leaves for garnish

In a medium saucepan, heat the butter and oil. Cook the onion, celery, and apple over medium heat until soft, about 6 minutes. Stir in the potato and stock. Bring to a boil, lower the heat, and simmer, partially covered, for 30 minutes.

Puree the mixture in a food processor or blender with the cheese. Return to the pan and stir in the cream. Season with salt and pepper and serve, garnished with celery leaves.

SERVES 6

Braised Celery with Black Forest Ham and Cheese

2 tablespoons butter
2 tablespoons oil
2 ounces Black Forest ham,
   diced
1 tablespoon chopped shallot
1 clove garlic, minced
8 stalks celery, trimmed and
   cut into 4-inch pieces
1 cup chicken stock
   (page 343)
2 ounces shredded white
   cheddar cheese

In a medium sauté pan, heat the butter and oil. Add the ham, shallot, and garlic; cook for 3 minutes over medium heat. Add the celery and cook for another 3 minutes, stirring gently. Add the stock; bring to a boil, lower the heat, and simmer, covered, for 30 minutes.

Sprinkle with cheese and place under a preheated broiler until the cheese is bubbly.

SERVES 4

Mustard Shrimp with Two Celeries

1 pound bay shrimp
1 stalk celery, finely diced or
   chopped
½ cup celery leaves, finely
   chopped
2 green onions, thinly sliced

Dressing

⅓ cup mayonnaise
⅓ cup plain yogurt
1 tablespoon balsamic
   vinegar
2 tablespoons mild mustard
½ teaspoon Worcestershire
   sauce
2 teaspoons celery seed

Salt and pepper

SERVES 4

In a medium bowl, combine the shrimp, celery, celery leaves, and green onion. Combine the dressing ingredients until well blended and toss with the shrimp mixture. Season with salt and pepper. Use for sandwiches or serve in lettuce cups as a salad.

CORN

CORN IS A TRIBUTE to one of the basic attributes of human nature: no matter how good it gets, we can always find something to complain about. We used to regret that corn lost flavor minutes away from its warm earthy crib; we had scientists explain the reasons in terms of sugars and starches and hydrocarbon chains. As a remedy, some few of us even dragged pots of boiling water to the cornfields to partake of the raw and the cooked simultaneously.

Meanwhile, back at the genetics lab, they were working on a type of corn with a double sugar gene that would taste as sweet as sugar and stay that way for several days after picking. And when they were done, we had our choice of supersweet hybrids like Sugar Dots, Honey and Cream, Kandy Korn, and How Sweet It Is. While it's hard to complain about these perfectly formed, ivory-smooth, candy-kerneled specimens, it's not impossible. "They're too sweet," some say, "too sugary," corn just doesn't taste "corny" anymore.

Even those who cavil over these annoying refinements can seldom resist the taste of fresh summer corn, no matter how unnaturally succulent it now threatens to be. The current season is always all too short, the next season always too far distant, and our collective corn memories too urgent and complex and evocative.

Corn is part of us, just as we are part of the New World from which it sprang. It was the very salvation of the earliest settlers, who learned its mysteries from Native Americans across the land. The Algonquians in Virginia taught Jamestown settlers how to plant it and then how to turn it into corn pone; the Mohawks pressed the oil from walnuts and dribbled it onto the cooked, hot corn kernels; Florida Seminoles made it into relishes; and the Shawnees made johnny cakes from cornmeal. Corn was so important to most of the Native American peoples that their year started with its planting, and the greatest summer feasts centered around its harvest. Corn represented fertility and power, while the variously colored kernels symbolized different tribes or families. The names of many types of corn memorialize this heritage: Seneca Chief, Black Aztec, Hopi Bantam.

From the Native American *msíckquatash*, a Narragansett recipe of dried beans and corn, the Pilgrims adapted one of their first dishes, succotash, and served it annually on December 22—Forefathers' Day—to celebrate the day of their landing. Plymouth's Governor Bradford praised a few kernels of corn as being "[as] good as a feast." Even today there is a place in New Bedford, Massachusetts, called Johnnycake Hill where Pilgrim travelers once stopped to eat their johnny cakes (also called journey cakes) on their journey between Plymouth Colony and the garrison at Russell's Mill in Dartmouth.

Corn, according to Harold McGee *(On Food and Cooking)*, "is the New World's single most important contribution to the human diet." One of its first-discovered, and most appreciated, properties was its fermentability. To this we owe corn whiskeys, especially our most famous indigenous liquor— bourbon—made from ground corn and barley malt. By the War of 1812, the British soldiers who found corn growing in Thomas Jefferson's fields at Monticello knew what to do with it: they fed it to their horses. By 1850 the eating of corn on the cob was a fairly common sight in this country, although it looked positively barbaric to some uninitiated observers. One of them, Frederika Vremer, described her shock at seeing people gnawing on what she called the "whole stem" of the vegetable. Currently, corn is second only to rice as the earth's most widely consumed cereal grain.

Corn comes in many fashion colors, from white, yellow, red, purple, blue, brown, and black to calico. The cobs range in size from two feet down to two-inch miniatures with tender edible cores. Corn may be transformed into everything from breakfast muffins to midnight snack crackers; from grilled baby-corn appetizers to polenta-cake desserts. In the form of popcorn (which is a special plant variety), corn is the only vegetable anyone would ever eat in the movies. Appreciative corn lovers once proposed the humble corn tassel as our national flower. Granted, its beauty doesn't approach that of some of the other contenders for the honor—the rose, the daisy, and the marigold—but, as one of its more fervent proponents, Margo Cairns of Minnesota, argued: ". . . let that most American and most useful of all the plant kingdom be enshrined as nationally emblematic." And that means corn.

CONSUMER AND COOKING GUIDE: Corn

Market Selection: Yellow, white, and calico. Ears should appear fresh, with green husks and silk ends that are free of decay. Peel back a bit of husk and silk to make sure the ear is free of worm infestation. Taste a kernel for sweetness.
Availability: June through September
Storage: Store in the refrigerator, wrapped in plastic bag or wrap, for up to 2 days.
Flavor Enhancers: Chili powder, curry, freshly ground pepper
Equivalents: 1 large ear = 1 cup kernels
Nutritional Value: Good source of Vitamin A
 75 calories per medium ear
Cooking and Handling Notes: To cut kernels from corn: Stand an ear of corn upright and with sharp knife, cut downward, rotating the corn until the cob is clean. Separate the kernels with your fingers.
Basic Cooking Methods: Cook in boiling salted water for 3 minutes.
 Steam for 4 minutes.

Curried Corn Soup

2 tablespoons butter or oil
½ small onion, chopped
1 stalk celery, chopped
1 medium tomato, seeded
   and chopped
1 clove garlic, minced
1 tablespoon curry powder,
   or to taste
½ teaspoon ground cumin
2 tablespoons flour
4 cups chicken stock
3 cups corn kernels
3 tablespoons fresh cilantro
   leaves

SERVES 4

In a saucepan, heat the butter. Cook the onion, celery, tomato, and garlic for about 3 minutes. Stir in the curry, cumin, and flour and cook for another minute. Add the chicken stock and bring to a boil. Add the corn, lower the heat, and simmer for 10 minutes. Stir in fresh cilantro and serve.

Corn "Risotto" with Prosciutto

2 tablespoons butter or oil
2 ounces prosciutto, diced
1 small onion, chopped
1 small red bell pepper,
   seeded and diced
1 cup chicken stock
   (page 343)
¼ cup heavy cream
2 cups fresh corn kernels
½ cup grated dry Monterey
   Jack cheese

SERVES 6

In a sauté pan, heat the butter. Add the prosciutto, onion, and pepper; cook for 5 minutes, or until soft. Stir in the chicken stock and cream and bring to a boil. Add the corn, lower the heat, and cook for 8 minutes, or until soft and creamy. Stir in the cheese and serve.

"Corn"acopia Chicken Salad

3 cups corn kernels, cooked
  and cooled
1 cup cooked black beans
1 small red bell pepper,
  diced
1 small green bell pepper,
  diced
1 bunch green onions, thinly
  sliced
1 medium tomato, seeded
  and coarsely chopped
2 cups diced cooked chicken
1 small bunch fresh cilantro,
  chopped

DRESSING

1 clove garlic, minced
½ jalapeño pepper, seeded
  and minced
½ teaspoon ground cumin
1 teaspoon honey
5 tablespoons red-wine
  vinegar
⅓ cup oil
  Salt and pepper

12 lettuce leaves

SERVES 12 AS AN
APPETIZER, 6 AS A MAIN
COURSE

In a large bowl, mix the vegetables with the chicken and cilantro. Combine the dressing ingredients until well blended and toss with the corn mixture. Spoon onto lettuce leaves and serve.

Sweet Corn and Chili Roulade

9 tablespoons (1 stick plus
　1 tablespoon) butter
1 or 2 jalapeños, seeded and
　chopped
3 green onions, chopped
1 cup fresh corn kernels
½ cup flour
2 cups hot milk
4 eggs, separated
1 cup grated Monterey Jack
　cheese
¼ teaspoon salt
　Tomato salsa (optional)

SERVES 8

Preheat the oven to 400°F. Line a 10 x 15-inch jelly-roll pan with foil and grease the foil with 2 tablespoons of the butter.

In a skillet, heat 2 tablespoons of the butter. Sauté the jalapeño, onion, and corn over medium heat for about 3 minutes. Set aside.

In a medium saucepan, melt the remaining 5 tablespoons of butter. Add the flour and cook for about 3 minutes, stirring constantly. Gradually add the milk; cook, stirring, until the mixture is thick and smooth. Beat in the egg yolks one at a time and stir in ½ cup of the cheese. Set aside.

Beat the egg whites with the salt until stiff peaks form. Fold them into the cheese mixture; pour the batter evenly into the prepared pan.

Bake for about 18 minutes, or until the batter pulls away from the pan slightly. Turn the roulade out onto a dish towel and remove the foil. Sprinkle with the remaining ½ cup cheese. Spread the corn mixture over the cheese and roll up, starting with the short end. Allow the roulade to cool before slicing. Serve with salsa if desired.

Grilled Corn with Ginger-Lime Butter

4 tablespoons (½ stick)
    butter
1 tablespoon grated fresh
    ginger
1 tablespoon fresh lime juice
½ teaspoon salt
6 ears of corn, in husks

SERVES 6

Preheat the grill. In a small saucepan, melt the butter with the ginger, lime juice, and salt. Peel the corn husks back and remove the silks. Brush the corn with the butter mixture and rearrange the husks over the corn. Tie the ends with nonflammable kitchen string to keep them from opening.

Place the husks on the preheated grill and cook for about 15 minutes, turning every so often.

Fresh Corn and Maple Muffins

1 cup yellow cornmeal
1 cup unbleached all-purpose
    flour
1 cup fresh corn kernels
½ teaspoon salt
2 eggs
3 tablespoons corn oil
⅓ cup maple syrup
1 cup buttermilk

MAKES 1 DOZEN MUFFINS

Preheat the oven to 400°F. Grease 12 muffin cups.

In a large bowl, combine the cornmeal, flour, corn, and salt. In a small bowl, beat the eggs with the oil, maple syrup, and buttermilk. Stir the liquid mixture into the dry ingredients and mix just until blended. Spoon the batter into the prepared muffin cups; bake for about 20 minutes, or until brown.

CUCUMBERS

AMONG THE PROOFS of Thomas Wolfe's surpassing literary skills is the fact that he was once able to write lustily about the cucumber. In his description of Eugene Gant's raiding the refrigerator in *Of Time and the River*, he writes of a man who can't wait to sink his teeth into "a speared forkful of those thin-sliced cucumbers—ah! what a delicate and toothsome pickle they do make—what sorcerer invented them. . . ."

In fact, over the centuries, the services of sorcerers have often been required to make cucumbers taste like anything. One of the oldest cultivated plants, cucumbers were discovered in Asia by the Romans, who brought them home and successfully transplanted them. However, when they attempted to extract some flavor from their purloined produce, they realized that their work had just begun. Records describe Roman cooks seasoning cucumbers with everything from sun-made wine and pennyroyal to "a little sylphium," an expensive and highly esteemed flavoring. They boiled the bland vegetable with precooked brains (presumably animal brains) and added honey and cumin at serving time. Something must have worked because we know that Emperor Tiberius like cucumbers so much, he had them grown in carts that could be wheeled out for a daily sit in the sun to help them thrive, even off-season.

Tiberius wasn't the only cucumber lover, according to the ancient Sumerian legend of Gilgamesh, which describes people eating wild cucumbers, among other things too squirmy to mention. Columbus brought cucumber seeds to Haiti, possibly in an attempt to get rid of them once and for all. As luck would have it, the seeds thrived and spread over North America, where Native Americans, especially the Pueblo Indians, became the cucumber's biggest fans to date.

Early American cooks seemed no less determined than their Roman antecedents to enjoy cucumbers and began developing recipes for frying, stewing, battering, creaming, pickling, steaming, and stuffing the vegetable. In the late 1700s the Shaker religious communities included in their Manifesto the proclamation that cucumbers "can be dressed in more palatable and suitable ways than most any other vegetable except tomatoes." Our present heritage of preparations, raw and cooked, is rich and universal. There are the Indian condiment raita and the Finnish salad *kurkkusalaatti*, as well as Japanese steamed cucumbers. True fanatics may wish to revive the once-popular three-week cucumber diet, which promised various cures and nice skin to boot. Current scientific analysis has lent support to some of these claims, showing that the vegetable is exceptionally high in vitamin E.

Along with regular green cucumbers, we are seeing unusual varieties, like the pale seedless Armenian (or Turkish or Syrian) type, an intriguing-looking ivory-white variety, and the lemon-shaped, yellow-green lemon cucumber. Although a staggering quantity of cucumbers—600 million pounds—is grown annually in California, Florida, and Texas, the United States imports 300 million pounds a year from Mexico. That's a lot of toothsome pickles.

CONSUMER AND COOKING GUIDE: Cucumbers

Market Selection: Field-grown slicing cucumbers are the most common, all-purpose variety. In addition, one can also find long hothouse or English cucumbers (usually packaged in a tight wrap of plastic), bumpy-skinned pickling cucumbers, extra-slender Japanese cucumbers, and squat, pale, lemon cucumbers. All types should be firm and unblemished.

Availability: Year-round but best in spring and early summer

Storage: Seal in a plastic bag in the refrigerator for up to 1 week.

Flavor Enhancers: Dill, chives, tarragon, mint

Equivalents: 2 medium cucumbers (8 inches) = 1 pound
        1 pound, peeled and seeded = 2 cups, sliced

Nutritional Value: Good source of vitamins A and E
        45 calories per medium cucumber

Cooking and Handling Notes: If cucumbers are waxed, make sure to peel them. To seed a cucumber, cut it in half lengthwise and scrape out the seeds with a small spoon.

   Cucumbers should be cooked briefly, either by blanching or sautéeing.

Lemon, Cucumber, and Cantaloupe Soup

2 lemon cucumbers, peeled,
seeded, and sliced
1 small cantaloupe, peeled,
seeded, and sliced
2 tablespoons honey
¼ cup fresh lime juice
¼ cup fresh orange juice
1 cup plain yogurt
2 tablespoons chopped fresh
mint

SERVES 4

Combine the cucumber, cantaloupe, honey, lime juice, and orange juice in a food processor; process until smooth. Stir in the yogurt and mint. Serve over ice or very well chilled.

Spicy Oriental Pickled Cucumbers

1 pound small pickling
cucumbers, each cut
lengthwise into 6 wedges,
seeded
2 teaspoons salt
1½ tablespoons sugar
2 tablespoons rice vinegar
¼ cup sesame oil
1 slice fresh ginger, peeled
8 small dried red chili
peppers, seeded
1 teaspoon Szechuan
peppercorns (optional)

MAKES 3 CUPS

Toss the cucumber with the salt and let stand for 20 minutes. Drain, rinse in a colander, and pat dry.

In a bowl, dissolve the sugar in the vinegar. Add the cucumber and toss to coat.

In a small skillet, heat the sesame oil. Add the ginger, chili peppers, and peppercorns. Cook for about 30 seconds, or until the peppers are dark red and the spices are fragrant. Let cool completely and combine with the cucumber mixture.

Let marinate at room temperature for 3 hours, or cover and refrigerate overnight.

Cucumber-Pineapple Salsa

2 pickling cucumbers or
   1 English cucumber,
   peeled and seeded
   Flesh of 1 small pineapple
3 jalapeño peppers, seeded
   and deveined
1 slice fresh ginger, peeled
¼ small red onion, peeled
½ cup fresh cilantro leaves
3 tablespoons brown sugar
2 tablespoons fresh lemon
   juice
   Salt and pepper

MAKES 2 CUPS

Combine all of the ingredients in a food processor; process to a medium-fine texture. Season to taste with salt and pepper. Let stand for at least 2 hours before using for flavors to develop fully. Delicious with grilled meats, fish, or poultry.

Scallop Sauté with Cucumber-Tomato Sauce

1 tablespoon butter
4 tablespoons oil
1½ pounds sea scallops
   Flour for dredging
1 English cucumber, peeled,
   seeded, and sliced ¼ inch
   thick
1 cup chopped tomato
1 teaspoon fresh tarragon
   leaves or ½ teaspoon dried
¼ cup sour cream
   Salt and pepper

SERVES 6

In a large skillet or sauté pan, heat the butter and 2 tablespoons of the oil. Dredge the scallops in flour and sauté them for about 2 minutes. Remove and reserve.

Add the remaining 2 tablespoons of oil to the skillet and sauté the cucumber until lightly browned. Reserve with the scallops. Add the tomato, tarragon, and sour cream to the pan and bring to a boil. Reduce the heat and simmer for about 5 minutes, or until the sauce has thickened. Return the scallops and cucumber to the sauce and heat through. Season to taste with salt and pepper.

Cucumber and Snap Pea Sauté with Cumin

2 tablespoons butter or oil
2 tablespoons chopped
   shallot
2 English cucumbers,
   peeled, halved lengthwise,
   seeded, and thinly sliced
½ pound sugar snap peas,
   strings removed
   Pinch sugar
½ cup chicken or vegetable
   stock
½ teaspoon ground cumin
   Salt and pepper

SERVES 4

In a medium skillet, heat the butter. Add the shallot and cook until soft. Add the cucumber, peas, and sugar. Cook over high heat for about 1 minute. Add the stock; bring to a boil, lower heat, and simmer for 2 minutes. Stir in the cumin and season with salt and pepper.

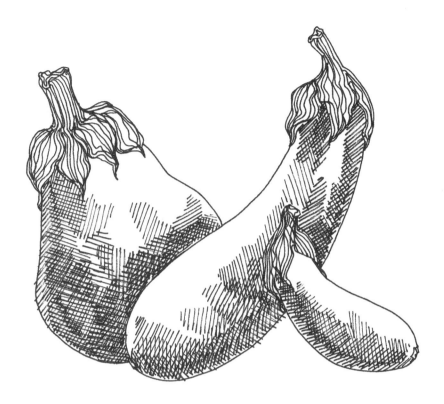

EGGPLANT

WHAT'S ROUND and oblong and big and small and white and purple and green and striped and orange and lavender and mottled and black? What else but eggplant? Or more precisely a dozen eggplants. True, most supermarkets are unlikely to feature eggplants on such a chromatic scale, but ethnic markets often offer colorful varieties that are downright ostentatious.

There is, for example, the lavender and white–striped Listada de Gandia, or the heart-shaped Rosa Bianco, the white-skinned Long White Sword, the Pink Bride, and the provocative Black Beauty. You may even come across the rare, tomato-colored Small Ruffled Red, a bitter variety popular in Oriental sauces and in Thai and Cambodian dishes. You will soon discover, however, that beneath their alluring exteriors, most eggplants taste pretty much the same. Size and shape are probably more important considerations than color in selecting a specimen appropriate to your eggplant intentions.

Syrians and Turks insist that there are more than a thousand ways of preparing eggplant. It seems like a good idea to have at least one of them in mind when buying an eggplant, since it does not, despite its versatility, make very good crudités. Nor can it be tossed raw into a salad or even briefly cooked, al dente style. Eggplant can, however, be sautéed, baked, broiled, roasted, grilled, stuffed, and stewed, all of which makes it a major ingredient in many of the world's cuisines.

In the classic French ratatouille, the globe is surrounded by garlic-scented tomatoes, onions, peppers, and zucchini, essentially the same ingredients found in Italy's caponata. In other cuisines, it becomes eggplant Parmesan, Greek moussaka, and Romanian caviar. And there is the pickled eggplant of Almagro, the Castilian town that became known throughout Spain for this one culinary contribution. Simmered for hours in olive oil, eggplant can become *imam bayeldi*, the legendary dish of Turkey, as famous for its flavor as for the following tale. As the story goes, a bride prepared this dish every night for her new husband because he loved it so much. One night, when she finally ran out of oil and informed him she could not make *imam bayeldi*, he collapsed from dismay. Putting aside for a moment the obvious Freudian implications, this tale is a testimony to true eggplant fervor. With this same level of enthusiasm, the inhabitants of Mediterranean countries greeted Arab traders who first brought them eggplant in the Middle Ages. In fact the word *aubergine*—used in France, Germany, and England—is Arabic in origin: *al-badinjan*, which became the Catalan *alberginera*, and later evolved into *aubergine*. The word *eggplant* derives from the white species, which closely resembles a hen's egg.

From the Mediterranean, the eggplant soon traveled to the New World. At Monticello, Jefferson planted seeds and cuttings in the late eighteenth century. The famous New York restaurant Delmonico's is often credited with introducing eggplant to the country's more serious eaters in the late 1800s. Although many nineteenth-century American cookbook writers mentioned eggplant, most of them did not know what to make of it—literally. Miss Leslie, author of *Seventy Five Receipts* (1827) and the *New Cookery Book* (1857), warned of the bitter flavor and commented that though often served at dinner, eggplant was more properly a breakfast dish. In her *Philadelphia Cook Book* (1886), Mrs. Rorer's recipe for the unceremonious-sounding "Fried Egg-Plant No. 1" ends with the counsel, "Tomato catsup should be served with it." Fanny Farmer's first edition (1896) includes only two halfhearted suggestions. Such reticence had a formidable predecessor in John Gerard's

1597 *Herball,* which warned of the eggplant's "mischievous quality; the use whereof is utterly to be forsaken."

The eggplant, a native of India, is a member of the deadly nightshade family, which includes many poisonous plants as well as potatoes, bell peppers, tomatoes, tobacco, and a potent hallucinogen called jimson weed. Because of eggplant's tendency to discolor when exposed to air, its flesh should be cut with a stainless-steel blade and the cooked vegetable mashed with a wooden utensil. Raw eggplant has a spongy texture and absorbs enormous amounts of oil. But the patient cook knows that eventually the sponginess begins to break down from the heat of cooking; at that point, much of the excess oil is expelled.

Finally, we have the recommendation of many of the world's eggplant authorities that chopped or sliced eggplant be rinsed and salted to draw out bitterness and excess moisture. On the other hand, there is the informed opinion of James Beard, who unequivocally condemned such advice as nothing more than an old wives' tale.

CONSUMER AND COOKING GUIDE: Eggplant

Market Selection: Pear-shaped (purple); Italian or baby (small, globe-shaped, purple); white (often egg-shaped); Oriental or Japanese (small, narrow, purple); Thai (round, white or green). All types should be firm, with smooth, unblemished skin.

Availability: Year-round; peak—July through October

Storage: Refrigerate in a plastic bag for up to 5 days.

Flavor Enhancers: Garlic, basil, parsley, lemon juice, hot peppers, fresh cilantro

Equivalents: 1 medium eggplant = 1 pound
      1 pound = 4 cups, diced

Nutritional Value: 1 cup cooked eggplant = 38 calories; eggplant contains some
      protein and provides vitamins A, B complex, and C, as well as
      phosphorus, potassium, and calcium.

Cooking and Handling Notes: To bake an eggplant: pierce the skin in several places with a fork and place the eggplant on a baking sheet. Bake in a preheated 400°F oven until the eggplant collapses (about 40 minutes for large and 20 minutes for Oriental eggplant). Let cool and use as recipe directs.

Eggplant and Tomato Soup Gratin

3 tablespoons olive oil
1 clove garlic, minced
1 large sweet onion, diced
1 pound eggplant, unpeeled,
   cut into 1-inch cubes
2 large ripe tomatoes, seeded
   and cut into 1-inch cubes
2 tablespoons tomato paste
1 teaspoon dried oregano
1 cup tomato juice
4 cups chicken stock
   (page 343)
¼ cup chopped fresh parsley
   Salt and pepper
6 slices toasted country-style
   bread
6 ounces grated dry
   Monterey Jack cheese

SERVES 6

In a saucepan, heat the oil. Cook the garlic and onion until wilted, about 3 minutes. Add the eggplant and tomato and cook for 5 minutes. Stir in the tomato paste, oregano, tomato juice, stock, and parsley. Bring to a boil, lower the heat, and simmer, partially covered, for 15 minutes. Season with salt and pepper.

Sprinkle the bread slices with cheese, and toast or broil them until the cheese is melted and lightly browned. Ladle the soup into bowls and top with cheese toasts.

Eggplant Salad Agridolce

2 tablespoons olive oil
2 cloves garlic, minced
1 small onion, chopped
½ red bell pepper, chopped
½ cup balsamic vinegar
4 Oriental eggplants, baked
  until soft (see Cooking Note,
  81), and cut into strips
½ cup Greek black olives,
  pitted and coarsely
  chopped
¼ cup toasted pine nuts
  (see page 347)
  Pinch cayenne
  Salt

MAKES 2 CUPS

In a medium skillet, heat the oil. Cook the garlic, onion, and pepper for 5 minutes. Add the vinegar and continue cooking until the mixture is thick and syrupy.

Add the eggplant with the remaining ingredients. Cook for another 3 minutes and taste for salt. Serve warm or at room temperature with crackers or bread or as part of an antipasto platter.

Thyme and Lime–Marinated Grilled Eggplant Slices

MARINADE

2 tablespoons fresh lime
  juice
2 cloves garlic, minced
1 teaspoon fresh thyme
  leaves or ½ teaspoon dried
½ teaspoon crushed
  red-pepper flakes
½ teaspoon salt
½ cup olive oil

1 medium globe eggplant,
  unpeeled, cut into ¼-inch
  slices

SERVES 6

Combine the marinade ingredients. Pour the marinade into a large, shallow glass bowl.

Place the eggplant slices in the bowl (two bowls may be needed) and turn them so that each side is coated with marinade. Let sit for 30 minutes; turn the eggplant again and let sit for another 30 minutes.

Meanwhile, preheat the grill. Place the eggplant slices close to the heat source and cook for about 4 minutes, or just until light char marks appear. Turn and cook on the other side. Serve immediately.

Rigatoni with Eggplant and Lamb

4 tablespoons olive oil
1 bunch green onions, white
   part only, thinly sliced
1 pound lamb cut from leg,
   cut into 1-inch cubes
1½ pounds eggplant (globe or
   Oriental), unpeeled, cut
   into 1-inch cubes
2 medium tomatoes, seeded
   and chopped
1 teaspoon dried oregano
½ cup chicken or beef stock
½ cup Greek black olives,
   pitted and halved
2 tablespoons capers, rinsed
   and drained
½ cup Feta cheese, crumbled
1 pound freshly cooked
   rigatoni

SERVES 4 TO 6

In a skillet, heat the oil. Add the onion and lamb and cook until the lamb loses its pink color. Add the eggplant and cook until lightly browned. Stir in the tomato, oregano, and stock. Bring to a boil, lower heat, and simmer for 8 to 10 minutes, or until the sauce thickens slightly.

Stir in the olives, capers, and cheese. Toss with the rigatoni and serve.

Eggplant Pockets Filled with Herbed Ricotta

¼ cup olive oil
1 large globe eggplant,
    peeled and cut into ¼-inch
    slices

FILLING

1 cup fresh basil leaves
3 cloves garlic
2 tablespoons olive oil
½ cup grated Parmesan
1 cup ricotta cheese
½ teaspoon dried oregano
    Salt and pepper

½ cup shredded Fontina
    cheese

MAKES ABOUT 12 POCKETS

Preheat the oven to 425°F.

Brush two baking pans with 2 tablespoons of the olive oil and lay the eggplant slices in the pans in one layer. Brush the eggplant with the remaining 2 tablespoons olive oil and bake for 15 minutes. Lower the oven temperature to 350°F.

Meanwhile, make the filling by processing all of the filling ingredients in a food processor until smooth. Remove eggplant from oven and spoon 2 to 3 tablespoons of filling onto each eggplant slice. Fold the sides over the filling and place the pockets, seam side down, on a greased shallow baking pan. Sprinkle Fontina cheese over the pockets and bake for 15 minutes.

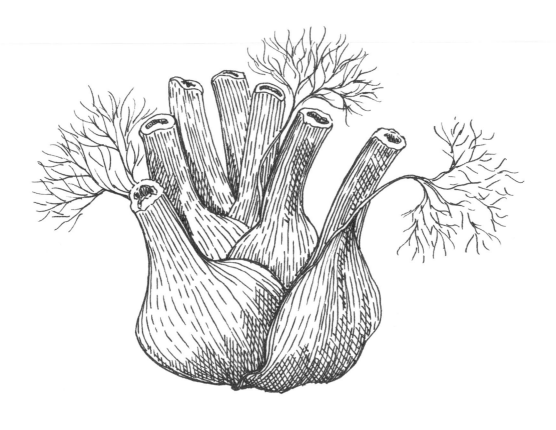

FENNEL

I<small>T MAY LOOK</small> like celery, taste like anise, and sound like "Pinocchio" in its native Italian, but the best thing about fennel is that it's not like anything else.

The proof? Walk over to your refrigerator crisper drawer in the middle of a day when you're tired of apples, and saltines, and leftover Brussels sprouts, and chocolate-chip cookies, and all the things you've been snacking on all afternoon. Snap off a crisp piece of fennel and bite into it. Everything's good about it: the crunch, the spicy smell, the satisfying sweetness. That's fennel: just what you wanted even when you didn't know you wanted it.

We in this country owe much to the Italians and their restaurants and produce shops for familiarizing us with Florentine fennel, the vegetable they call *finocchio*. They braise it and serve it anointed with olive oil and shaved Parmesan; they marinate it with seafood and vegetables; they cook it on the grill with fresh fish or sausages; they slice it raw for antipasto. The nineteenth-century writer Alexandre Dumas reports that in the Italy of his time, people often stuck "a head of fennel under one arm, munching it with bread for lunch or dinner." Another Italian custom of this time was described by the American consul in a letter to Thomas Jefferson: "It is eaten at dessert, crude, and with, or without dry salt, indeed I preferred it to every other vegetable, or to any fruit." Jefferson had also been introduced to fennel by his Monticello neighbor, Phillip Mazzei, a Florentine grape grower and expert on exotic plants.

Aside from Jefferson, perhaps only the Native Americans made much culinary use of fennel in our own country, consuming its seeds, leaves, and roots as well as its stems, which they ate raw like celery stalks. They also made a concoction with fennel and barley water, reputed to increase the flow of milk in nursing mothers. Not until the present century, with its increased Italian immigration, did a larger American audience develop for fennel.

Actually, fennel cultivation can be traced back to the Egyptians and to the Greeks, whose word for the vegetable, *marathon*, meaning "to grow thin," suggests the dietary use to which they put it. The famous Greek battle of Marathon was so called because the site was covered with fennel.

The French are fond of wrapping fish with fennel leaves or grilling fish over hot coals strewn with fennel stalks and using the leaves in bouquets garnis and courts bouillons for fish. Norwegians include it with other herbs and spices for pickling fish. Called "the fish herb," fennel has the effect of breaking down fats and aiding digestion.

High in protein, this low-calorie member of the carrot family can be prepared as a rich gratin or a garnish, as a salad or a dessert, and everything in between.

Market Selection: Fennel is sometimes known as finocchio and Florence or Florentine fennel, and is often confused with sweet anise. The bulbs should be white and firm, with crisp stalks and green feathery leaves.

Availability: October through April

Storage: Wrap in plastic bag or wrap, unwashed, and refrigerate for up to 1 week.

Flavor Enhancers: Garlic, parsley, basil, tomatoes

Equivalents: 1 medium bulb = 2 cups, chopped

Nutritional Value: Rich in vitamin A, calcium, and potassium
        30 calories per cup

Cooking and Handling Notes: Trim the root end of the bulb and the outer layer before cooking. Stalks should be discarded as they are tough and fibrous. Feathery leaves may be cooked or used as garnish.

Basic Cooking Methods: Cook in boiling salted water for about 7 minutes.
    Steam for 10 minutes.

Double Fennel and Carrot Bisque

3 tablespoons oil or butter

1 bunch green onions,
  chopped

1 fennel bulb, trimmed and
  chopped (reserve a sprig of
  leaves for garnish)

2 large carrots, peeled and
  chopped

2 tablespoons fennel seed

1 small potato, diced

4 cups chicken broth
  (page 343)

¼ cup heavy cream
  Salt and pepper

SERVES 6

In a medium saucepan, heat the oil. Sauté the onion, fennel, carrot, and fennel seed for about 5 minutes. Stir in the potato and chicken broth and bring to a boil. Reduce heat, cover, and simmer for 20 minutes.

Puree the mixture in a food processor with the cream. Reheat gently and season with salt and pepper. Garnish with a sprig of fennel leaves.

Fish Stew with Fennel

3 tablespoons olive oil
2 cloves garlic, minced
1 large onion, thinly sliced
2 fennel bulbs, trimmed and
    sliced
¼ cup chopped fresh parsley
    Finely grated zest of
    ½ lemon
½ teaspoon crushed red-
    pepper flakes
2 large tomatoes, seeded and
    chopped
1 teaspoon dried thyme
½ cup white wine or
    vermouth
1 cup fish stock (page 343)
    or clam broth
2 pounds assorted white-
    fleshed fish and shellfish
    Salt and pepper

SERVES 6

In a large sauté pan, heat the oil. Add the garlic, onion, and fennel; cook, covered, for 15 minutes, or until the vegetables are soft.

Stir in the parsley, lemon zest, pepper flakes, tomato, thyme, and wine. Bring to a boil and cook for about 5 minutes over high heat, or until the sauce thickens. Add the fish stock; bring to a boil, lower the heat, and simmer for 10 minutes.

Stir in the fish and cook over low heat for 5 minutes. Season with salt and pepper.

Fennel, Chicken, and Niçoise Olive Salad

1 large fennel bulb,
    trimmed, quartered, and
    thinly sliced
3 cups diced cooked chicken
1 cup Niçoise olives, pitted
½ cup chopped fresh chives

DRESSING

½ cup mayonnaise
    (homemade, page 346, or
    store-bought)
1 tablespoon Dijon mustard
1 tablespoon balsamic
    vinegar
½ cup sour cream or plain
    yogurt

1 head loose-leaf lettuce,
    torn into bite-size pieces

SERVES 6 AS A FIRST COURSE

Combine the fennel, chicken, olives, and chives in a mixing bowl. To make the dressing, combine the mayonnaise, mustard, vinegar, and sour cream. Toss with the fennel mixture and serve on lettuce.

Garlicky Fennel and Potato Gratin

3 large baking potatoes,
    peeled and diced
4 cloves garlic, peeled
2 large fennel bulbs,
    trimmed and sliced
4 tablespoons (½ stick)
    butter
½ cup chicken stock
    (page 343)
½ cup cottage cheese
    Salt and pepper
1 cup grated Gruyère cheese

Preheat the oven to 375°F. Grease a shallow 4-cup baking dish.

Cook the potato and garlic in salted boiling water for 15 minutes. While the potato is cooking, sauté the fennel in the butter for 5 minutes; add the stock and cook, covered, for 10 more minutes.

Drain the potato and garlic and place in a food processor with the fennel mixture and cottage cheese. Puree until smooth. Season with salt and pepper. Pour into the prepared baking dish and sprinkle with the Gruyère. Bake for 25 minutes, or until the top is golden-brown and bubbly.

SERVES 6

Smoked Salmon and Fennel Risotto

4 tablespoons (½ stick)
    butter
1 small onion, chopped
2 medium fennel bulbs,
    trimmed and chopped,
    fronds reserved
2 cups Arborio rice
5 to 6 cups simmering
    chicken stock (page 343)
3 ounces smoked salmon,
    cut into narrow strips
    Salt and pepper

In a large skillet, heat the butter. Sauté the onion and fennel over medium heat for 10 minutes.

Add the rice and stir to coat well with butter. Add the hot broth a ladleful at a time; stir until it is absorbed by the rice before adding the next ladleful. Continue until most of the broth has been added and the rice is just tender but not mushy.

Add the smoked salmon and cook for another minute. Season with salt and pepper and garnish with fennel fronds.

SERVES 6

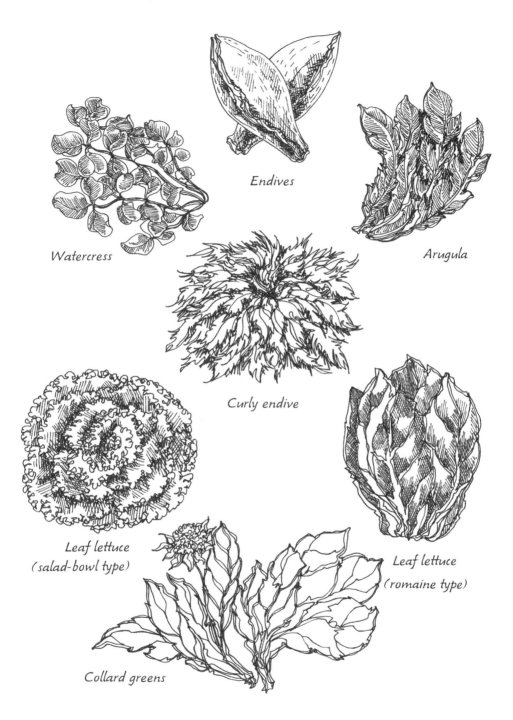

Endives

Watercress

Arugula

Curly endive

Leaf lettuce
(salad-bowl type)

Leaf lettuce
(romaine type)

Collard greens

GREENS

JUST A FEW YEARS AGO, the idea of eating greens—as in "mess o' greens"—signaled either an attempt at authentic Southern cooking or a radical-chic dinner party. The grocer at your corner supermarket could be counted on to look at you blankly, if not suspiciously, if you asked for collard, dandelion, or mustard greens, which were appreciated as weeds nobody would ever eat unless he had to. As for beet greens, if the store hadn't already disposed of them by the time you got through the checkout counter, you were instructed by most recipes to discard them yourself, except for an inch of stalk left on while cooking the "real" vegetable, the beets themselves.

Salad greens were viewed with a similarly narrow perspective. Iceberg, romaine—who could ask for anything more? A million American restaurants were able to take a million heads of lettuce, toss them with a million tablespoons of Thousand Island dressing, and come up, against all mathematical odds, with the same yawn-provoking salad. Could a million American restaurants be wrong?

Now, of course, the opinions have become a lot greener on every side. Salad greens are considered "light," which is the magic word of the day, guaranteeing success for everything from beer to mayonnaise. "Let them eat light," proclaimed the chefs and restaurateurs, the delis and gourmet groceries, thereupon devising green dishes that people could order with an almost aerobic lack of guilt.

Once in the throes of this enlightenment, those of us who really wanted our grilled ham and cheese on rye could change, ever so slightly, to warm curly endive with baked goat cheese, prosciutto, and garlicky croutons. Psychologically, dishes made with greens appeal to other contemporary inclinations as well: they are associated with newness, freshness, youth (what could be younger than a baby butter lettuce?); they are usually personal, made-for-the-moment dishes, individually prepared. And they are perfect for people who have little time to cook.

So it is no wonder that a certain craziness has crept into the country's produce departments. In the "greens" areas at farmers' markets or grocery stores, we may find ourselves lost in a confusion of leaves, both curly and smooth, green, yellow, and red. Easy-to-buy salad mixes do the choosing for us, but at prices that seem most unvegetable-like. It's nice to know, therefore, that all this foliage is pretty much interchangeable once you have decided whether you want cooking greens or salad greens. This chapter offers some guidance to mixing and balancing flavors and textures, from bitter to bland, spicy to nutty.

Consumer and Cooking Guide: Greens

Market Selection: The most common salad greens are lettuces, of which there are four basic varieties. The loose-leaf variety takes its name from the way it grows—from the stem, rather than forming a compact head. Oak-leaf, red-leaf, and green-leaf lettuce are in this category. Crisphead lettuces, such as iceberg, are large, compact, and crisp. Butterhead lettuces, such as Bibb (also called limestone) and Boston, have very soft leaves that are almost buttery in texture. Romaine lettuce (also known as Cos lettuce) is elongated and has crunchy leaves.

Chicory, escarole, Belgian endive, frisee, Lolla Rossa, and radicchio are all members of the endive family and have a slightly bitter taste. Arugula and watercress are small-leaved bunches that have a peppery taste. Mesclun, mache, and Mizuna are good choices for additional texture and taste. All greens should be crisp and fresh-looking, free of brown spots or decay.

Common cooking greens are beet greens, collards, mustard greens, turnip greens, and kale. Known for a tart, tangy flavor, they can be tossed in a salad, raw, but cooking them in soups, stews, or sautés pleasantly mellows their taste. Leaves should be deep green and free of blemishes.

Availability: Most greens are available year-round. The endive family's peak season is September through December. The peak season for cooking greens is winter through early spring.

Storage: Wrap, unwashed, in paper towels, then in plastic bag or wrap, and refrigerate for up to 5 days.

Flavor Enhancers: See "Salad Bar."

Nutritional Value: Good source of vitamins A and C and calcium

      20 to 30 calories per cup

Cooking and Handling Notes: All greens should be cleaned of grit just before using. Fill a large bowl with cold water and 2 tablespoons of vinegar. Swirl the greens in the water; remove and dry. (Grit will sink to the bottom of the bowl.) If salad greens are not properly dried, dressing will not adhere to the leaves. A spin-type salad dryer makes fast and easy work of this task.

Basic Cooking Methods: Wash greens and place them in a shallow saucepan with only the water that is clinging to the leaves. Cook, covered, over medium heat for about 3 minutes, or until the greens begin to wilt.

Steam for 3 minutes.

SALAD BAR

The following greens combine especially well with the foods listed after their names:

Arugula: butter lettuces, citrus fruits, berries, smoked meats. Dress with basic vinaigrette and garnish with toasted walnuts.

Belgian endive: watercress, apples, pears. Dress with creamy vinaigrette and garnish with a blue cheese.

Butterhead lettuces: arugula or watercress. Dress with mustard vinaigrette and garnish with chopped chives.

Chicory: radicchio, loose-leaf lettuces, citrus fruits. Dress with garlic vinaigrette and garnish with crumbled bacon or croutons.

Escarole: frisee, romaine. Dress with mustard-garlic vinaigrette and garnish with croutons.

Iceberg: butterhead, romaine, and loose-leaf lettuce, shrimp, crab, chicken. Dress with yogurt dressing or a creamy citrus dressing.

Loose-leaf lettuce: arugula, watercress, endive, red onions. Dress with herbed vinaigrette and garnish with toasted pine nuts or crumbled goat cheese.

Radicchio: butterhead and loose-leaf lettuces, smoked meats, Gorgonzola cheese. Dress with mustard-garlic vinaigrette and garnish with chopped fresh herbs.

Romaine: butterhead; or use alone with citrus fruits, spicy cooked sausage, anchovies. Dress with herbed garlic vinaigrette.

Watercress: butterhead, loose-leaf, romaine, endive, shrimp, and sweet cherry tomatoes. Dress with any vinaigrette and garnish with chopped chives.

DRESSINGS

Basic Vinaigrette
Combine ½ teaspoon each salt and pepper with 3 tablespoons red-wine
  vinegar and ½ cup olive oil until well blended.

Mustard-Garlic Vinaigrette
Combine ½ teaspoon each salt and pepper, 1 clove crushed garlic, 2
  tablespoons red-wine vinegar, and ½ cup olive oil until well blended.

Honey-Mustard Dressing
Combine 1 tablespoon honey, 1 tablespoon mustard, ½ teaspoon each salt
  and pepper, 2 tablespoons white-wine vinegar, 1 teaspoon lemon juice, and
  ½ cup olive oil until well blended.

Tomato-Basil Vinaigrette
In a food processor, combine 3 oil-packed sun-dried tomatoes, ¼ cup fresh
  basil leaves, 1 clove garlic, 1 tablespoon grated Parmesan, 3 tablespoons
  red-wine or balsamic vinegar, and ½ cup olive oil until smooth.

Low-Fat Yogurt Dressing
Combine ½ cup low- or nonfat yogurt, 1 tablespoon oil, 2 tablespoons hot-
  sweet mustard, 1 teaspoon lemon juice, and ½ teaspoon each salt and
  pepper.

Variations: A tablespoon or two of chopped fresh herbs may be added to any
  of these dressings. Toasted poppy seeds, sesame seeds, or sunflower seeds
  make an interesting addition to a vinaigrette. Substituting fruit vinegars for
  the wine vinegars can lead to dressings that go especially well over bitter
  greens.

Creamy Lemon Dressing
Combine ½ teaspoon each salt and pepper, 2 tablespoons heavy cream, 2
  tablespoons fresh lemon juice, 2 tablespoons white-wine vinegar, and ½
  cup vegetable oil until well blended.

Oriental Dressing
Combine 1 tablespoon sugar, 2 tablespoons soy sauce, 3 tablespoons red-wine
  vinegar, 3 tablespoons sesame oil, and 6 tablespoons peanut or vegetable
  oil until well blended.

Fusilli with Mustard Greens and Spicy Sausage

1 pound hot Italian sausage

1 red onion, chopped

1 small red bell pepper,
  chopped

2 pounds mustard greens,
  stems removed and
  coarsely chopped

½ pound freshly cooked
  fusilli (corkscrew pasta),
  drained

2 tablespoons olive oil

¼ cup grated Parmesan

**SERVES 4 AS A FIRST
COURSE OR 2 AS A MAIN
COURSE**

Prick the sausage and brown it well on all sides in a large skillet. Remove and reserve.

In the same skillet, cook the onion and pepper until wilted, about 5 minutes. Add the greens (in several batches, if necessary) and cook until wilted. Slice the sausage and stir into the greens. Cook another 5 minutes.

Toss the pasta with the oil and then with the greens mixture. Sprinkle with cheese and serve.

Beet Greens with Ricotta and Mushrooms

3 tablespoons oil

2 cloves garlic, minced

1 pound button mushrooms,
  quartered

2 pounds beet greens,
  chopped

½ cup ricotta cheese

½ cup grated Parmesan

2 eggs, lightly beaten

½ teaspoon salt

¼ teaspoon freshly ground
  pepper

SERVES 6

Preheat the oven to 375°F. Butter a shallow 2-quart baking dish.

In a large skillet, heat the oil. Sauté the garlic and mushrooms for about 3 minutes. Add the beet greens and cook until wilted, about 3 minutes.

Remove the pan from the heat and stir in the cheeses, eggs, salt, and pepper. Pour into the prepared dish and bake for about 30 minutes, or until bubbly and golden.

GREEN BEANS

"THE THREE SISTERS OF LIFE"—that's what the Native Americans called their trio of essential vegetables: beans, corn, and squash. Green beans are an old New World food, known in Mexico for some 7,000 years before the arrival of the conquistadors. The first European to see them growing may well have been Christopher Columbus. When the green bean was brought back to Europe, it was instantly accepted because of its similarity to an existing vegetable, the broad bean. Green beans were also welcome because they resembled asparagus and could be prepared similarly. In fact, one seventeenth-century dictionary writer, Randle Cotgrave, called them *'sperage beans.* In Tuscany, the green bean's popularity won the Tuscans the nickname *mangia fagioli,* or "bean eaters."

The word *haricot,* which originally referred to the newly arrived green bean, is clearly French, but it is actually a corruption of the Aztec word *ayacotl.* The connection with Native Americans is perpetuated in the names of bean varieties such as Hopi String Bean and Cherokee Trail of Tears.

Now enjoying near-universal popularity, fresh green beans are the main ingredient in many of the world's favorite dishes. German cooks make *blind Huhn* (blind hen), a savory combination of apples, carrots, bacon, and beans. A Bulgarian moussaka, called *mussakes selen fassul,* substitutes fresh beans and other vegetables for the eggplant and a yogurt mixture for the béchamel. Italians and Cajuns stew green beans a long time, smothered with onions and other vegetables; by contrast, beans prepared al dente, adorned with the pods and leaves of nasturtiums, come to us, not from the hot chef of the moment but from the eighteenth-century Shakers. Another delightful dish requires only a simple tossing of green beans with butter and savory, known as the "bean herb." Beans are also excellent pickled, a favorite treatment in Pennsylvania Dutch country.

Phaseolus vulgaris is the Latin name for the green bean plant. (*Phaseolus* means "boat" and refers to the pod that carries the beans.) Today's growers have developed different varieties depending on whether the vegetable is to be consumed fresh or grown to maturity and then dried. Several types of fresh and dried beans are often combined in salads and vegetable dishes for an interesting contrast of tastes and textures. Today's popular varieties include thin, round Blue Lakes and the flatter Kentucky Wonders, also called Old Homesteads; both have actually been around since the mid-1800s. Other choices include Italians or Romanos, those broad, flat, meaty beans that are either green or yellow, and another Italian coiled type, the green *anellini.* There is the slender *haricot vert* and the unusual purple beans called Royal burgundy, which are most interesting when served raw in salads, especially since they turn a more ordinary green when cooked. Finally, there are yellow wax beans and any number of varietals referred to as snap, string, or simply green beans. Although many people still call the vegetable "string beans," stringlessness has been bred into most of today's varieties.

CONSUMER AND COOKING GUIDE: Green Beans

Market Selection: Kentucky Wonder and Blue Lake are the most common varieties. Yellow wax, Romano, and Chinese long beans have recently been making more frequent appearances on the greengrocer's shelf. All types should be crisp, unblemished, and bright in color.

Availability: Year-round; peak—May through August

Storage: Will keep for about 4 days, wrapped in plastic bag or wrap, and refrigerated.

Flavor Enhancers: Dill, garlic, cumin, tarragon

Equivalents: 1 pound = about 4 cups

Nutritional Value: Good source of vitamin A and potassium
40 calories per cup

Basic Cooking Methods: Cook in boiling salted water for 4 minutes.
Steam for 5 minutes.

Green Bean and Barley Soup

3 tablespoons oil or butter
1 medium onion, chopped
2 stalks celery, chopped
1 red bell pepper, chopped
1 medium tomato, seeded
  and chopped
4 cups chicken stock
  (page 343)
1 cup barley
½ pound green beans, cut
  into 2-inch lengths
½ pound yellow beans, cut
  into 2-inch lengths
3 tablespoons fresh dill
  Salt and pepper

SERVES 6 TO 8

In a large pot, heat the oil. Sauté the onion, celery, pepper, and tomato for about 5 minutes. Add the stock and 2 cups water and bring to a boil. Add the barley, lower the heat, and simmer, covered, for 30 minutes.

Add the beans and dill and cook for 10 minutes. Season with salt and pepper and serve.

Green Bean–Walnut Pâté

4 tablespoons oil
1 large onion, chopped
½ cup walnuts
¼ teaspoon cayenne
1 hard-boiled egg, cut up
1 pound green beans, cooked
  until tender and cooled
2 tablespoons fresh lemon
  juice
2 tablespoons chopped fresh
  dill
  Salt and pepper

MAKES ABOUT 1½ CUPS

In a medium skillet, heat 2 tablespoons of the oil. Sauté the onion until it is golden in color. Add the walnuts and cook for another 2 minutes. Stir in the cayenne.

Place the onion-walnut mixture in a food processor with the egg, beans, lemon juice, and remaining 2 tablespoons of oil. Process until almost smooth. Stir in the dill. Taste for salt and pepper. Spoon into a crock and serve with bread or crackers.

Green and Yellow Bean Salad with Smoked Mozzarella

1 pound green beans, cut
    into 2-inch lengths
1 pound yellow wax beans,
    cut into 2-inch lengths
¼ pound smoked mozzarella,
    cut into ½-inch cubes
1 large ripe tomato, seeded
    and diced

DRESSING

1 clove garlic, minced
1 teaspoon Dijon mustard
3 tablespoons balsamic
    vinegar
1 tablespoon chopped fresh
    tarragon or ½ teaspoon
    dried
⅓ cup olive oil
    Salt and pepper

SERVES 6

Cook the beans in boiling salted water for about 2½ minutes. Refresh them under cold water and drain. In a large bowl, combine the beans with the cheese and tomato.

Whisk the dressing ingredients until well combined. Toss with the bean mixture and season with salt and pepper.

Sautéed Green Beans with Garlic, Sage, and Pancetta

¼ pound pancetta, diced or
    chopped
1 clove garlic, chopped
1 pound green beans, cooked
    until tender and drained
3 fresh sage leaves or 1
    teaspoon dried
    Salt and pepper

SERVES 4

In a large skillet, cook the pancetta until most of the fat is rendered. Add the garlic and beans and cook, stirring, for about 3 minutes. Add the sage and season with salt and pepper.

Green Beans with Garlic and Prawns

3 tablespoons vegetable oil
½ pound prawns, shelled and
  deveined
3 cloves garlic, minced
1 slice fresh ginger, minced
1 pound green beans, cut
  into 2-inch lengths
4 teaspoons soy sauce
1 teaspoon sugar
1 tablespoon dry sherry
2 tablespoons toasted sesame
  seeds (page 347)

SERVES 4

In a large skillet, heat the oil. Sauté the prawns until they are pink; remove them from the skillet and reserve. Add the garlic, ginger, and green beans to the same skillet. Cook, stirring, for about 2 minutes.

Combine the soy sauce, sugar, and sherry and add to the skillet. Cover and cook for about 5 minutes; add the prawns. Cook for another minute; sprinkle with sesame seeds and serve.

JERUSALEM ARTICHOKES (SUNCHOKES)

LIKE MOST FOODS, Jerusalem artichokes taste especially good when the alternative is starvation. This simple truth may explain their unbridled popularity with the members of the Lewis and Clark expedition, who, in the early 1800s, devoured Jerusalem artichokes with an appreciation that the vegetable has seldom generated since. Indeed, some people have never even heard of, or tasted, this crunchy root of the sunflower, and others are somewhat put off by its exotic name and appearance. And yet, Jerusalem artichokes are actually native to North America, one of the few vegetables, along with potatoes, tomatoes, and peppers, to originate in the New World.

Part of their unusual name can probably be traced to Samuel de Champlain, who first discovered the vegetables on Cape Cod, where they were being cultivated by the Abenaki Indians. He described them as "roots . . . which have the taste of artichokes." The city of Jerusalem had nothing to do with any of these New World peregrinations but somehow got mixed up in the naming process, possibly as a corruption of some other word, though no one is quite sure which. The theory that *Jerusalem* is a mispronunciation of *girasol*, or "sunflower," has been adequately challenged in Harold McGee's *The Curious Cook*, which contains an entire chapter on the subject. McGee credits the theory that the vegetables were originally called "Terneuzen artichoke," for the Dutch town that grew them commercially after their arrival from the New World.

At any rate, by now perhaps no vegetable has prompted more activity in the area of vegetable naming. If you don't like Jerusalem artichokes, you can eat whichever you choose: sunchokes, French *topinambours*, Italian *tartufi bianchi* (white truffles), Canadian potatoes, or Algonquin *kaishucpenauks*.

As for their appearance, they are no less promising than a sack of potatoes, or a gnarled-up mass of ginger root, or a pile of dusty-looking kiwis. The problems with Jerusalem artichokes (there are two) are more basic than any of these externals. Eating Jerusalem artichokes often results in stomach cramps caused by their undigestible carbohydrates. They also darken with cooking because of their high iron content. A solution to both problems, recently promulgated in McGee's book, is to give the tuber a preliminary fifteen-minute boil in acidulated water. The skin can then be easily removed, and the vegetable will be ready for marinating, pickling, deep-frying, roasting, or slicing into soups and salads.

Although there is nothing particularly new about Jerusalem artichokes, very few cookbooks include recipes for or information about them. An exception, strangely enough, is Amelia Simmons' *American Cookery*, the first American cookbook, published in 1796. It said: "Artichokes: The Jerusalem is best."

CONSUMER AND COOKING GUIDE: Jerusalem Artichokes

Market Selection: Jerusalem artichokes should be firm and crisp-looking.
Availability: October through March
Storage: Use as soon as possible. May be refrigerated, unwashed, in a plastic bag for up to 3 days.
Equivalents: 1 pound = 2 cups, sliced
Nutritional Value: Good source of vitamin B and iron
        20 calories per cup
Cooking and Handling Notes: If not using immediately after peeling, submerge in acidulated water until ready to use, to prevent discoloration. Boiling in acidulated water (unpeeled) for 15 minutes will remove some of the unpleasant gases and also retain the color.
Basic Cooking Methods: See individual recipes.

Sunchoke Soup with Chilies and Corn

3 tablespoons oil
1 medium onion, chopped
2 jalapeño peppers, seeded
 and chopped
1 teaspoon ground cumin
1 pound Jerusalem
 artichokes, peeled and
 sliced
5 cups chicken broth
 (page 343)
¼ cup cream
2 cups corn kernels
 Salt and pepper
1 small red bell pepper,
 diced, for garnish

In a saucepan, heat the oil. Cook the onion and jalapeño until soft. Stir in the cumin. Add the artichoke and chicken broth and bring to a boil. Reduce the heat and simmer, partially covered, for about 25 minutes.

Puree the mixture in a food processor or blender until smooth. Stir in the cream and corn and cook gently for 5 minutes. Season with salt and pepper. Serve garnished with diced red pepper.

SERVES 6

Sunchoke and Shallot Puree

1 pound sunchokes, peeled
 and sliced
1 potato, peeled and diced
3 shallots, peeled and halved
1 clove garlic, peeled and
 halved
2 tablespoons butter
2 tablespoons cream or
 whole milk
1 teaspoon fresh lemon juice
 Salt and pepper

Bring a large pot of water to a boil. Add the sunchoke, potato, shallot, and garlic. Reduce the heat and simmer, partially covered, for 30 minutes. Drain in a colander, being careful not to lose the shallots and garlic.

Place the vegetables in a food processor with the remaining ingredients and puree until smooth. Season with salt and pepper; serve hot.

SERVES 6

Sunchoke and Carrot Slaw with Dill

1 pound sunchokes, peeled
   and shredded
1 pound carrots, peeled and
   shredded
1 bunch green onions, cut
   into julienne
½ cup mayonnaise
1 tablespoon fresh lemon
   juice
1 tablespoon mild mustard
2 tablespoons chopped fresh
   dill
¼ cup plain yogurt or sour
   cream
   Salt and pepper

SERVES 6

In a large bowl, combine the sunchoke, carrot, and green onion. Mix the remaining ingredients until well blended and toss with the sunchoke mixture. Season with salt and pepper.

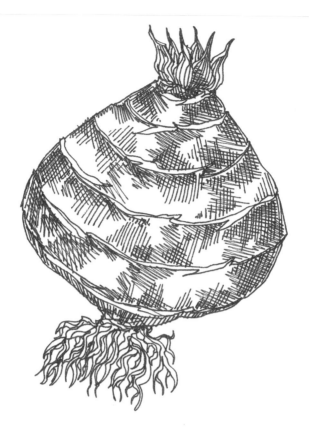

JÍCAMA

"A STRANGER . . . in the produce section." These are the words that cookbook author Laurel Robertson used to describe a lumpy, odd-looking creature she discovered one day at the grocery store. Although it appeared about as promising as a dusty old stone, she followed her instincts and brought the inert-looking blob home for dinner. If she hadn't, she concludes her happy tale, she would "never have met the jícama."

For those who still haven't met the jícama (pronounced *he*-come-a), it is a vegetable humble, if not homely, in appearance. For some reason it is never described for itself but is always compared to something else: a deflated turnip or an oversized rutabaga or a jowly potato. It doesn't even get much credit for its own crisp, just-sweet-enough taste, which is also usually likened to that of other vegetables. Use it like water chestnuts, some say, or grate it as a passable substitute for daikon. It is also characterized as a cross between an apple and a potato.

And yet nothing is quite like the jícama, a member of the morning-glory family that hails from Mexico and South America. A cousin of the sweet potato, this underground tuber comes in two types: *agua* (watery juice) and *leche* (milky juice). Like the hot pretzels on the sidewalks of New York, jícama is street food in its native habitat, sold with a squeeze of lime and a shake of fiery chili powder.

Also called the yam bean root, jícama ranges in weight from a few ounces to 6 pounds. Its crispy white flesh is hidden under a fibrous dust-brown skin, which must be completely stripped off. Like potatoes, jícamas can be steamed, baked, boiled, mashed, or fried; unlike potatoes, however, they can also be eaten raw. Sliced into wide sticks, jícama makes a crunchy carrier for guacamole and highly seasoned salsas and dips. Cut up into squares, it enhances fresh fruit salad, absorbing and reflecting surrounding flavors. It is equally versatile as a cooked vegetable—sautéed with carrots or green beans, stir-fried with chicken or shrimp, or simmered in curries and savory stews. Low in starch and calories, jícama is satisfying, flavorful, and nowhere near as strange as it looks.

CONSUMER AND COOKING GUIDE: Jícama

Market Selection: Choose medium-size jícamas with smooth, unblemished skins.
Availability: Year-round
Storage: Store in a cool dry place, uncovered, for up to 3 weeks. Cut pieces may be wrapped in plastic bag or wrap, and stored in the refrigerator for up to a week.
Flavor Enhancers: Hot pepper, citrus juices
Equivalents: 1 medium jícama = 2 cups, cubed
Nutritional Value: Good source of potassium and vitamin C
      50 calories per cup
Cooking and Handling Notes: Rub a cut lemon or lime on the cut surface of jícama to maintain whiteness.
Basic Cooking Methods: See individual recipes.

Jícama and Watercress Salad with Fried Pancetta

¼ pound pancetta, diced
1 small jícama, peeled and
   cut into matchsticks
2 tablespoons fresh lime
   juice
1 teaspoon salt
1 teaspoon crushed red-
   pepper flakes
2 bunches watercress, stems
   removed
½ cup olive oil
¼ cup sherry vinegar
1 clove garlic, minced
1 teaspoon Dijon mustard

SERVES 6

In a small skillet, cook the pancetta until golden-brown and crisp. Drain on paper towels and set aside.

Place the jícama in a shallow bowl and sprinkle with the lime juice, salt, and red-pepper flakes. Let marinate for 30 minutes. In a serving bowl, toss the jícama with the watercress.

To make the dressing, combine the oil, vinegar, garlic, and mustard until smooth. Toss with the jícama mixture and sprinkle with pancetta.

Beef, Snow Pea, and Jícama Salad

One 2-pound flank steak,
   cooked and sliced into
   strips
½ pound snow peas,
   blanched and drained
1 small jícama, peeled and
   cut into matchsticks
¼ cup fresh lemon juice
3 tablespoons soy sauce
2 tablespoons vegetable oil
1 tablespoon sesame oil
1 tablespoon grated fresh
   ginger
Salt and pepper

SERVES 6

In a large bowl, toss the flank steak with the snow peas and jícama. Combine the remaining ingredients until well blended and toss with the jícama mixture.

Grilled Jícama

1 medium jícama, peeled,
  quartered, and cut into
  ¼-inch-thick slices
Olive oil
Fresh lime juice

SERVES 4 TO 6

Preheat the grill.

Brush both sides of the jícama slices with a small amount of olive oil. Place them on the hot grill and cook for about 1 minute per side. Remove from the heat and sprinkle with lime juice.

Jícama, Shiitake, and Scallop Stir-Fry

1 teaspoon balsamic vinegar
2 teaspoons sesame oil
1 pound bay scallops or sea
  scallops (if using sea
  scallops, cut them in half)
2 tablespoons vegetable or
  peanut oil
2 cloves garlic, minced
1 tablespoon minced fresh
  ginger
¼ teaspoon crushed red-
  pepper flakes
¼ pound shiitake
  mushrooms, stemmed,
  caps cut into strips
½ medium jícama, peeled
  and cut into matchsticks
2 green onions, thinly sliced
¼ cup chicken stock (page
  343) or water

SERVES 4

Sprinkle the vinegar and sesame oil over the scallops and let them marinate for about 30 minutes.

In a wok, heat the vegetable oil. Cook the garlic, ginger, and pepper flakes for about 30 seconds. Add the mushrooms and jícama and stir-fry for 2 minutes. Add the scallops and green onion and stir-fry for 2 more minutes. Stir in the stock and cook for 2 more minutes. Serve immediately.

MUSHROOMS

"NOT BEING AMBITIOUS of martyrdom, even in the cause of gastronomical enterprise, especially if the instrument is to be a contemptible, rank-smelling fungus, I never eat or cook mushrooms."

So wrote Marion Harland in her 1873 classic, *Common Sense in the Household: A Manual of Practical Housewifery*. At the time she was writing, Mrs. Harland did not have the option of selecting her wild mushrooms from several contiguous baskets at the produce market. Instead, she had to trust the mushroom gatherer, have confidence in her own judgment, and take certain precautions against the possibility of poisonous varieties. Boil mushrooms with a white onion and stir them with a silver spoon, she cautioned; if the onions turn black or the spoon darkens, throw everything away "and be properly thankful for your escape." Though she offers several recipes, she remains suspicious, insisting that the poisonous types "sport all colors and are usually far prettier than their virtuous kindred."

Even such an appreciative mushroom fancier as Alexandre Dumas, who early in the nineteenth century had praised *cèpes* for their "warm and aphrodisiac . . . effects" and extolled morels for stimulating the appetite, fortifying and restoring the stomach, and being "very useful in sauces," often had second thoughts. "I confess," he wrote with a regretful tone, "that nothing frightens me more than the appearance of mushrooms on the table, especially in a small provincial town."

The safety issue was Mrs. Rorer's concern when she wrote, in her 1886 cookbook, "It is always safe to use the canned mushrooms, which are convenient and cheap, but tough and indigestible. . . . It is said that one poisonous mushroom among a pint of good ones will turn a silver spoon black, if stirred with it while they are stewing; this, however, is not true." Fannie Farmer, in her 1909 edition, seems more adventurous than usual when she urges that, since mushrooms "grow about us abundantly," they therefore "should often be found on the table."

These days, as we approach the twenty-first century, the basic nature of mushrooms hasn't changed—the poisonous characters are as deadly poisonous as ever; what *has* changed is the basic nature of marketing mushrooms. The ones that make it into the contiguous baskets have been preapproved and have passed scrupulous inspections. They are often, however, mislabeled, though nothing tragic will ensue should one be substituted for another in the myriad preparations that await them.

Bisques, stir-fries, sauces, soufflés, soubises, purees, duxelles, stuffings, pickles, raw salads—infinity must be the final number for mushroom dishes. Alice B. Toklas even made sandwiches out of them, while Americans in the nineteenth century enjoyed a popular concoction called "mushroom catsup." Practically nothing is the best thing to do to most types, such as the fleshy fresh morels with their spongy honeycomb caps, so adept at sucking in the garlicky butter of a quick sauté. Matsutake mushrooms, named for the Japanese pine tree *(matsu)* near which they grow, are at their aromatic best in slow-cooked stews and soups. Just a bit of cream heightens the flavors in Martha Washington's recipe "To Dress a Dish of Mushrumps."

Not everyone is so minimalist, however. The 1909 *Fannie Farmer* suggests that mushrooms be served under a bell-shaped glass cover "which may be bought at first-class kitchen furnishers." Even more foreplay is required in Pierre Blot's 1867 *Handbook of Practical Cookery*, which suggests that "you may make, with common white note-paper, as many little square boxes as you have mushrooms to broil; grease them with butter, put the mushrooms in, set them on the gridiron, and on a moderate fire, and serve them in the boxes when done.''

Some varieties, like shaggy manes and beefsteak mushrooms, have been likened to meat, while oyster mushrooms are prized for their resemblance to fish or seafood. There is even something called a chicken mushroom, named for obvious reasons.

Mushrooms are often the mysterious ingredient in stories and folktales as well as in recipes. They stand accused in the deaths of such eminent personages as the real Emperor Claudius and the fictional Trimalchio, the central and symbolic character of Petronius' satire on the excesses of Roman life. By the Middle Ages their toxic qualities were harnessed into an effective fly killer. Fame at the box office came with the starring role in Andy Warhol's *Eat,* a forty-five-minute movie of a man eating a mushroom.

Mushrooms are an ancient food, some varieties traceable to the Stone Age. They were the food of the Pharaohs in ancient Egypt, and they remained the food of the rich throughout nineteenth-century France. For all their haughty associations, mushrooms are a most primitive plant—a fungus, as are molds and yeasts. Not really a vegetable, they are incapable of photosynthesis for sustenance, but rather derive nourishment from feeding on other organisms. Some varieties are successfully cultivated in caves; in underground quarry tunnels, as in seventeenth-century France; and in abandoned limestone mines, as in present-day Pennsylvania.

Those who insist on foraging for mushrooms in the wild should join mycological societies or enlist the companionship of an expert when deciding on edible specimens. They would also be wise to read Jane Grigson, who lived in a cave herself and offers any mushroom lover a wealth of information in *The Mushroom Feast.* Her most poignant advice about mushroom hunting, however, is gleaned from a private letter that she wrote in 1975 to M. F. K. Fisher: ''Perhaps a gift for finding mushrooms is like a gift for music— sometimes it skips a generation or two and then bobs up again.''

With almost 40,000 varieties of mushrooms in existence, no marketplace is likely to adequately reflect the supply. In downtown Barcelona's Boquería Market, however, the mushroom man always displays with pride one of the world's most incredible arrays. Called the king of the mushrooms, Señor Petras can explain everything in his stand, which he calls Fruits del Bosc (the fruits of the woods). During a recent visit, Señor Petras was extolling the virtues of some particularly magnificent, exotic-looking morels. *"Son extraordinarias!"* he said with a characteristic Catalan pride that prompted the question "Where are they from?"

"Oregon," he answered with a shrug, as if he couldn't quite believe it himself.

CONSUMER AND COOKING GUIDE: Mushrooms

Market Selection: Button or cultivated, chanterelle, enoki, morel, oyster, and shiitake are the most common varieties. All should be blemish free, with no signs of decay.

Availability: Year-round

Storage: Wrap in paper towels and then in plastic bag or wrap, and refrigerate for up to 5 days. To dry mushrooms for soups or sauces, place them directly in a paper bag and refrigerate for 2 to 4 weeks.

Flavor Enhancers: Tarragon, parsley, dill, coriander

Equivalents: 1 pound = 4 cups, sliced
       1 pound = 3 cups, chopped

Nutritional Value: Good source of potassium
       20 calories per cup

Cooking and Handling Notes: Because most varieties have such a high water content, mushrooms should be cooked over medium or medium-high heat until they are just brown, to develop a deep mushroom flavor.

Chanterelles, morels, shiitake, and porcini can be found in dried form. Their flavor is intense—a little goes a long way. These dried mushrooms should be soaked in hot water until soft and rinsed of grit and sand before being added to a dish.

Basic Cooking Methods: See individual recipes.

Enoki Mushrooms in Mushroom Broth

2 tablespoons butter
1 onion, chopped
1 clove garlic, minced
2 pounds button
  mushrooms, chopped
½ pound shiitake
  mushrooms, chopped
1 large tomato, seeded and
  chopped
1 teaspoon fresh thyme or
  ½ teaspoon dried
  Salt and pepper
2 packages enoki mushrooms

In a large pot, heat the butter. Cook the onion, garlic, button and shiitake mushrooms, and tomato for about 10 minutes. Stir in the thyme and 6 cups of water. Bring to a boil, reduce heat, and simmer for 30 minutes.

Pass the mixture through a food mill to extract all the flavor. Return to the pot and season with salt and pepper. Cut the root ends from the enoki mushrooms and add to the broth. Reheat for 5 minutes and serve.

SERVES 6

Crisp Veal and Oyster Mushroom Salad

2 tablespoons butter
2 tablespoons oil
¼ pound veal cut from the
  leg, cut into ½-inch-wide,
  ¼-inch-thick strips
  Salt and pepper
  Flour for dredging
1 pound oyster mushrooms,
  cut into strips
1 teaspoon chopped sage
¼ teaspoon crushed red-
  pepper flakes
3 tablespoons balsamic
  vinegar
2 cups mixed greens

In a medium skillet, heat the butter and oil. Sprinkle the veal with salt and pepper and dredge in flour. Cook the veal until browned on both sides. Remove and reserve.

In the same pan, cook the mushrooms with the sage and pepper flakes for about 5 minutes. Add to the veal. Pour the vinegar into the skillet and bring to a boil. Toss the greens with the veal and mushrooms and dress with warm vinegar.

SERVES 6

Poached Sole with Chanterelle Sauce

6 large sole fillets
  Salt and pepper
6 fresh dill sprigs
1 tablespoon butter
½ cup dry white wine

SAUCE

6 tablespoons (¾ stick)
  butter
2 tablespoons chopped
  shallot
½ pound chanterelles, sliced
3 tablespoons heavy cream
  Salt and pepper

SERVES 6

Preheat the oven to 375°F.

Blot the fish dry and sprinkle with salt and pepper. Place a dill sprig on each fillet and fold the fillets in half, skin-sides in, point to point. Butter a shallow baking dish that will hold the fish in one layer. Place the fish in the dish and pour in the wine. Cover with foil and bake in the preheated oven for 15 minutes.

In a skillet, heat the butter. Cook the shallot until soft; add the chanterelles. Cook over high heat for about 5 minutes. Add the liquid from the poached fish and cook until most of the liquid has evaporated. Add the cream and cook for 2 more minutes. Season with salt and pepper and pour over the fish.

Chicken Sauté with Mushrooms and Carrots

4 tablespoons (½ stick)
  butter
½ pound button mushrooms,
  coarsely chopped
1 large chicken, cut into
  serving pieces
  Salt and pepper
2 cloves garlic, minced
¼ cup sherry vinegar
½ cup chicken stock (page 343)
2 carrots, peeled and diced
1 tablespoon fresh dill
2 tablespoons heavy cream
  Chopped watercress for
  garnish

SERVES 4 TO 6

In a large skillet, heat 2 tablespoons of the butter. Cook the mushrooms over high heat until they are brown. Remove and reserve.

Add the remaining 2 tablespoons of butter to the skillet. Sprinkle the chicken pieces with salt and pepper and add them to the skillet. Cook until brown on all sides. Remove and reserve.

Add the garlic to the pan and cook for about 1 minute. Pour in the vinegar and reduce until it just glazes the bottom of the pan. Return the chicken and accumulated juices to the skillet, along with the stock, carrot, and dill. Cover and simmer for 30 minutes.

Add the cream and the reserved mushrooms to the pan and cook for another 3 minutes. Remove the chicken to a serving dish and top with sauce. Garnish with watercress.

Mixed Mushroom and Lentil Chili

2 tablespoons oil

1 red bell pepper, diced

1 Anaheim chili, roasted, peeled, and chopped

2 jalapeño peppers, seeded and chopped

1 large onion, chopped

4 cloves garlic, chopped

2 ounces dried porcini, soaked in hot water

1 pound button mushrooms, coarsely chopped

½ pound oyster mushrooms, coarsely chopped

½ pound shiitake mushrooms, stems discarded and caps sliced

2 tomatoes, seeded and chopped

½ cup chopped fresh parsley

1 teaspoon ground cumin

1 teaspoon dry oregano

2 tablespoons chili powder

1 cup lentils, preferably green, rinsed and picked over

Salt and pepper

Cilantro for garnish

SERVES 8

In a large pot, heat the oil. Cook the peppers, onion, and garlic until soft, about 10 minutes. Drain the porcini; strain and reserve the liquid. Chop the porcini and add to the pot with the other mushrooms. Cook over high heat, stirring, for 8 minutes.

Add the tomato, parsley, cumin, oregano, chili powder, 1 cup water, and the reserved porcini liquid. Bring to a boil and add the lentils. Lower the heat and simmer for 30 minutes.

Season with salt and pepper and garnish with cilantro. Serve with warm tortillas.

Mixed Mushroom Ratatouille

4 tablespoons olive oil
1 onion, chopped
2 cloves garlic, chopped
1 rib celery, chopped
2 pounds mixed mushrooms, chopped
2 tomatoes, seeded and chopped
1 teaspoon dried oregano
¼ cup chopped fresh parsley
¼ teaspoon crushed red-pepper flakes
1 cup dry white wine
½ cup Niçoise olives, pitted and chopped
Salt and pepper

SERVES 6 AS A SIDE DISH OR 12 AS AN APPETIZER WITH CRACKERS

In a large skillet, heat the oil. Cook the onion, garlic, and celery until tender, about 8 minutes. Layer the mushrooms over the celery mixture and cook until tender, about 8 minutes.

Add the tomato, oregano, parsley, pepper, and wine; bring to a boil. Reduce the heat, cover, and simmer for about 30 minutes, or until very little liquid remains. Stir in the olives and season with salt and pepper. Serve hot, warm, or at room temperature.

OKRA

IN BAHIA, the state of Brazil most suffused with its African past, the night air throbs with the heartbeat sounds and rhythmic chanting of the Candomblé. Among the rituals of this cult, whose deities are combinations of African gods and Christian saints, is one in which okra pods are ceremoniously cut up and prepared with liberal amounts of voodoo magic. The next day, at the outdoor waterfront marketplace, okra sits quietly beside the other vegetables—the manioc and hot peppers and sweet potatoes—but it never quite regains its innocence. There's something exotic about okra, now and forever.

Halfway around the earth, at a spice shop in Turkey, long strings of shriveled okra pods crisscross the roof beams, waiting for winter. In the Caribbean, Jamaicans prepare their favorite pepperpot soup using such exotic ingredients as okra and pigs' tails, cut in precise two-inch lengths. In the

South Carolina low country, folks make an okra pilaf they call "limping Susan." There is nothing ordinary about this international vegetable, whose tapered green or red pods, sometimes called "lady's fingers," look like elves' hats or the pointy toes of some miniature mythological monster.

A member of the hibiscus family, okra produces bright yellow flowers like the cotton plant to which it is also related. Okra was brought to the New World from Africa along with watermelons and pigeon peas as part of the slave trade. Its African name—*kingumbo,* or *ochinggombo* from Angola's Umbundu language—became identified with the dish in which it was used (gumbo) both for its taste and for its thickening properties. The word *okra* comes from the Twi language on Africa's Gold Coast, where the vegetable is called *nKurama.* Some people object to okra's mucilaginous quality, but this can be diminished by cooking the vegetable in acidulated water.

Okra remains an important ingredient throughout the American South, where it is blanched and sauced, made into succotash with ham hocks, cornmeal-coated and deep-fried, pickled, cooked with tomatoes and corn, steamed, and frittered. When it is sliced, its starlike cross-sections look unique and inviting in salads.

Even outside the South, okra is found fresh in many produce markets throughout the country these days, especially in Middle Eastern, Greek, or Indian specialty markets. With a paste of garlic and coriander, it makes a famous Lebanese hors d'oeuvre, *bamieh bi zayt.* An Indian variety, *bendi-kai,* is often cooked like asparagus or made into a pickle. Okra is used in Greek pilafs, chopped meat dishes, and lamb stews. The seeds, which can be roasted and brewed for a coffeelike drink, are crushed for oil in some parts of the world.

By far the easiest-to-pronounce okra dishes come from the Caribbean: these are *foo-foo,* an African word for the color of the mixture; and *coo-coo,* from the African word for "mush."

Consumer and Cooking Guide: Okra

Market Selection: Green and red. Okra should be deep green or red in color, firm, unblemished, and 2 to 3 inches long.

Availability: Year-round; peak—June through August

Storage: Refrigerate, unwashed, in a plastic or paper bag for up to 5 days.

Flavor Enhancers: Garlic, thyme, sun-dried tomatoes, parsley, oregano

Equivalents: 1 pound = 2 cups, sliced

Nutritional Value: Good source of vitamin C and potassium
45 calories per cup

Cooking and Handling Notes: If okra is to be cooked whole, cut the stems without piercing the pods, to lessen sliminess.

Basic Cooking Methods: Cook in boiling salted water for about 10 minutes, or until tender.

Fried Okra with Spicy Tomato Sauce

SAUCE

4 large ripe tomatoes, seeded
    and chopped
2 tablespoons olive oil
½ teaspoon ground cumin
1 to 2 jalapeño peppers,
    seeded, deveined, and
    diced
½ teaspoon dried oregano
3 sprigs fresh cilantro
    Salt and pepper

1½ pounds okra, sliced into
    rounds
½ cup milk
    Cornmeal for dredging
½ cup vegetable oil

SERVES 6

In a medium saucepan, combine all of the sauce ingredients. Cook over medium-high heat until thick, about 20 minutes.

Dip the okra into the milk and then dredge in cornmeal. In a large skillet, heat the oil; add the okra. Cook for about 2 minutes. Remove with a slotted spoon to a paper towel. Serve warm, with tomato sauce.

Okra, Corn, and Tomato Gratin

3 tablespoons oil
2 cloves garlic, minced
1 small onion, chopped
1 small green bell pepper,
   seeded and diced
½ pound okra, sliced
2 cups corn kernels
3 medium tomatoes, seeded
   and diced
1 teaspoon dried thyme
   Salt and pepper
1 cup bread crumbs
½ cup grated Parmesan
2 tablespoons butter or
   margarine

SERVES 6 AS A SIDE DISH

Preheat the oven to 375°F. Grease a 10-inch round baking dish.

In a large skillet, heat the oil. Sauté the garlic, onion, and pepper until wilted, about 5 minutes. Add the okra and corn; cook for another 8 minutes. Add the tomato and thyme; cook until the tomato breaks down a bit, about 4 minutes.

Season with salt and pepper and pour the mixture into the prepared baking dish. Combine the bread crumbs and cheese and sprinkle over the vegetables. Dot with butter and bake for about 20 minutes, or until golden-brown and bubbly.

Gumbo with Tasso Ham, Seafood, and Tiny Shells

3 tablespoons oil
¼ pound Tasso ham or any
  well-seasoned ham, diced
1 small onion, chopped
2 cloves garlic, minced
2 stalks celery, chopped
1 carrot, chopped
1 teaspoon dried thyme
1 tablespoon paprika
2 tablespoons flour
2 tablespoons tomato paste
2 cups chicken broth
  (page 343)
½ pound okra, trimmed and
  cut into chunks
1 cup tiny pasta shells
1 pound prawns, shelled
½ pound cooked crabmeat
  Salt and pepper
½ cup chopped fresh parsley

SERVES 6

In a large saucepan, heat the oil. Cook the ham, onion, garlic, celery, and carrot until soft, about 10 minutes. Stir in the thyme, paprika, flour, and tomato paste and cook for another minute. Add the broth; bring to a boil, reduce heat, and add the okra and shells. Simmer, partially covered, for about 15 minutes.

Add the prawns and crabmeat and cook for 3 minutes. Season with salt and pepper and stir in the parsley. Serve.

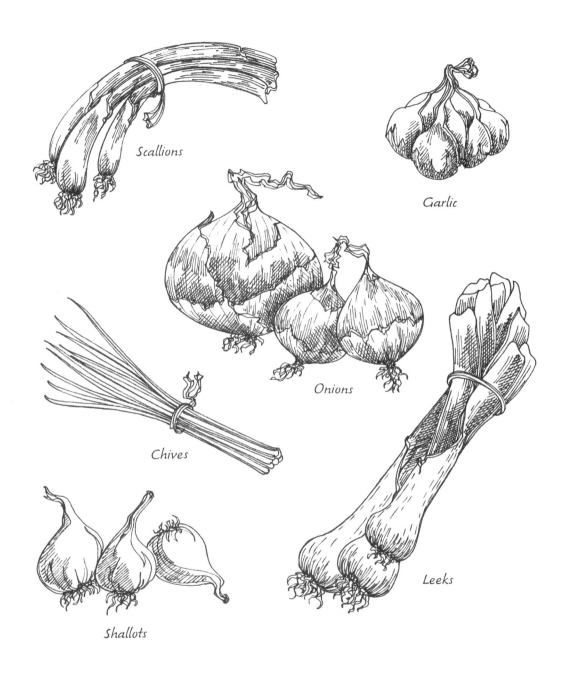

Scallions

Garlic

Onions

Chives

Shallots

Leeks

ONIONS

"THERE ARE TWO TYPES of onions, the big white Spanish and the little red Italian. The Spanish has more food value and is therefore chosen to make soup for huntsmen and drunkards, two classes of people who require fast recuperation."

Things have gotten considerably more complicated, at least in terms of onions, since Alexandre Dumas wrote these words a century ago. Onions have become overwhelming, not only because there are so many kinds but also because the categories are arbitrary. Should onions be grouped by color (red, yellow, white, green)? Or by shape (round, oval, slender)? Or by personality traits (sweet, assertive, tear-jerker)? Or should we invent yet another category, say "rollability"? This would probably serve most purposes as well as any other and would provide a practical method of distinguishing a scallion from a baseball-shaped yellow globe.

Among the onions that don't roll particularly well are leeks—mild, elegant, and ivory-toned, with a way of aristocratizing the simplest mélange; and green onions (also called scallions). Ramp, however, popular in parts of the South and Appalachia, is derived from an Elizabethan word for wild leek. Chives and garlic, species related to the onion, are like botanical opposites in terms of their edibility: we eat the bulbs of garlic and the green shoots of chives, which have hardly any bulb at all. The Ascalonian onion, named for the ancient Palestinian town with which it was associated, is known to us today as the shallot.

As for the "rollables," they can vastly improve any meal—from soups to stuffed roasts to sautéed vegetables—and they can be a meal all by themselves: baked, stuffed, creamed, boiled, or fried into rings. An old Creole recipe for onion juice mixed with sugar is supposed to be good for just about anything, especially colds; it is, according to the *Picayune Creole Cook Book,* "almost an infallible remedy."

Although all onions become sweeter when cooked (but not overcooked), some varieties of sweet onions can taste as sweet as oranges. These include Georgia Vidalias, Texas Supersweets, California Imperials, Hawaiian Maui Sweets, and Washington State Walla Wallas.

Raw or cooked, all these sweet onions taste identical and can be used interchangeably in recipes. The appearance and quality of all sweet onions is generally excellent, because they are hand-selected for packaging. This personal attention, combined with their short season and abbreviated shelf life, contributes to their high cost.

Compared with regular onions, sweet onions have a higher sugar content and are low in the sulfur-containing compounds that make ordinary onions pungent and irritating to the eyes.

Merchandisers are trying to do to sweet onions what nature did not: give them designer logos and distinguishing characteristics so that consumers will develop brand loyalty. These efforts do not affect taste but do affect prices.

At the center of all this merchandising are onions like the Texas Grano 1015 Y Supersweet. It was developed in the early 1980s by Dr. Leonard Pike, a professor of horticulture at Texas A & M University at College Station. The 1015 Y is named for its optimum planting date, October 15. It is nicknamed the "million-dollar baby" because of the money spent to develop it.

Mountain-grown Maui Sweets are large yellow or yellow-white onions cultivated in Hawaii's volcanic soil. Vidalias date to the early 1940s, when Dr. Henry A. Jones, a research director at the Desert Seed Company in El Centro, California, developed the F1 Hybrid Yellow Granex, which was named Vidalia after the Georgia town where it was subsequently grown commercially. By Georgia law, only onions produced in designated areas of nineteen southeastern counties may be marketed as Vidalias. Texans are quick to point out, however, that because of their state's milder climate and earlier growing season, Vidalias are often planted in South Texas, then transplanted in Georgia when the weather warms.

The round golden onions known as Walla Wallas are grown in Walla Walla County in southeastern Washington and in part of adjacent Umatilla County in northeastern Oregon. Walla Wallas include a few strains like the French onion, whose seeds were planted in the Walla Walla area around 1900 by a Frenchman, Peter Pieri—he had imported the seeds from Corsica, where he had served in the French army—and the Arbini, named for John Arbini, who developed this mild, sweet onion in 1925.

Most experts agree that the taste of onions depends on growing conditions, the sulfur content of the soil, and the weather; type, appearance, size, and shape give few clues to quality. In recent years, onion rivalry has resulted in official Onion Challenges, one of which was held in McAllen, Texas, a few years ago. Entries were judged under categories like "marinated," "baked," "rings," "appearance," and "raw." (Rollability, it seems, was not even a consideration.)

As for the question of sociability, the onion family comes complete with both problem and solution:

If Leekes you like, but do their smell dis-like,
Eat Onyons, and you shall not smell the Leeke;
If you of Onyons would the scent expell,
Eat Garlicke, that shall drowne the Onyons' smell.

—Dr. William Kitchiner, The Cook's Oracle

CONSUMER AND COOKING GUIDE: Onions

Market Selection: Dry onions include red, yellow, and white Italian torpedo, Bermuda, Vidalia, Maui, Walla Walla, granex, pearl, and boiling onions. Other varieties that are part of the onion family include shallots, leeks, garlic, chives, and green onions (scallions). Dry onions and shallots should be firm to the touch with a dry, brittle outer skin. Green shoots indicate an old onion. Leeks and green onions should have white bottoms and crisp, green-looking tops. Garlic should be firm and unblemished. Chives should be bright green and unwilted.

Availability: Year-round for most varieties. Sweet onions are available in the spring.

Storage: Shallots, garlic, and dry onions should be stored, unwrapped, in a cool dry place. Chives, leeks, and green onions should be wrapped in paper or plastic and stored in the refrigerator up to 1 week.

Equivalents: 2 medium dry onions = 1 cup, chopped
    1 pound = 3 medium onions

Nutritional Value: Dry onions are a fair source of vitamin C. Shallots are high in iron.
    36 calories per cup

Cooking and Handling Notes: To minimize "crying" refrigerate onions for 2 hours before cutting.

Basic Cooking Methods: See individual recipes.

Triple Onion and Potato Soup

3 tablespoons butter or oil
3 cloves garlic, minced
3 large yellow onions,
   chopped
1 medium tomato, seeded
   and chopped
2 teaspoons chopped fresh
   dill
3 potatoes, peeled and diced
5 cups chicken stock
   (page 343)
¼ cup cream
   Salt and pepper
½ cup chopped fresh chives

SERVES 6

In a large saucepan, heat the butter. Cook the garlic, onion, and tomato for about 5 minutes. Stir in the dill, potato, and stock. Bring to a boil; reduce heat, cover, and simmer for 15 minutes.

In a food processor, puree about one-third of the soup mixture with the cream. Return to the pot, reheat gently, and season with salt and pepper. Sprinkle with chives and serve.

Green-Onion Cocktail Biscuits

1 cup all-purpose flour
½ cup yellow cornmeal
½ teaspoon baking soda
   Pinch salt
½ teaspoon freshly ground
   pepper
1 teaspoon sugar
2 tablespoons cold butter,
   cut into bits
4 green onions, minced
½ cup cottage cheese
5 tablespoons milk

MAKES ABOUT 20 BISCUITS

Preheat the oven to 425°F. Grease a baking sheet.

In a large bowl, combine the dry ingredients. Cut in the butter until the mixture is crumbly. Stir in the remaining ingredients until a soft dough forms.

Knead the dough gently on a floured surface and roll into a 10 x 16-inch rectangle. Cut into rounds with a 2-inch cutter and place on the prepared sheet.

Bake for 12 to 15 minutes, or until golden-brown. Split and fill with your favorite spread or cold meat and mustard.

Sweet Onion and Zucchini Relish

1 large sweet onion, diced
2 yellow or green zucchini, diced
½ cup raisins
3 tablespoons catsup
2 tablespoons light brown sugar
3 tablespoons balsamic vinegar
½ teaspoon crushed red-pepper flakes
1 teaspoon salt

MAKES ABOUT 2 CUPS

Place all of the ingredients in a medium saucepan with 1 cup of water; bring to a boil. Reduce heat, partially cover, and simmer for about 40 minutes, or until slightly thick, stirring occasionally. Allow to cool and store in an airtight container in the refrigerator. Great with hot dogs and hamburgers.

Leek, Red Pepper, and Goat Cheese Frittata

4 tablespoons (½ stick) butter
2 tablespoons oil
2 leeks, white parts only, thinly sliced
½ red bell pepper, seeded and thinly sliced
¼ pound goat cheese
6 eggs
½ teaspoon dried thyme
Salt and pepper

SERVES 6 TO 8

In a 12-inch skillet, heat 2 tablespoons of the butter and the oil. Cook the leek and pepper until very soft, about 8 minutes. Stir in the goat cheese, until melted. Remove the mixture to a large bowl and let it cool for a few minutes.

Add the eggs, thyme, salt and pepper to the leek mixture and whisk together until combined. Add the remaining 2 tablespoons of butter to the skillet and heat. Pour the egg mixture into the skillet and cook over medium heat until the eggs are partially set. Slide the frittata onto a large platter; flip it back into the skillet with the uncooked side down. Cook for another 3 minutes.

Let cool and serve warm or at room temperature, cut into wedges.

Pan-Fried Hamburgers with Burgundy-Shallot Sauce

1½ pounds ground sirloin or
    ground round
3 tablespoons plus ½ cup
    burgundy
1 tablespoon Dijon mustard
2 tablespoons chopped fresh
    chives
1 teaspoon salt
½ teaspoon pepper
3 tablespoons butter
½ cup chopped shallot
2 tablespoons balsamic
    vinegar
Salt and pepper

SERVES 6

Combine the ground meat with 3 tablespoons of wine, mustard, chives, salt, and pepper. Form into six patties. In a large skillet, heat 2 tablespoons of butter. Cook the hamburgers to desired doneness; remove and keep warm.

In the same skillet, cook the shallot for about 2 minutes over high heat. Add the vinegar and ½ cup of wine, lower the heat, and simmer for about 2 minutes. Stir in the remaining butter and taste for salt and pepper. To serve, pour sauce over hamburgers.

Rigatoni with Caramelized Pearl Onions and Mushrooms

2 pounds pearl onions
3 tablespoons butter or oil
2 cloves garlic, minced
½ pound mushrooms, sliced
¼ cup balsamic vinegar
2 tablespoons dry sherry
½ cup chicken stock
    (page 343)
½ cup chopped fresh parsley
    Salt and pepper
1 pound freshly cooked
    rigatoni
½ cup grated Parmesan

SERVES 4 TO 6

Cook the onions in boiling water for 2 minutes. Drain. When cool enough to handle, peel and remove the roots. In a medium skillet, heat the butter. Cook the onions over high heat until lightly browned. Lower the heat, cover, and cook for about 20 minutes, or until soft.

Add the garlic and mushrooms and cook for another 5 minutes, until the mushrooms are slightly browned. Add the vinegar and sherry; cook over high heat until almost all the liquid evaporates.

Stir in the stock, bring to a boil, and add the parsley. Season to taste with salt and pepper. Toss with rigatoni and sprinkle with cheese. Serve.

Braised Lamb Shanks in Red Onion and Olive Sauce

2 tablespoons butter
2 tablespoons oil
6 lamb shanks, cut into
    2-inch pieces (have your
    butcher do this)
    Salt and pepper
½ cup flour
6 red onions, thinly sliced
3 cloves garlic, minced
1 tablespoon grated lemon
    zest
3 tablespoons chopped fresh
    parsley
2 cups beef stock (page 344)
½ cup dry red wine
2 cups Greek or Italian black
    olives, pitted and coarsely
    chopped
    Salt and pepper

SERVES 6

In a large Dutch oven or a sauté pan, heat the butter and oil. Sprinkle the lamb with salt and pepper and dredge it in flour, shaking off any excess. Brown the lamb on all sides. Remove it from the pan and reserve.

Add more oil if necessary, and in same pan, cook the onion and garlic until soft. Place the lamb shanks over the onion, sprinkle with lemon zest and parsley, and add the stock and wine. Bring to a boil; reduce the heat, cover, and simmer for 1½ to 2 hours, or until the lamb is very tender.

Remove the lamb from the pan and keep it warm. Puree the onion sauce in a food processor and return it to the pan. Stir in the olives and season with salt and pepper. Serve the lamb shanks with sauce.

PEAS

Once upon a time ago, there was a miser, or so this pea-studded story goes. He had invited such a large number of people to a dinner party one evening that he was obliged to serve not one big bowl of peas, but two. Inspired by basic frugality, he devised a creative solution to this expensive dilemma. Instead of two bowls of peas, he arranged to have his cook prepare one bowl of peas and one of asparagus. Just before setting the latter on the dinner table, the server was instructed to trip on the rug, or whatever they used as a floor covering in those days, and drop the bowl of asparagus. At this point the host was to express regret for having only one bowl of peas left to distribute among his guests. Predictably, however, the peas, and not the asparagus, came crashing to the floor, thwarting the miser's plans and exposing his ungenerous intentions. Given the current price of asparagus, today's miser would do just the opposite—spare the asparagus and spill the peas.

Nevertheless, the tale points up the popularity of peas as a subject of light literature. There is, for example, the fairy tale of the princess and the pea, the nursery rhyme about "pease porridge hot," and quite a few moral allegories, such as the above. There are even some Ripleyesque strange-but-true tales. It is said, for example, that England's King William III, in a losing battle to contain his passion for the vegetable, once scooped up an entire royal platterful and shoveled it into his mouth with his bare hands.

Peas have been eaten in dried form since 6000 B.C. The Greeks and Romans snacked on an unappetizing-sounding variety called gray peas, which were sold to theater and circus audiences like peanuts at a ball game. The prominent Piso family of Rome took its very name from the beloved vegetable for some unknown reason; it was probably the same reason that the Ciceros named themselves after the chick-pea. In those early days, only the Chinese enjoyed the succulent secret of fresh peas, including the delicate sweetness of the young shoots. Nobody else ever considered eating the vegetable fresh until the Italians developed some tender varieties in the 1500s.

It was these fresh garden peas that incited avarice and downright gluttony. Even the daintiest of women, according to a 1696 account from Madame de Maintenon (wife of Louis XIV), "having supped, and supped well at the King's table, have peas waiting for them in their rooms to eat before going to bed." Aristocrats dipped the vegetable, unshelled, into various sauces and popped them into their mouths, pods and all.

Anyone who has studied biology is acquainted with the most intimate genetic details about peas, thanks to Gregor Mendel's research into the mysteries of heredity. But for our purposes, there are two categories of peas: shelling peas and edible-pod peas, both known by the Latin binomial *Pisum sativum.* The former category includes garden peas, English peas, and the French *petit pois,* with pods less than ⅓ inch in diameter. Shelling varieties have either smooth or wrinkled pea seeds. *Mange tout,* or "eat all," is the French name for edible podded peas; these include the flat snow pea and the sugar snap pea, with thicker pods and larger peas. Since these peas do not have the parchmentlike membranes of shelling peas, they are also called *pois sans parchemin.*

Some peas have interesting names: Ringleader, Ne Plus Ultra, the Daniel

O'Rourke, the Shah, and even Tall Telephone. In addition, there are some rare specimens that can add unexpected color and flavor to a salad or mixed vegetable dish. These include the Golden Sweet, a lovely, sun-yellow podded pea; and the eggplant-colored shelling variety called Blue Podded, with lavender blossoms.

Nutritionally, peas are pearl-sized powerhouses of nutrients which retain their potency even when canned. Early in this century, peas became so popular as a canned vegetable that special machinery was developed to process them as quickly as possible. Even now, 95 percent of the peas harvested in the United States go directly to the canneries.

There are all kinds of procedures for the proper eating of peas. One wonderfully tactile *modus mangerandi* is to put them into the mouth whole and pull along the pod with the teeth, artichoke style. But perhaps the best advice, as so often happens in these cases, comes from M. F. K. Fisher: "The best way to eat fresh [peas] is to be alive on the right day, with the men picking and the women shelling, and everybody capering in the sweet early summer weather, and the big pot of water boiling and the table set with little cool roasted chickens and pitchers of white wine. So . . . how often does this happen?"

Consumer and Cooking Guide: Peas

Market Selection: Two types are widely available—garden or English peas (green peas); and edible-pod peas (sugar snaps, snow peas, and Chinese peas). Color should be bright and texture firm in all types.
Availability: April through August for garden peas; February through June for edible-pod peas
Storage: Refrigerate in plastic bags for up to 4 days.
Flavor Enhancers: Mint, tarragon, chervil
Equivalents: 1 pound unshelled peas = ½ cup shelled
Nutritional Value: Good source of vitamins A and C
　　　　95 calories per cup—garden peas
　　　　60 calories per cup—edible-pod peas
Basic Cooking Methods: Cook shelled peas in boiling salted water for 5 minutes. Cook pod peas in boiling salted water for 2 minutes.

Steam pod peas for 3 minutes.

Salmon-Stuffed Snow Peas

20 snow peas

FILLING

¼ pound smoked salmon
2 tablespoons cream cheese
1 teaspoon fresh lemon juice
1 tablespoon minced fresh
   dill

MAKES ABOUT 4
APPETIZER SERVINGS

Blanch the snow peas in boiling salted water for 1 minute. Drain and refresh under cold water. Slit each pod open on one side.

Combine all of the filling ingredients in a food processor; process until smooth. Spoon or pipe the filling into the prepared peas.

Snappy Sugar Snap Soup

2 tablespoons oil
1 tablespoon minced fresh
   ginger
1 clove garlic, minced
1 tablespoon finely grated
   orange zest
¼ teaspoon cayenne
3 cups chicken broth
   (page 343)
2 pounds sugar snap peas,
   strings removed
½ cup cream
   Salt and pepper
   Chopped mint for garnish

SERVES 4

In a large saucepan, heat the oil. Sauté the ginger, garlic, orange zest, and cayenne until fragrant, about 2 minutes. Add the stock; bring to a boil and add the peas. Reduce the heat and simmer for about 10 minutes.

Puree the mixture in a blender or food processor with the cream. Season with salt and pepper and serve hot or chilled, garnished with mint.

Pilaf with Peas, Prosciutto, and Parmesan

2 tablespoons butter or oil
2 shallots, finely minced
¼ pound prosciutto, in one
    piece, diced
1 cup Arborio rice
1 cup chicken stock
    (page 343)
1½ pounds peas, shelled
2 tablespoons chopped fresh
    chervil
2 tablespoons freshly grated
    Parmesan
Salt and pepper

In a medium saucepan or sauté pan, heat the butter. Cook the shallot and prosciutto for about 5 minutes. Stir in the rice and cook until the rice becomes translucent. Add 1 cup of water and the stock. Bring to a boil, lower heat, and simmer, covered, for 15 minutes.

Stir in the peas and chervil; cook for 3 more minutes. Stir in the Parmesan and season with salt and pepper.

SERVES 6

Three-Pea Sauté

2 tablespoons butter
1 tablespoon oil
½ pound snow peas, strings
    removed
½ pound sugar snap peas,
    strings removed
1 pound English peas,
    shelled
¼ cup chicken stock
    (page 343)
1 teaspoon fresh lemon juice
1 tablespoon fresh tarragon
    or 1 teaspoon dried
Salt and pepper

In a skillet, heat the butter and oil. Cook the snow peas and sugar snaps for about 3 minutes, tossing well. Add the English peas and stock. Cover and cook for 2 more minutes. Stir in the lemon juice and tarragon and cook for another minute. Season with salt and pepper; serve.

SERVES 6

Warm Potato Salad with Peas and Bacon

2 pounds small red potatoes,
    unpeeled
1 pound garden peas, shelled
½ pound bacon, cooked and
    crumbled
½ cup chopped fresh chives
3 tablespoons red-wine
    vinegar
1 tablespoon fresh lemon
    juice
2 teaspoons Dijon mustard
½ cup olive oil (some of the
    bacon drippings may be
    used in place of some of
    the oil)
    Salt and pepper

SERVES 6

Cook the potatoes in boiling salted water for about 12 minutes. Drain and slice. Combine with the peas, bacon, and chives. Whisk the remaining ingredients together and pour over the potato mixture, tossing gently to combine.

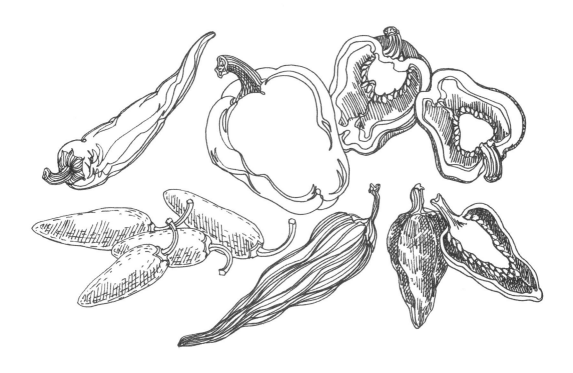

PEPPERS

ALL PEPPERS—sweet to hot—belong to the genus *Capsicum.* In attempting to trace the word to its origin, one group of imaginative etymologists suggests that *capsicum* comes from the Greek *kapto,* "to bite." While this explanation takes care of the snappiness that characterizes the hottest varieties, it completely excludes the milder, more sociable sweet peppers. Another group of imaginative etymologists, therefore, contends that the word derives from the Latin *capsa,* meaning "box," supposedly suggestive of the shape of many bell peppers. Clearly, neither of these explanations appeases all of the peppers all of the time, but they do serve to illustrate one of the main problems in discussing peppers: their mind-boggling numbers and varieties, types, shapes, and sizes. For our purposes, we simply divided them into two categories: sweet and hot.

Sweet Peppers

THE MOST COMMON sweet pepper is, of course, the innocent, waxy, indestructible-looking, year-round green bell pepper that everyone has (at least once) eaten stuffed. These are the most prevalent peppers in America, not necessarily due to culinary preference but because they have a long shelf life and travel well. Green peppers are, in fact, the pepper's first stage. If left unpicked, they proceed through various shades of yellow-green, on to bright red. Although sweet peppers were originally elongated, wrinkled, and much smaller than they are today, they eventually were bred into their current, more marketable, configurations. The Dutch have even produced an attractive deep-purple pepper that is green inside and turns green outside when cooked. Other color choices include white, salmon, and chocolate-brown.

In addition to these many-colored bell peppers, other types of sweet peppers commonly available include the curved bull's horn; the bright red or yellow Cubanelle; the dark red, heart-shaped, thick-walled pimiento; the tapered Lamayo; and the Japanese Green. Except for the last, which is mildly spicy, the main differences among sweets are their shapes, colors, and relative "meatiness." Sweet peppers are found in all the world's cuisines, from Middle Eastern lamb dishes, to Cantonese stir-fries with shrimp and ginger, to Basque *pipérade* and Hungarian goulash.

Hot Peppers

LIKE THEIR SWEET COUSINS, hot peppers are New World vegetables, and since they probably date from 7000 B.C., very old New World vegetables at that. Their incendiary presence has become central to many of the world's cuisines, from Thailand, China, and India to Africa and the Caribbean. Unlike sweet peppers, the hot varieties contain a highly pungent substance called *capsaicin,* which is the power behind such products as anti-mugger aerosols, warming back plasters, postmen's dog-dissuader sprays, and even powdered foot warmers. The hotter the pepper, the more capsaicin it contains, most of it concentrated in the membrane or rib. Removing both this membrane and the seeds can significantly reduce the overall heat level (see Cooking and Handling Notes). Among the more scientific methods for measuring a pepper's heat is the Scoville scale, developed in 1912 by Parke-Davis pharmacologist Wilbur L. Scoville. On this scale, jalapeños rack up 10,000 units, compared to the habañeros' grand total of 100,000. But most people can judge a pepper's heat simply by cutting off a sliver and touching it to the side of the tongue.

New Mexico is this country's main producer of chili peppers, followed by California, Louisiana, Mississippi, South Carolina, Florida, and Colorado. Pepper addicts attribute all kinds of powers to their favorite scorchers, from lowering cholesterol to removing warts. While scientific evidence for these claims is lacking, we do know that for those who can stand the heat, capsicums provide six to nine times more vitamin C than tomatoes. But as Frederick Turner explains in *Of Chiles, Cacti and Fighting Cocks,* true addicts believe that their beloved capsicums "induce a sense of spiritual and physical well-being that transcends analysis."

Because there are more than 300 varieties of capsicums, we describe only the most commonly available ones, though even these will vary by region. Your neighborhood greengrocer will be your best local guide. More information can be found in such specialized works as Elizabeth Schneider's *Uncommon Fruits and Vegetables: A Commonsense Guide* and Jean Andrews' *Peppers: The Domesticated Capsicums.*

Anaheim: 5 to 8 inches long; green to red; mild to hot. Also called New Mexico chili or California chili.

Ancho: 3 to 6 inches long; green to black, often with red spots; mildly hot and sweet; a type of poblano pepper also called pasilla.

Banana: 2 to 3 inches long; tapered; red and yellow; mild to hot; the almost identical Hungarian wax chili is very hot.

Cayenne: 4 to 12 inches long; thin, sharp-tipped; red or green; very hot. Similar to the Thai pepper and the *chile de árbol;* may be substituted for jalapeños or serranos, which are less hot, and for the hotter habaneros.

Chimayo: 2 inches long; curved; very hot.

Habañero: 1 to 2 inches long; orange to green and yellow; reputedly the hottest pepper in the world!

Jalapeño: 2 inches long, cone-shaped; red to green; hot to very hot; often used raw.

Serrano: 2 inches long; green (immature) to yellow, orange, and red (mature); very hot; often eaten fresh.

Consumer and Cooking Guide: Peppers

Market Selection: Commonly found sweet peppers include green, red, yellow, and purple bell peppers and pimientos. Hot peppers include jalapeños, Anaheims, anchos, poblanos, and serranos. All types should be glossy, unblemished, and firm.
Availability: Year-round; peak—July through October
Storage: Refrigerate, unwashed, wrapped in plastic, for up to 1 week.
Flavor Enhancers: Cilantro, ground coriander, parsley, garlic
Equivalents: 1 medium bell pepper = ¾ cup, chopped
Nutritional Value: Good source of vitamins A and C
          35 calories per cup
Cooking and Handling Notes: To roast peppers: place whole peppers over a direct flame or in a preheated 400°F oven and cook until skin is charred. Seal in a plastic bag and let cool. Peel under running water.

Be sure to wash your hands thoroughly after working with hot peppers to remove the volatile and often abrasive oils from your skin. Wearing thin rubber gloves is an alternative. The seeds and veins of hot peppers should be removed, as they are the hottest parts of the pepper. (If you want your dish extra hot—do not remove.)

Roasted Red Pepper and Tomato Soup

6 large red bell peppers,
   roasted (page 348)
2 tomatoes, roasted at 400°F
   in foil for 20 minutes
1 teaspoon fresh thyme or
   ½ teaspoon dried
2 cups chicken stock
   (page 343)
1 cup heavy cream
   Salt and pepper
1 small yellow or green bell
   pepper, diced, for garnish

SERVES 4 TO 6

Seed the peppers and tomatoes and puree them. Pass them through a food mill to make smooth. In a medium saucepan, simmer the mixture with the thyme and chicken stock for 15 minutes. Add the cream and cook for 5 more minutes. Season with salt and pepper. Serve hot or cold, garnished with diced pepper.

Baked Peppers Stuffed with Confetti Couscous

2 tablespoons butter
3 green onions, thinly sliced
1 carrot, chopped
½ teaspoon paprika
¾ cup quick-cooking
   couscous
¼ cup golden raisins
¼ cup toasted pine nuts (see
   page 347)
¼ cup minced fresh parsley
3 ounces goat cheese
6 small red, green, or yellow
   bell peppers, stem ends
   and seeds removed
   Olive oil

SERVES 6

In a sauté pan, heat the butter. Sauté the onion and carrot until soft, about 5 minutes. Stir in the paprika and 2 cups water. Bring to a boil and add the couscous. Remove the pan from the heat and let stand, covered, for 5 minutes, or until the liquid has been absorbed. Stir in the raisins, pine nuts, parsley, and goat cheese.

Preheat the oven to 375°F. Brush a baking pan with olive oil.

Stuff the peppers loosely with the couscous mixture and sprinkle with olive oil. Place the peppers on the prepared pan and cover loosely with foil. Bake for 30 minutes; remove the foil and bake for 10 more minutes. Serve warm or room temperature.

Warm Scallop Salad with Bell Pepper Dressing

DRESSING

½ green bell pepper, chopped
1 small tomato, seeded and
    chopped
1 tablespoon chopped fresh
    parsley
1 tablespoon fresh lemon
    juice
1 tablespoon white-wine
    vinegar
3 tablespoons butter or oil
1 tablespoon chopped shallot
½ red bell pepper, chopped
1 pound sea scallops (halved
    if large)
½ cup toasted pecans (see
    page 347), finely chopped
Salt and pepper

SERVES 4

Combine the dressing ingredients in a blender or food processor until smooth.

Heat the butter in a skillet and sauté the shallot and pepper until soft. Stir in the scallops and cook over medium-high heat for about 3 minutes, or until the scallops are cooked through. Stir in the pecans and season with salt and pepper. Toss with dressing and serve.

Pick-a-Peck-of-Peppers Barbecue Sauce

1 each red, green, and
  yellow bell peppers,
  roasted (page 348)
1 Anaheim pepper, roasted
  (page 348)
2 to 3 jalapeño peppers
2 cloves garlic
3 tablespoons fresh lime
  juice
3 tablespoons fresh lemon
  juice
1 tablespoon ground cumin
4 tablespoons firmly packed
  dark brown sugar
4 tablespoons vegetable oil
Salt

MAKES 2 CUPS

USE THIS SAUCE for basting fish, beef, or chicken. It will keep for about 2 weeks.

Remove the seeds and veins from all of the peppers (see page 146). Place all of the ingredients in a food processor or blender and puree. Salt to taste. Store in the refrigerator in an airtight jar.

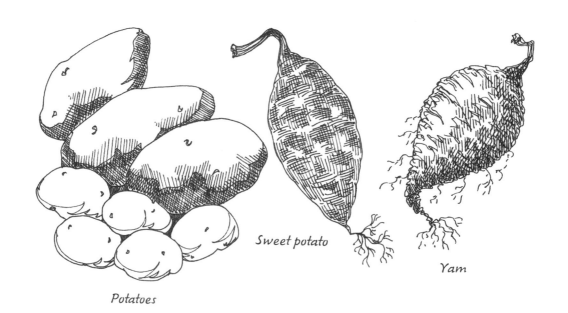

Potatoes

Sweet potato

Yam

POTATOES, SWEET POTATOES, AND YAMS

Potatoes

"THEY ARE GOOD for boys' cold fingers at supper-time on winter nights."

What could "they" possibly be? Bowls of oatmeal? Cups of hot cocoa? Gloves? The suggestion, which comes from an 1873 advice book entitled *Common Sense in the Household*, by Marion Harland, refers to—what else?—baked potatoes.

We all know the feeling: take a hefty, hot Idaho off the coals, split it open, sneak a bit of butter (a big bit) into it, and grind some pepper over it. It's comfort, it's warmth, it's manna, it's earth, it's heaven. And, as with all things, it's not the only way to do it.

Even on such a simple theme as baked potatoes, variations abound. Some cooks butter and salt the skins before baking to prevent them from becoming too crisp and to enhance their flavor for the skin-nibblers (isn't that everybody?). Others let the baked potato rest before eating it, or wrap it in a napkin, or put it in a saucepan and shake it around a bit before serving. By substituting olive oil for butter and performing a few abracadabras, some of today's "special occasion" restaurants have elevated the humble tuber to the heights of fashion and priced it accordingly.

Of course, baking isn't the only way to cook what has been called the Houdini among vegetables. As M. F. K. Fisher says, "There are several thousand things to do with potatoes," and some of them have names that reveal their universal appeal: Irish colcannon, Catalan Amanida de Patates, scalloped potatoes Jefferson (said to be the president's invention), potatoes aïoli, gnocchi, *gratin Parmentier, frigideira,* and *krupnik,* not to mention a plethora of *pommes de terre:* Anne, Annette, Georgette, and Dauphine. There is even a potato layer cake that James Beard considered "one of the best of that type of cake in the whole gamut of pastries."

Although the potato is an American vegetable, cultivated for centuries in Peru and South America, it was first brought to this country in the 1700s. Records show that the first plantings were made in the early 1700s by newly arrived Irish Presbyterians in Londonderry, New Hampshire. Soaked in vinegar, potato slices were used as a remedy for scurvy. Their most honorable mention in those early years comes from Harvard College, where potatoes were on the dinner menu for the installation of its new president.

Today, the tubers are grown just about everywhere, although the most important potato states are Idaho, Washington, Maine, and Oregon. Among the most colorfully named types are Russet Burbank, White Baker, Rose Fir, Blue Carib, Yukon Gold, and Yellow Finnish. Depending on the statistician cited, each person in this country annually consumes either 75 or 120 pounds of potatoes, or somewhere in between.

It must be conceded here that the great gastronome Brillat-Savarin had a discouraging word for potatoes—three words in fact—when he said "None for me." But most culinary writers and chefs defend them with descriptions of paean proportions.

"I have always been fascinated by the potato," admitted James Beard. Sheila Hibben wrote, somewhat protectively, "the potato, like man, was not meant to dwell alone." Rosalind Creasy sighs, "Potatoes, comforting potatoes." And M. F. K. Fisher reveals that "For me, a plain baked potato is the most delicious one . . . It is soothing and enough."

But perhaps it is the Irish who should have the last word. "Only two things in this world are too serious to be jested on," say the Irish, "potatoes and matrimony."

Market Selection: The thick-skinned russets (Idahos) have dry, mealy flesh and are best for baking, mashing, and frying. The thinner-skinned types (White Rose, reds, creamers) are waxy-textured and are well suited for boiling, roasting, and steaming. Finnish Yellows and Yukon Golds are new on the produce scene. Their yellow flesh yields a buttery flavor, and they may be used like the waxy types. Skins should be free of wrinkles, green spots, and sprouts or shoots.

Availability: Year-round

Storage: Potatoes will keep in a cool dark place for at least a month. Do not store with apples or onions as they give off gases that can spoil potatoes. Refrigeration gives potatoes an unpleasant sweetness.

Flavor Enhancers: Garlic, dill, parsley, chives

Equivalents: 2 large potatoes = 1½ pounds
  2 medium potatoes = 1 pound
  10 small potatoes = 1 pound

Nutritional Value: Good source of potassium. Potato skins contain vitamin C.
  145 calories per large potato

Cooking and Handling Notes: Do not use a food processor to puree or mash potatoes. Excessive starch will be released, making the potatoes pasty in taste and texture.

Basic Cooking Methods: Cook potatoes in boiling salted water for 16 minutes. Steam for 20 minutes.

To bake: pierce whole thick-skinned (russet, Idaho) potatoes with a fork and bake in a preheated 450°F oven for 45 minutes, or until tender.

Potato-Carrot Vichyssoise

5 cups chicken stock
  (page 343)
1 bunch green onions, sliced
1 pound carrots, peeled and
  sliced
1 large russet potato, peeled
  and diced
Salt and pepper
¼ cup chopped fresh chives

SERVES 6

In a large saucepan, bring the stock to a boil. Add the onion, carrot, and potato and cook for 15 minutes. Remove half of the mixture to a food processor and puree. Return to the pan and reheat with the remaining soup. Season with salt and pepper and sprinkle with chives. Serve.

Potato and Asparagus Salad with Smoked Salmon

3 pounds small red potatoes,
  cooked, cooled, and sliced
  ⅛ inch thick
2 pounds asparagus, peeled,
  cut into 1-inch pieces, and
  cooked just until tender
½ pound smoked salmon, cut
  into strips
¼ cup chopped fresh dill
1 cup plain yogurt
2 tablespoons mustard
2 teaspoons fresh lemon
  juice
2 tablespoons mayonnaise
Salt and pepper

SERVES 12

In a large bowl, combine the potato, asparagus, and smoked salmon. In a small bowl, mix 2 tablespoons of dill with the remaining ingredients. Toss with the potato mixture and season with salt and pepper. Sprinkle with the remaining dill.

Roasted Lamb on a Bed of Onions and Potatoes

3 tablespoons olive oil
2 pounds onions, peeled and
  sliced
6 cloves garlic, chopped
1 bunch fresh parsley,
  chopped
2 pounds russet potatoes,
  peeled and sliced
About 1½ cups chicken
  broth
Salt and pepper
One 5-pound leg of lamb,
  butterflied

SERVES 8

Preheat the oven to 400°F.

In a large skillet, heat 2 tablespoons of the oil; sauté the onion until tender. Combine half the garlic and parsley with the sliced potatoes. Grease a baking dish with the remaining tablespoon of oil. Place a layer of potatoes in the dish, followed by a layer of sautéed onion. Pour in just enough broth to cover. Loosely cover with foil and bake for about 25 minutes. Uncover and bake for 30 minutes more, checking to see if the mixture is still moist. (Add more broth if dry.)

Meanwhile, make slits in the lamb with the point of a knife. Coat the lamb with the remaining garlic and parsley; massage into the lamb. Place the lamb over the potato mixture and bake for another 25 minutes. (A meat thermometer should register 135°F.) Remove from the oven and let rest for 10 minutes before slicing. Serve slices of lamb on a bed of onions and potatoes.

Chicken and Potato Sauté with Sage

3 tablespoons oil
1 tablespoon butter
6 sage leaves
2 cloves garlic, minced
6 skinless, boneless chicken-
  breast halves, cut into
  strips
1 pound small red potatoes,
  quartered
⅓ cup chicken broth
  (page 343)
Salt and pepper

SERVES 6

In a large skillet, heat the oil and butter. Add the sage and garlic and cook for about 2 minutes. Add the chicken and potato; cook over medium-high heat for about 3 minutes. Cover, turn heat to low, and cook for another 10 minutes.

Add the chicken broth and cook, uncovered, for 3 minutes more. Season to taste with salt and pepper.

Trout Stuffed with Potatoes and Spinach

STUFFING

2 tablespoons oil
1 clove garlic, minced
½ pound fresh spinach,
    chopped
4 medium red potatoes,
    diced and cooked 10
    minutes
2 tablespoons grated
    Parmesan
Salt and pepper

6 small trout, boned and
    butterflied
Salt and pepper
2 tablespoons oil
1 shallot, chopped
½ cup white wine
2 tablespoons butter

SERVES 6

To make the stuffing: Heat the oil and sauté the garlic and spinach for about 3 minutes. Combine with the potatoes and cheese. Season with salt and pepper.

Blot the trout dry and sprinkle the cavities with salt and pepper.

Preheat the oven to 400°F.

Oil a baking dish and sprinkle with shallots. Fill the trout with the stuffing mixture and place them side by side on the baking dish. Sprinkle with wine and cover with parchment or foil. Bake for 15 minutes; uncover, dot with butter, and bake for another 5 minutes.

Potatoes Steamed in White Wine

1 cup white wine
½ cup broth or water
1 pound yellow Finns or
    fingerling potatoes
1 tablespoon good olive oil
1 tablespoon chopped fresh
    tarragon
Salt and pepper

SERVES 4

Bring the wine and broth to a boil in the bottom of a steamer. Place the potatoes in one layer in the top of the steamer and cover. Cook for about 13 minutes. Remove the potatoes and sprinkle them with oil and tarragon. Season to taste with salt and pepper.

Sweet Potatoes and Yams

IT IS POSSIBLE to make an enormous fuss over the difference between sweet potatoes and yams. Botanically speaking, the two vegetables share nothing except for some flowery associations. The yam, a tuber, is a member of the lily family, while the sweet potato is a member of the morning glory family. Yams are usually sweeter, moister, plumper, denser, and a deeper orange color than sweet potatoes—though not always. The two plants also come from different parts of the world. The yam probably originated in Africa (although it *may* be the same plant that had been cultivated in Asia since 8000 B.C.); the sweet potato is a New World plant discovered by Columbus (although it *may* have mysteriously traveled to Polynesia hundreds of years prior to Columbus's first voyage). Slaves in the American South called the sweet potato *nyamis* because of its similarity to a vegetable of that name that they knew from their homeland. This African word brought the two vegetables together, probably for all eternity, despite botany, archaeology, plant pathology, and the like. And that's probably just as well.

For all practical purposes, it might be more intriguing to think of the yam and the sweet potato as twins separated at birth, growing up with different quirks and twitches but retaining the essential sweet nature that makes them virtually interchangeable from a culinary perspective. Furthermore, the yams generally available in this country are really a variety of sweet potato. (True yams do offer one element missing from sweet potatoes; they contain a compound from which the sex hormone estrogen was first manufactured.)

The value of the sweet potato as a main-course vegetable as well as a dessert has been proven in most cultures and at every American Thanksgiving. The European acceptance of the sweet potato following Columbus's return to Spain was immediate and enthusiastic. The Spanish potato, as it became known, was also soon elevated to the status of aphrodisiac, assuring it an entree to the highest levels of society. Henry VIII had sweet potatoes imported from Spain and made into many types of confections. The distinguished culinary writer and chef Antonin Carême assured the vegetable immortality when he included it in his classic *The Art of French Cooking in the Nineteenth Century*. Perhaps less well known is the vegetable's popularity both in China, where it is sun-dried and used for noodle making, and in Japan, where it has been a staple for hundreds of years, especially when typhoons have decimated the rice crop.

But it is the American Thanksgiving that is the true test of the sweet potato's versatility. It is transformed into pies, puddings, and muffins, as well as candied vegetables, biscuits, and even ice cream. The wonder is that, like so many of the foods associated with Thanksgiving, from cranberries and chestnuts to the turkey itself, sweet potatoes are packed away, psychologically speaking, until the next Thanksgiving comes along. Not only can sweet potatoes be substituted in almost any recipe for white potatoes with unexpected and sprightly results, but they make tasty and unusual combinations when sautéed with garlic and tomatoes, layered in gratins with various types of cheese, or fried in tempura batter and served with dipping sauces.

In Louisiana Creole country, any day might begin with sweet potatoes in the form of waffles, fritters, or pone. But when there is world enough and time, people look forward to one of the oldest Creole specialties, *patates douces*. As originally prepared, sweet potatoes are buried in ashes at the end of a meal and left to cook slowly until the next. The almost century-old *Picayune Creole Cook Book* issued this word of warning in 1901: "[preparing] the sweet potato is an art, for the delicate flavor of the potato is lost if it is not properly cooked."

Homage to the sweet potato/yam is an institution in parts of Louisiana, where an annual October festival, the Yambilee, culminates in a colorful procession called the Grand Louisiana Parade.

Market Selection: The two basic varieties of sweet potatoes are moist-fleshed and dry-fleshed. The moist-fleshed types, with dark skins and bright orange flesh, are now known as yams. They are sweeter than the dry-fleshed variety, which has a lighter-color skin and flesh. Choose sweet potatoes that are firm to the touch and have unblemished skins.

Availability: Year-round; peak—October through March

Storage: May be stored, unwrapped, at room temperature for about 10 days or in a cool, dark place for up to 2 months.

Equivalents: 3 medium = 1 pound
      1 pound, diced = 4 cups

Nutritional Value: Excellent source of vitamin A and potassium
      165 calories per potato

Basic Cooking Methods: Cook in boiling salted water for 20 minutes.
  Steam for 25 minutes.
  To bake: Pierce the skin in several places with a fork. Bake in a preheated 450°F oven for 45 minutes.

Hot Sweet-Potato Chowder

4 tablespoons oil
1 leek, white part only,
    chopped
2 stalks celery, chopped
2 jalapeño peppers, seeded,
    deveined, and chopped
½ cup chopped fresh parsley
1 teaspoon ground cumin
½ pound mushrooms,
    coarsely chopped
2 tablespoons tomato paste
4 medium sweet potatoes or
    yams, peeled and cut into
    ½-inch cubes
6 cups chicken stock
    (page 343)
2 cups corn kernels (fresh,
    frozen, or canned)
    Salt and pepper
½ cup fresh cilantro leaves
    for garnish

SERVES 8

In a large saucepan, heat the oil. Cook the leek, celery, and jalapeño until soft, about 8 minutes. Stir in the parsley, cumin, and mushrooms and cook for 2 more minutes. Add the tomato paste and sweet potato and stir well to combine. Pour in the stock and bring to a boil. Reduce the heat, partially cover, and simmer for 15 minutes.

Add the corn and cook for another 5 minutes. Remove about 1 cup of the vegetables to a food processor and puree with about ½ cup liquid from the soup. Return to the pot, season with salt and pepper, and sprinkle with cilantro.

Sweet Potato and Chive Pancakes

1 pound sweet potatoes,
    cooked, peeled, and
    mashed
⅓ cup flour
1 teaspoon cornstarch
1 whole egg
2 egg yolks
½ cup milk
½ teaspoon salt
½ teaspoon freshly ground
    black pepper
½ cup chopped fresh chives
4 tablespoons butter or oil
    for frying
1 cup plain yogurt or sour
    cream
1 teaspoon ground cumin

MAKES ABOUT 12
PANCAKES

In a food processor, combine the potato with the remaining ingredients, except the butter, yogurt, and cumin, until smooth.

In a large skillet, heat the oil. Spoon the batter into the pan to form 2-inch pancakes. Fry for about 45 seconds per side, or until golden-brown. Serve immediately. Combine the yogurt with the cumin and serve over the pancakes.

Sautéed Sweet Potatoes and Greens

4 strips bacon
4 sweet potatoes, peeled,
    quartered, and sliced
2 cloves garlic, minced
6 ounces spinach, Swiss
    chard, or other seasonal
    greens, coarsely chopped
Salt and pepper

SERVES 6 TO 8

In a large skillet, cook the bacon until crisp. Drain it on paper towels and crumble. Pour out all but 5 tablespoons of bacon fat from the skillet.

Cook the sweet potato, covered, for about 10 minutes. Uncover, add the garlic, and cook for another 8 minutes. Add the greens and cook just until wilted. Season with salt and pepper and sprinkle with crumbled bacon.

RADISHES

NOSES KNOW MORE about radishes than mouths. Even unbitten, the radish cannot disguise its personality from the all-wise nose, which can sniff out the aggressive radish from the mild, the rugged individualist from the congenial. At first bite, it is the nose that detects the radish's sweet sting, head-rinsing pungency, bright attention-getting tingle. Confronting a radish is seldom a passive experience.

And yet there is more to radishes than meets the nose, especially now that they are beginning to show up in interesting and unexpected colors and shapes. The marble-sized, cherry-red regulars are moving over and making room for distant cousins that are long and white, round and white, multicolored, scarlet, green, or black, thin as a finger or heavy as a watermelon. The wonders of modern technology have nothing to do with the production of the large varieties, which, according to historians, were once big enough for foxes to burrow into and set up as permanent headquarters.

Radishes' enchanting names are often a clue to their appearance: Cherry Belle, Easter Egg, China Rose, Round Black Spanish, White Icicle, and the surprising, though rare, Shantun Green. Each color and size has its own degree of heat, which is produced by an enzyme in the skin. Some people go to the trouble of peeling radishes in order to mitigate these peppery effects, but others, including the Chinese, use the peel as a braised vegetable in itself.

This brings us to the mouth, which is, after all, the ultimate arbiter in most gastronomic decisions. The pleasures of radish consumption increase with our appreciation of the many ways these versatile members of the cabbage family can be enjoyed. They can be stir-fried, pickled, or grated into soups and salads; their seed pods can be pickled or eaten fresh; their leaves can be boiled like greens or added like cress to salads. The long white Chinese radishes or Japanese daikons are used to make a pudding called *lo bok go,* to spice sauces, and to make Korean *kim chee.* Ancient Egyptians even made use of radish-seed oil before the olive came around. And, in any culture, there is nothing better to cleanse the palate than a dose of fresh radish in almost any form.

An ancient vegetable, the radish was one of the seven basic foods—the others were wheat, beans, peas, turnips, onions, and cabbage—cultivated in primitive Europe. Its festive connections have permeated many cultures: the Chinese, for example, reserve it for a special New Year's dish of julienned radish and dried apricots, accompanied by a sweet-and-sour sauce. Germans look forward to eating thin-sliced spiral-cut radishes served with dark bread and butter, during *Oktoberfest.* They also enjoy *Rettichsalat,* a white-radish salad popularly paired with steak. In Mexico, in the black-pottery town of Oaxaca, large radishes are carved into animal shapes as part of the Christmas Eve festivities known as Night of the Radishes. England once greeted spring with a Radish Feast on May 11 which included brown bread and butter, lots of radishes, and English ale in festive quantities.

Though the United States at present claims no particular radish-oriented holiday, its citizens do consume no less than 400 million pounds of the vegetable annually. The following suggestions may help us preserve that hefty-sounding quota.

Market Selection: White Icicle; red button; daikon; Easter Egg; French Breakfast. Tops should be bright green and fresh-looking. Radishes should be firm, with smooth skins.

Availability: Year-round

Storage: Clip the tops, wrap in plastic, and refrigerate for up to 1 week. Daikon may be stored as above for up to 2 weeks.

Flavor Enhancers: Chives, parsley, chervil

Equivalents: 1 cup, sliced = about 15 radishes

Nutritional Value: Good source of vitamin C
　　　　　20 calories per cup

Basic Cooking Methods: See individual recipes.

Red Radishes on Black Bread

2 tablespoons chopped fresh
  parsley
1 small clove garlic, minced
¼ teaspoon salt
2 tablespoons butter,
  softened
4 thin square slices of dense
  pumpernickel, crusts
  removed
  About 10 red radishes,
  thinly sliced

MAKES 16 CANAPÉS

Combine the parsley, garlic, salt, and butter until smooth. Spread on the bread; cut the bread into four even strips. Arrange the radish slices, overlapping, on the bread.

Radish and Carrot Salad with Honey-Lemon Vinaigrette

3 carrots, coarsely shredded

2 cups radishes, coarsely shredded

2 green onions, thinly sliced

2 tablespoons fresh lemon juice

1 tablespoon honey

½ teaspoon Dijon mustard

4 tablespoons olive oil

3 tablespoons chopped fresh parsley

Salt and pepper

Combine the carrot, radish, and green onion in a salad bowl. Mix the remaining ingredients until well blended. Toss with the radish mixture and season with salt and pepper.

SERVES 4

Daikon and Mushroom Sauté

2 tablespoons oil

1 tablespoon butter

1 clove garlic, minced

1 bunch green onions, thinly sliced

½ pound button mushrooms, thinly sliced

¼ pound shiitake mushrooms, thinly sliced

1 cup shredded daikon

4 tablespoons balsamic vinegar

2 tablespoons toasted sesame seed (page 347)

2 tablespoons chopped fresh parsley

In a skillet, heat the oil and butter. Cook the garlic and onion until soft, about 3 minutes. Add the mushrooms and cook over medium-high heat until brown, about 5 minutes.

Stir in the daikon; cook for 1 minute and add the vinegar. Cook for about 3 minutes, or until the vinegar has almost evaporated. Sprinkle with sesame seeds and parsley; serve.

SERVES 4

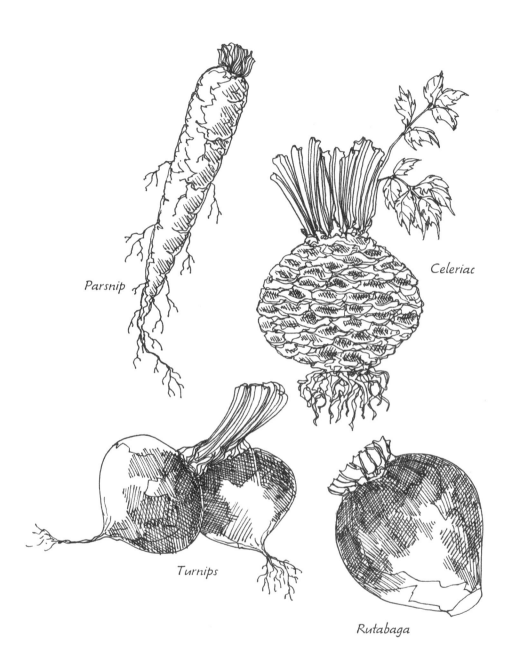

Parsnip

Celeriac

Turnips

Rutabaga

ROOT VEGETABLES

Celery Root

DESPITE ITS ASSOCIATION with root vegetables, celery root (or celeriac, as it is sometimes called) has a certain panache. Perhaps this is due to its honored place in the French specialty *céleri-rave rémoulade*, or because it makes such luxurious pairings with dried *cèpes* or with tender artichoke hearts. In the form of a distinctive salad or soup, celery root is often served apart from the meal, either first or as a separate course. As one old American cookbook suggests: "Serve . . . after the roast-piece of the dinner."

Most cookbooks, however, simply ignored the vegetable—also called soup-celery, celery knob, and turnip-rooted celery—by any name. In fact, it enjoys wide popularity in this country only in German communities, where it is eaten pureed and in stews. Celery root has a pungent celerylike flavor and is, in fact, a special variety of celery, developed by gardeners during the Renaissance. In recipes calling for cauliflower, fennel, or cardoon, celery root makes an interesting and unexpected substitute if not a quantum improvement.

Parsnips

"FINE WORDS BUTTER no parsnips" said Sir Walter Scott, in what might have been the high point of parsnips' literary career. Certainly the low point was a remark by journalist Alexander Woollcott, whose search for a deprecatory comment once culminated in these words: "The play left a taste of lukewarm parsnip juice." Such insults have long been the lot of this ignored taproot, whose generous sweetness is belied by an albinolike, bloodless appearance.

A native of Eurasia, the parsnip was enjoyed from Greek and Roman times through the Middle Ages. English cooks served parsnips, baked or roasted, alongside roast pork, while Germans included them in deer-meat stews. New Englanders, who believed the vegetable helped prevent scurvy, used them as a flavoring in soups, as honey-covered sweets, and as a garnish for salt fish.

Parsnips were also boiled, fried, baked in casseroles, and made into fritters and griddle cakes. North American Indians grew them in abundance. Because of their high sugar content, parsnips have been used in wine making and as a syrup substitute for sugar. André Simon's *Concise History of Gastronomy* refers to a recipe for parsnips cooked with lettuce and seasonings, which supposedly tastes like lobster, but even a confirmed parsnip fan finds this hard to believe.

In Italy the pig population was always a major consumer of parsnips, whereas in this country, as Fannie Farmer observed a century back, parsnips were "raised mostly for feeding cattle." The truth is that for roughly 400 years, parsnips have been underappreciated, ever since they were all but elbowed out by the arrival of the potato. Recently, more attention has been paid to harvesting the vegetable when it is ripe and sweet, which is causing a mini-comeback for this ancient cousin of celery. Its charms become perhaps most apparent when it is cooked in partnership with some of its fellow winter roots.

Rutabagas

THERE'S SOMETHING intrinsically unromantic about the rutabaga. It does not connote the exotic or mysterious; so far as we know, the rutabaga has never inspired a candlelight dinner, a flight of shameless self-indulgence, or an uncontrolled flirtation with decadence. Perhaps, to paraphrase Juliet to Romeo, 'tis but its name that is the enemy.

Rutabaga sounds rooted, workaday, even clunky. The almost indiscriminate vegetable lover M.F.K. Fisher had only three words for the rutabaga in her gastronomical masterwork, *With Bold Knife and Fork:* "Down with it."

And yet, with our renewed appreciation for honest, nutritious food, a rutabaga renaissance may be at hand. The vegetable developed in the Middle Ages, possibly in Bohemia, as a cross between wild cabbage and turnip. A member of the mustard family, it has the appearance of a large yellow turnip with a fat neck, though its taste is more cabbagelike and somewhat starchy. Its hearty nature made the rutabaga popular on the American frontier, where it was often the first root vegetable sown in the newly planted soil.

Though the largest specimens can be fibrous and woody, medium-sized rutabagas have a fresh, mustardy spiciness that makes them unexpected and unusual salad ingredients and crudités for spreads or dips. The Laurentian rutabaga, one of the most widespread varieties, cooks up a tempting orange and makes an attractive puree, soup, or gratin.

CONSUMER AND COOKING GUIDE: Celery Root, Parsnips, and Rutabagas

Market Selection: Vegetables should be firm; sprouting tops should be bright green.
Availability: October through April
Storage: Wrap celery root and parsnips in plastic and refrigerate for up to 1 week. Rutabagas should be stored unwrapped in a cool dry place up to 1 month.
Flavor Enhancers: Nutmeg, garlic, cilantro, cinnamon, cloves
Equivalents: 1 small celery root, sliced = 2 cups
      1 rutabaga, diced = 2 cups
      1 parsnip, sliced = 1 cup
Nutritional Value: Celery root is rich in phosphorus and potassium. Parsnips and rutabagas are good sources of vitamin A and potassium.
      40 calories per cup—celery root
      60 calories per cup—rutabaga
      102 calories per cup—parsnip
Cooking and Handling Notes: Best cooked cubed rather than whole.
Basic Cooking Methods: Cook celery roots in boiling salted water 7 minutes; steam for 8 minutes.

Cook parsnips in boiling salted water for 5 minutes; steam for 7 minutes.

Cook rutabagas in boiling salted water for 13 minutes; steam for 15 minutes.

Celery Root and Apple Salad with Toasted Walnuts

2 medium celery roots,
  peeled and cut into
  matchsticks
2 medium Red Delicious
  apples, cored and cut into
  matchsticks
2 tablespoons lemon juice
3 green onions, thinly sliced
1 bunch watercress leaves

DRESSING

2 tablespoons red-wine
  vinegar
1 tablespoon mustard seed
1 tablespoon mustard
1 tablespoon honey
½ cup oil
  Salt and pepper
1 cup walnut halves, toasted
  (see page 347)

SERVES 4

Combine the celery root and apple in a bowl and sprinkle with the lemon juice. Toss with the green onion and watercress.

Whisk the vinegar, mustard seed, mustard, honey, and oil until well combined. Toss with the celery-root mixture and season with salt and pepper. Garnish with walnuts.

Parsnip and Zucchini Soup

4 tablespoons olive oil
1 large leek, thinly sliced
1 large onion, thinly sliced
1 jalapeño pepper, seeded
 and minced
6 cups chicken stock
 (page 343)
1½ pounds parsnips, peeled
 and sliced
1 pound zucchini, sliced
1 medium potato, peeled and
 diced
1 bunch cilantro, chopped
 Salt and pepper

SERVES 6 TO 8

In a large saucepan, heat the oil. Cook the leek, onion, and jalapeño until wilted. Add the stock, bring to a boil, and add the parsnip, half the zucchini, and the potato. Lower the heat and cook, partially covered, for 15 minutes.

Puree the mixture with the remaining zucchini and half the cilantro. Season with salt and pepper and reheat gently. Garnish with the remaining cilantro.

Parsnip Fritters

5 parsnips, peeled and
 cooked until tender
1 tablespoon flour
1 teaspoon mustard
1 teaspoon honey
2 eggs
4 tablespoons oil or butter
 Salt and pepper

SERVES 4 AS A SIDE DISH

Mash the parsnips and combine them with the remaining ingredients except the oil, salt, and pepper.

Heat the oil in a large skillet. Form the parsnip mixture into hamburger-sized patties and fry until golden-brown on each side. Season to taste with salt and pepper.

Mashed Medley of Winter Roots

1 celery root, peeled and cut
   into eighths
1 baking potato, peeled and
   cut into chunks
1 rutabaga, peeled and cut
   into chunks
1 parsnip, peeled and thickly
   sliced
6 cloves garlic, peeled
4 tablespoons (½ stick)
   butter
½ cup milk
¼ teaspoon cayenne
   Salt and pepper
½ cup chopped fresh chives

SERVES 6

In a large pot of boiling water, cook the celery root, potato, rutabaga, parsnip, and garlic until tender, about 40 minutes.

With a slotted spoon, remove the vegetables to a food processor and puree with the butter and milk. If the consistency is too thick, add some vegetable cooking water until you have the desired consistency. Season with salt and peppers. Place in a flat serving dish and sprinkle with chives.

Smothered Chicken and Winter Roots

4 tablespoons olive oil
1 large chicken, cut into
    serving pieces
    Salt and pepper
    Flour for dredging
2 cloves garlic, minced
1 large onion, thinly sliced
1 cup chicken stock (page
    343)
½ cup white wine
1 medium rutabaga, peeled
    and cut into matchsticks
1 small celery root, peeled
    and cut into matchsticks
1 parsnip, peeled and sliced
1 carrot, peeled and sliced
1 bay leaf
½ teaspoon dried oregano

SERVES 4 TO 6

In a large sauté pan, heat the oil. Sprinkle the chicken with salt and pepper and dredge it in flour. Sauté the chicken over medium-high heat for about 5 minutes per side, or until golden-brown. Remove and reserve.

In the same pan, cook the garlic and onion until wilted. Add half the stock and the wine; stir, scraping up bits from the bottom of the pan, and bring to a boil. Add the remaining vegetables, bay leaf, and oregano.

Lower the heat and simmer, partially covered, for 10 minutes. Return the chicken to the pan and cook for another 20 minutes. Add the remaining stock if necessary. Season to taste with salt and pepper.

Turnips

MANY PEOPLE think of turnips as woody, leaden spheres, the color of baseballs and with about as much culinary appeal. Yet now, with more and more varieties available, it is possible to eat tender spring turnips very lightly cooked or even raw. Another amazement in the turnip universe is the array of available colors: red-skinned, purple-tipped, pearl-white, golden-yellow. A salad of all these, thinly sliced in rounds, can be as bright and festive as a basket of confetti.

No one would suspect that turnips are the same vegetable once ranked, by whole nations, too low for edible consideration. Even hungry New Englanders disdained them as plebeian, though they ate them to prevent scurvy, preferably with mutton. Early New Yorkers ate them in a Dutch combo: boiled and mashed with potatoes and smeared with butter. The Pennsylvania Dutch often made coleslaw with turnips instead of cabbage, a concept similar to turnip kraut, a variation on cabbage sauerkraut. The Scottish actually ate turnips willingly with their haggis (which they also ate willingly), but they referred to them by the rather pugnacious name "bashed neeps." (Turnips were originally called "neeps," from the Latin word for turnip, *napus*, which also gave rise to the French word *navet*. The prefix *turn* refers to their spherical shape.)

Perhaps the apotheosis of turnipdom is the French stew *navarin à la printanière*, made with young turnips and spring lamb. Escoffier may have paid turnips their highest compliment by turning them into his lyrical stuffed turnips *(navets farcis)*; but perhaps even more surprising, Goethe himself had a favorite turnip recipe: "Turnips are good," he proclaimed in his *Prose Maxims*, "but they are best mixed with chestnuts."

A member of the cabbage family, turnips are similar in appearance to such root vegetables as rutabagas and swedes (originally Swedish turnips). In general, turnips are smoother than these cousins and have several circles of ridges at the base of their leaves. For cooking purposes, they can all be used interchangeably.

Turnips have been around a long time: they were enjoyed by Greek epicures (who favored those from Thebes) and by Roman gourmets (their turnips had to be from Amitermes). In one Roman dish, turnips were presented in sixteen different colors, though the favorite, by far, was purple. In the Orient, tender strips of turnip make a quick and delicious stir-fry.

But no discussion of turnips is complete without due homage to the man they called "Turnip" Townshend, who, in the early 1700s, introduced a bevy of unknown Dutch turnip varieties to England. Although his efforts had beneficial effects on the way people thought about turnips, they also (unfortunately for "Turnip") changed the way people referred to the man who brought them. He had been known previously as "Lord" Townshend.

Consumer and Cooking Guide: Turnips

Market Selection: The variety generally available is the white globe-shaped turnip. Red, purple, and pink turnips can be found in some markets, and very young, walnut-sized turnips are being harvested in early spring for the consumer. If you want sweet, tender turnips, select smaller roots. Turnips should be no larger than 3 inches in diameter, with unblemished skins and fresh-looking greens (if they are attached).

Availability: While turnips are available year-round, young turnips are prevalent only in spring.

Storage: Because of their high water content, turnips deteriorate quickly. Store, unwashed, in a plastic bag in the refrigerator up to 1 week.

Flavor Enhancers: Lemon juice, vinegar, curry powder, chives, oregano, marjoram, thyme

Equivalents: Six 3-inch turnips = 1 pound

      1 pound = 4 cups, chopped

      2 turnips = 1 serving

Nutritional Value: Turnips contain potassium and iron and are a good source of vitamin C.

      36 calories per cup

Basic Cooking Methods: Cook in boiling salted water for 10 minutes.

   Steam for 12 minutes.

Curried Turnip and Apple Soup

3 tablespoons butter or oil
1 small onion, chopped
2 ribs celery, chopped
1 pound turnips, peeled and
  chopped
2 small tart apples, cored
  and chopped
1 tablespoon curry powder
¼ cup chopped fresh parsley
4 cups chicken stock
  (page 343)
⅓ cup raw rice
Salt and pepper
Chopped fresh chives

SERVES 6

In a large saucepan, heat the butter. Add the onion, celery, turnip, and apple. Cook until wilted. Stir in the curry powder and parsley; cook for another minute. Add the stock, bring to a boil, and add the rice. Lower the heat and simmer, covered, for 20 minutes.

Puree the mixture in a blender or food processor. Season with salt and pepper and sprinkle with chopped chives.

Duck Breasts Braised with Young Turnips

4 boneless duck-breast halves
Salt and pepper
3 tablespoons chopped
  shallot
1 pound very small turnips,
  peeled
⅓ cup raspberry vinegar
½ cup chicken stock
  (page 343)
16 fresh raspberries, for
  garnish

SERVES 4

Remove any excess fat from the duck. Sprinkle with salt and pepper. With the tines of a fork, pierce the skin in several places.

Heat a skillet and place the duck in it, skin-side down. Cook until the fat begins to render. Turn and cook on the other side for about 8 minutes, or until browned. Remove and reserve.

In the same skillet, cook the shallot until soft. Add the turnips and cook on all sides for a total of 3 minutes. Add the vinegar; bring to a boil and add the stock. Boil for about 2 minutes. Return the duck to the skillet; cover and cook for 10 minutes over medium heat. Uncover and cook for another 5 minutes.

Slice each duck breast thinly. Arrange in a petal-like formation on four plates. Spoon the sauce over the duck, surround with turnips, and sprinkle with raspberries.

Garlic-Mashed Turnips and Potatoes

1 pound turnips, peeled and
cut into ½-inch pieces
1 pound potatoes, peeled and
cut into ½-inch pieces
4 cloves garlic, peeled
3 tablespoons butter
2 tablespoons sour cream or
plain yogurt
Salt and pepper

In a large pot of salted boiling water, cook the turnip, potato, and garlic for 10 minutes, or until the vegetables are tender. Drain and puree the vegetables and garlic through a food mill. (A food processor is not recommended, as it can turn potatoes very starchy.) Beat in the butter and sour cream and season with salt and pepper.

SERVES 6

Sautéed Turnips with Spinach and Raisins

2 tablespoons olive oil
1 clove minced garlic
3 medium turnips, peeled
and cut into matchsticks
½ cup raisins
3 tablespoons fresh lemon
juice
10 ounces fresh spinach,
coarsely chopped
Freshly ground nutmeg
Salt and pepper

In a sauté pan, heat the oil with the garlic. Add the turnip and raisins and cook for about 1 minute. Add the lemon juice; cover and cook for 3 more minutes. Stir in the spinach and cook just until wilted. Sprinkle with nutmeg and salt and pepper to taste.

SERVES 6

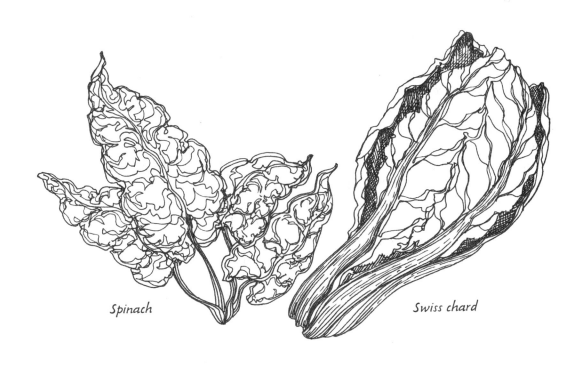

Spinach

Swiss chard

SPINACH AND SWISS CHARD

EVEN THOSE OF US who admit to loving spinach may never be able to like it. It is not spinach the vegetable that we resent, it is spinach the authority figure. Spinach reminds us of all the "supposed-to's" of childhood. Through no fault of its own, spinach has become a didactic vegetable, used for symbolic value as the good and the true, never the beautiful and certainly not the delicious. Memories of spinach are inseparable from this message: spinach is not just a good idea; it's the law. Other vegetables, like corn on the cob or potatoes, may have happy or even neutral connotations, but spinach means business. Food, it lectures us, is a system of nourishment: there are some things you must eat and spinach is one of them.

When we discover, therefore, that spinach isn't perfect because its oxalic acid blocks the absorption of calcium and iron, we can't help feeling vindicated. We always knew that spinach wasn't so great, we congratulate ourselves; we were right about that. We might have been right about some other things too.

Strong opinions have always been the lot of this emotion-charged vegetable. The famous seventeenth-century botanist and salad maker, John Evelyn, wrote that spinach was not often included in salads and "the oftener kept out, the better." In his ensuing series of backhanded compliments, he went on to praise spinach as useful in a "Sick Man's Diet" and also "profitable for the Aged." According to one old French proverb, "spinach is the broom of the stomach." Another traditional view, which likens spinach to sealing wax, comes close to being a compliment. Like wax, spinach takes on the tastes and characters of its surrounding ingredients, reflecting and preserving their virtues. It has long been a favorite of innovative chefs, who know how to take advantage of this trait. Perhaps one of the nicest images of spinach can be found in the pages of Thackeray's *Pendennis,* where his fictitious but adventurous chef, Alcide, describes one of his creations: "a little roast lamb, which I laid in a meadow of spinaches."

It might be possible to fill a real meadow with the diverse greens that bear the name spinach but that are not, in fact, in the same family. New Zealand spinach, a warm-weather green, came to England in 1770 with the scientist Sir Joseph Banks. Chinese spinach is a slightly sweet, highly nutritious green, known in India for centuries. Its other names are amaranth, Jacob's coat, and tampala. Ceylon spinach is a mucilaginous green, similar to okra, whereas water spinach, also called swamp cabbage, has young leaves that can be used like spinach.

Swiss chard, also known as spinach beet, is actually an offshoot of the beet family. It is one of the most successful substitutes for spinach. The big, ruffled leaves can be used to wrap around stuffings or small fish for steaming or roasting on the grill. Its firm, crisp stems, which may be cooked separately, range in color from white to pink to ruby red.

But none of these spinach stand-ins is the real thing—the leafy member of the goosefoot family that first grew in southwestern Asia, though no one knows exactly when. Some clues as to its age do exist: the Greeks didn't know about spinach, nor is there a Hebrew term for it, but the Persians called it *aspanakh.* Because some botanists have proposed Spain as its place of origin, it has also been referred to as "the Spanish vegetable."

Bloomsdale, Melody, and Wolter are some of today's spinach varieties. All have graceful slender stems and tender leaves, the essence of green. All spinach really needs is a vigorous swish through cold water to remove the almost intractable dirt and it is ready for action, as well as interaction, in salads, stir-fries, soufflés, stuffings, soups, pies, gratins, pasta, purees, and casseroles.

The greatest challenge to spinach popularity in this country came a century ago, when its nutritional values were extolled not only by dietitians but also by politicians. Certain members of Congress, perhaps attempting to associate themselves with something wholesome, began distributing spinach seeds to their constituents. Fortunately for spinach, along came Popeye.

CONSUMER AND COOKING GUIDE: Spinach and Swiss Chard

Market Selection: Smooth-leaf, curly-leaf, and New Zealand spinach may be used interchangeably. Swiss chard can be found with red or white stems. Spinach should have deep green, unblemished leaves. Swiss chard leaves should be glossy, with heavy white or red stems.

Availability: Year-round

Storage: Wrap spinach and chard in paper towels and enclose in plastic wrap. Refrigerate for up to 4 days.

Flavor Enhancers: Garlic, nutmeg, oregano, tarragon

Equivalents: 1 bunch = approximately 10 ounces

Nutritional Value: Both are excellent sources of vitamins A and C, potassium, and iron.

60 calories per cup

Cooking and Handling Notes: The best way to clean spinach and chard is to fill a large bowl with cold water and 2 tablespoons of vinegar or lemon juice. Hold the bunch by the stems and swish the leaves in the water several times. Grit will sink to the bottom of the bowl. Pat dry and use. The stems of Swiss chard should be allowed a longer cooking time than the leaves.

Basic Cooking Methods: Wash spinach or Swiss chard and shake off any excess water. Place in a shallow saucepan with only the water that is clinging to the leaves. Cook, covered, for about 3 minutes, or until wilted.

Steam for about 3 minutes.

Prawns and Prosciutto Wrapped in Chard

½ cup plain yogurt
¼ cup mayonnaise
¼ cup mustard
2 tablespoons honey
2 tablespoons chopped fresh
   dill

12 unblemished large chard
   leaves
12 large prawns, shelled and
   deveined
12 thin slices prosciutto
3 tablespoons fresh lemon
   juice

SERVES 4 AS A FIRST COURSE

Combine all of the sauce ingredients until well blended. Cover and refrigerate until ready to use.

Blanch the chard leaves in a large pot of boiling water for 3 minutes. Drain them and spread them out. Wrap each prawn in a slice of prosciutto. Sprinkle with lemon juice. Place the prawn on the upper part of a chard leaf. Fold the sides in and roll the prawn in the leaf; place it in the steamer basket. Repeat the procedure with the remaining prawns.

Steam, covered, for 8 minutes. May be served hot, warm, or chilled with a mustard-dill sauce.

Curried Spinach and Apple Bisque

2 tablespoons butter or oil
1 small onion, chopped
1 celery stalk, chopped
½ teaspoon ground coriander
1 teaspoon curry powder
2 small apples, peeled,
    cored, and diced
10 ounces fresh spinach,
    chopped, or one 10-ounce
    package, frozen
4 cups chicken stock
    (page 343)
3 tablespoons raw rice
    Salt and pepper

In a medium saucepan, heat the butter. Sauté the onion and celery until soft, about 5 minutes. Stir in the coriander, curry, and apple; cook for 5 more minutes. Add the spinach; stir and cook until wilted. Add the stock and rice. Bring to a boil; reduce the heat, partially cover, and simmer for 15 minutes.

Puree in the food processor and season with salt and pepper.

SERVES 4

Chard Chowder with White Beans and Bacon

½ pound bacon, diced
1 bunch chard
2 cloves garlic, minced
1 small red onion, chopped
1 teaspoon fresh rosemary or
    ½ teaspoon dried
2 medium red potatoes,
    diced
6 cups beef or chicken stock
    (pages 344 and 343)
1 can cannellini (white
    kidney beans), drained
    Salt and pepper
½ cup chopped flat-leaf
    parsley

In a large pot, cook the bacon until most of the fat is rendered but the bacon is not crisp. Remove some of the fat with a baster, if necessary.

Remove the stems from the chard leaves and chop them coarsely. Cut the leaves into chiffonade. In the same pot, cook the chard stems with the garlic, onion, and rosemary until the vegetables are soft, about 6 minutes. Stir in the chard leaves and potato and cook for 3 more minutes. Add the stock and bring to a boil.

Partially cover and reduce to a simmer. Cook for 10 minutes; add the beans. Cook for another 10 minutes and season with salt and pepper. Stir in the parsley and serve.

SERVES 6

Spinach-Pear Soup with Roquefort Cream

3 tablespoons butter
4 green onions, chopped
2 Bosc pears, peeled, cored,
  and diced
1 bunch spinach, stemmed
  and coarsely chopped
¼ teaspoon grated nutmeg
4 cups chicken stock
  (page 343)
½ cup cream
  Salt and pepper
2 ounces Roquefort cheese

In a medium saucepan, heat the butter. Cook the green onion until wilted; stir in the pear, spinach, and nutmeg. Cook for 2 minutes. Add the stock and bring to a boil. Lower the heat and simmer, partially covered, for 15 minutes.

Puree the soup with half of the cream and season with salt and pepper. Combine the remaining cream with the Roquefort until smooth. Reheat the soup gently and serve with a dollop of Roquefort cream on each serving.

SERVES 6

Sautéed Spinach with Hot Peppers and Raisins

3 tablespoons olive oil
1 shallot, minced
½ teaspoon crushed red-
  pepper flakes
1 cup golden raisins
¼ cup low-sodium soy sauce
2 tablespoons balsamic
  vinegar
1 bunch spinach, coarsely
  chopped
  Salt and pepper
3 tablespoons toasted sesame
  seeds (page 347)

In a skillet, heat the oil. Sauté the shallot with the pepper flakes for about 2 minutes. Add the raisins, soy sauce, and vinegar. Bring to a boil and cook until almost all of the liquid has evaporated. Add the spinach and cook just until wilted. Season with salt and pepper and sprinkle with sesame seeds.

SERVES 4

Penne with Spinach and Lamb Sausage

2 tablespoons olive oil

½ pound spicy lamb sausage,
  sliced

1 bunch green onions, thinly
  sliced

8 ounces spinach leaves, cut
  in chiffonade

½ teaspoon dried oregano

1 cup chicken stock
  (page 343)

3 ounces feta cheese,
  crumbled

½ cup Kalamata olives,
  pitted and halved

1 large ripe tomato, seeded
  and coarsely chopped

½ pound freshly cooked
  penne, drained

¼ cup chopped fresh parsley

SERVES 6 TO 8 AS A FIRST
COURSE; 3 TO 4 AS A MAIN
COURSE

In a medium skillet, heat the oil. Sauté the sausage until the raw color disappears. Remove and reserve. In the same skillet, cook the onion and spinach until wilted. Add the oregano and stock and bring to a boil. Stir in the feta, olives, tomato, and reserved sausage and heat through. Toss with pasta and sprinkle with parsley.

Spinach and Tomato Gratin

3 tablespoons olive oil
1 onion, thinly sliced
2 cloves garlic, minced
1 pound spinach leaves,
    coarsely chopped
2 medium tomatoes, seeded
    and coarsely chopped
½ teaspoon dried oregano
    Salt and pepper

TOPPING

½ cup bread crumbs
½ cup grated Parmesan
1 teaspoon grated lemon zest
1 clove garlic, minced
2 tablespoons olive oil

SERVES 4

In a skillet, heat the oil. Sauté the onion and garlic for about 5 minutes. Add the spinach and tomato and cook for another 4 minutes. Stir in the oregano and season with salt and pepper. Remove the mixture to a shallow 2-quart baking dish.

Preheat the oven to 425°F.

Combine all of the topping ingredients except the oil. Sprinkle the topping over the spinach mixture and drizzle the oil over the topping. Bake for about 15 minutes, or until the topping is golden-brown and crisp.

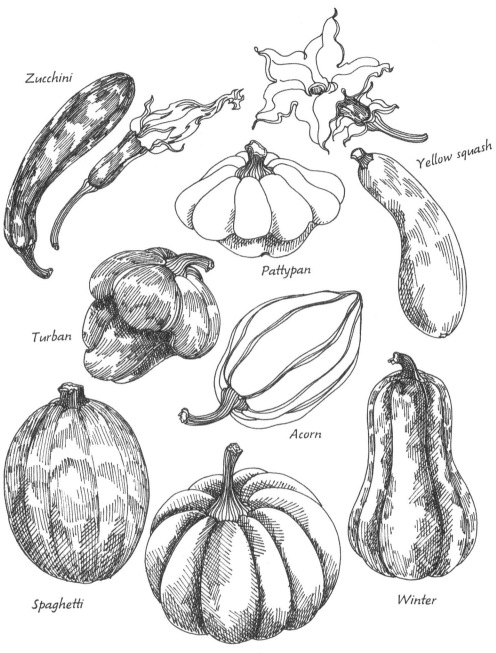

Zucchini

Yellow squash

Pattypan

Turban

Acorn

Spaghetti

Pumpkin

Winter

SQUASH

Summer Squash

*S*QUASH SEEMS LIKE just the right name for some of the more porous examples of this summer vegetable, which exhibit the "soak-up" qualities of a sponge. But like a good listener, squash has a knack for absorbing and reflecting, for making everything around it seem more interesting. Cooked with their natural summertime companions, garlic, tomatoes, and peppers, the various summer squashes can produce anything from a meaty-tasting vegetable stew to a flash-in-the-pan stir-fry.

In fact, summer squash is the essence of versatility—it can be grated raw in salads and pastas, pureed for sauces and soups, or cut into chunks for kebabs or for tempura-battered hors d'oeuvres. It can also be marinated, marmaladed, pickled, baked, fried, or stuffed. It even makes some interesting desserts, from this country's common zucchini breads to the Mexican *dulces*, which are slices of squash boiled in sugar, cooled, and served as candy. In Provence, the tender bright-yellow zucchini blossoms are swept through a batter, fried, and showered in powdered sugar. In Italy, *zuccato* is the sweet result when the plumpest of summer's harvest is preserved in sugar.

This brings up the question of size. Although baby squashes, hopefully with flowers attached, make intriguing-sounding menu items, the larger vegetables have equal virtues and often more fully developed nutlike flavors. Italians, for example, prefer to pick white marrow squash when they are hefty as an arm. In this country we can count on optimum flavor when zucchini are four to nine inches in length, with healthy green, yellow, or mottled skins. Patty pan squash, also called bush scallop or custard marrow, is best when four inches or smaller. This bumpy-skinned squash ranges in color from ivory to light green to the speckled green scallopini. Crooknecks and straightnecks, with yellow skin and flesh, are at their best at five to ten inches in length, as are Cocozelles and Casertas. The Latin American chayote, a pear-shaped, light green, furrow-skinned member of the gourd family sometimes grouped with summer squash, varies in length from three to eight inches. Used like most other summer squashes, it has a crisp, cucumberlike flesh and a large flat seed that is edible after cooking. Also known as vegetable pear, mirliton, mango squash, christophine, and chocho, this ancient tropical vegetable was a favorite of the Aztecs and Mayans long before the arrival of the Spaniards.

In fact, all squashes were a surprise to the first Europeans, who noted their ubiquitous use among the Indian groups of North and South America. Preparations ranged from drying the squash on sticks to preserve it for winter use, to an Iroquois soup that included the vegetable itself as well as its delicate blossoms. The word *squash* comes to us from the Narragansett Indian word *askoot-as-quahs*. Squash was one of three basic Native American foods (the other two were maize and beans) that had long been cultivated in the Western Hemisphere—estimates range from 2,000 to 9,000 years! It later became popular in all Mediterranean countries, where it was cultivated almost immediately upon arrival.

But perhaps squash's greatest conquest was among the early rough-and-tough California *rancheros,* who had no use at all for most vegetables. Even they deigned to eat squash as part of a vegetable mix called *colache,* which also included corn, beans, and tomatoes.

Of the varieties generally available, there are the summery-sounding Gold Rush and Sunburst and the color-coded White Lebanese, Greyzini, and Small Green Algerian. As for the blossoms, there is a more or less equal opportunity to select them by gender, if you are so inclined. When the flowers attached to the plant contain tiny squash, they have to be female, since only they produce fruit. When the flowers are empty or sold in elaborate bouquets, they are usually male. But, to be perfectly honest, only your produce manager will know for sure.

Consumer and Cooking Guide: Summer Squash

Market Selection: Green and golden zucchini; Sunburst; patty pan; scallopini; yellow crookneck; chayote. All varieties should be firm, with smooth, glossy skin.
Availability: Year-round; peak—July through September
Storage: Refrigerate in plastic for up to 5 days.
Flavor Enhancers: Garlic, oregano, basil, chervil, tarragon
Equivalents: 1 pound = 3 cups, sliced or diced
Nutritional Value: A good source of vitamin C
      25 calories per cup
Basic Cooking Methods: Cook in boiling salted water for about 3 minutes.
  Steam for 5 minutes.

Golden Squash and Black Bean Chowder

3 tablespoons oil
¼ pound pancetta, diced
1 small onion, chopped
1 large carrot, chopped
1 celery stalk, chopped
2 cups diced yellow squash
1 teaspoon fresh thyme or
  ½ teaspoon dried
¼ cup chopped fresh parsley
⅛ teaspoon cayenne
6 cups chicken stock
  (page 343)
1 large red potato, diced
1 cup cooked black beans
  Salt and pepper

In a large saucepan, heat the oil. Sauté the pancetta until the fat is rendered and the pancetta crisps slightly. Remove and reserve.

In the same pan, sauté the onion, carrot, celery, and squash until slightly softened. Stir in the thyme, parsley, and cayenne. Add the stock, bring to a boil, and add the potato. Reduce the heat and simmer, partially covered, for 15 minutes.

With a ladle, remove one-fourth of the soup to a food processor and puree. Return it to the pan with the reserved pancetta and the black beans. Cook for 5 minutes and season with salt and pepper.

SERVES 6

Zucchini and Potato Pancakes with Chived Yogurt

1 egg, lightly beaten
2 tablespoons flour
¼ teaspoon salt
¼ teaspoon freshly ground
  pepper
2 medium baking potatoes,
  peeled and coarsely grated
2 medium zucchini, coarsely
  grated
2 tablespoons butter
2 tablespoons oil
½ cup chopped fresh chives
½ cup plain yogurt
  Pinch cayenne

Combine the egg with the flour, salt, and pepper. Squeeze any excess water from the potato and zucchini and stir into the egg mixture.

In a large skillet, heat the butter and oil. Spoon tablespoons of the batter into the skillet and flatten with the back of a spoon. Cook over medium heat for about 4 minutes; turn and cook on the other side until golden-brown and crisp. Remove to paper toweling to drain excess oil.

Combine the chives with the yogurt and cayenne and serve with the pancakes.

SERVES 4 TO 6

Summer Squash Crumble

7 tablespoons olive oil

3 cloves garlic, minced

1 red bell pepper, thinly
sliced

6 zucchini, thinly sliced

6 crookneck squash, thinly
sliced

4 patty pan squash, diced

½ cup fresh basil leaves

2 medium tomatoes, thinly
sliced

¾ cup fresh bread crumbs

¾ cup grated Monterey Jack
cheese

¼ cup grated Parmesan

SERVES 6 TO 8 AS A SIDE
DISH

Preheat the oven to 375°F. Brush a 10-inch baking dish
with 2 tablespoons of the oil.

In a large skillet, heat 3 tablespoons of oil. Sauté the
garlic, pepper, and squashes over medium-high heat
for about 6 minutes, or just until the vegetables begin
to soften. Stir in the basil and transfer the mixture to
the prepared baking dish.

Arrange the tomato slices over the squash. Combine
the bread crumbs with the cheeses and sprinkle over
the tomatoes. Drizzle the remaining 2 tablespoons oil
over the crumb mixture. Bake for about 40 minutes, or
until golden-brown.

Rosemary-Scented Grilled Squash

½ cup olive oil
1 tablespoon minced fresh
 rosemary
2 cloves garlic, minced
½ teaspoon salt
½ teaspoon freshly ground
 black pepper
3 medium yellow zucchini,
 sliced in thirds lengthwise
3 medium green zucchini,
 sliced in thirds lengthwise
1 tablespoon fresh lemon
 juice
3 tablespoons balsamic
 vinegar

SERVES 6

Preheat the grill.

Combine the oil with the rosemary, garlic, salt, and pepper. Brush both sides of the zucchini slices with the oil and place them on the grill. Cook for about 3 minutes per side, or just until grill marks appear on the zucchini.

Whisk the lemon juice and vinegar into the remaining oil until well blended. Pour over the grilled zucchini and let marinate for about 1 hour at room temperature.

Corn and Chile–Stuffed Squash

1 tablespoon oil
8 patty pan squash

FILLING

½ cup corn kernels
½ cup diced tomato
1 jalapeño pepper, seeded,
 deveined, and minced
1 egg, lightly beaten
½ cup shredded cheddar
 cheese
Salt and pepper

SERVES 8

Preheat the oven to 400°F. Oil a baking pan with the 1 tablespoon oil.

Steam or boil the squash for 7 minutes. Let cool; scoop out the centers and discard.

Combine the corn, tomato, jalapeño, egg, and cheese, salt, and pepper until well blended. Spoon the mixture into the squash shells. Place the squash in the prepared pan and cover with foil. Bake for 15 minutes; remove the foil and bake for another 5 minutes, or until the filling is golden-brown and bubbly.

Spicy Stuffed Chayote with Mushrooms and Almonds

2 chayotes, halved
  lengthwise

STUFFING

3 tablespoons olive oil
1 small onion, finely
  chopped
½ red bell pepper, seeded and
  finely chopped
1 jalapeño pepper, seeded,
  deveined, and finely
  chopped
2 cloves garlic, minced
¼ pound mushrooms, finely
  chopped
¼ cup coarsely chopped fresh
  cilantro
½ cup bread crumbs
¼ cup coarsely chopped
  almonds
  Salt and pepper
1 cup shredded Monterey
  Jack cheese

SERVES 4

In a covered pot, boil the chayotes, in just enough water to cover, for about 20 minutes. Drain them and set them in a greased baking dish.

In a medium skillet, heat the oil. Sauté the onion, both peppers, garlic, and mushrooms until soft, about 8 minutes. Stir in the cilantro, bread crumbs, and almonds and cook for another minute. Season with salt and pepper and stir in the cheese.

Preheat the oven to 400°F.

Fill the chayote halves with stuffing and bake for 10 minutes.

Winter Squash

"IN ALEXANDRE DUMAS'S distinguished *Grand Dictionnaire de Cuisine*, he includes directions on how to cook an elephant. (You can look it up.) For many people, elephant cookery is less daunting than dealing with the mammoth category of winter squash. Not only do winter squashes come in quite a few major varieties, each with its own subtypes, they all differ drastically in shape, size, and color: there are long, pale boomerangs, golden-yellow footballs, grooved orange spheres, and multicolored turbans. There are even enormous—some would say elephantine—quarter-ton pumpkins, as any devotee of pumpkin festivals can attest. But perhaps the strangest aspect of winter squashes is that, with few exceptions, they are all handled alike for cooking purposes.

They can be baked whole and peeled for purees and soups; or cut in half, scooped of their seeds, stuffed, and baked. In the Philippines, thick slices of peeled firm-fleshed squash are fried with garlic and onion. Latin Americans cook the sweetest varieties into a crystallized confection. Italians use pumpkin puree not only as an ingredient in making pasta dough but also as a filling for ravioli. In Japan, kabocha squash symbolizes good health and luck on Christmas and New Year's Day. Spaniards mix sugar with the pastalike strands of spaghetti squash and boil it to make a sweet called *cabello de ángel* ("angel's hair").

For all their versatility, squashes were not universally appreciated when the Spanish first brought these New World discoveries back to Old World kitchens. The French had little use for them, especially their great seventeenth-century agriculturalist Olivier de Serres, who dubbed them "Spain's revenge." Yet they were the salvation of the early colonists in North America, who used them in every conceivable way. Besides roasting and steaming them, they mixed the pulp with corn flour for breads, puddings, and pancakes. They followed the Indian example of sun-drying the flesh to preserve it and also eating it raw. Pumpkin seeds—which are 29 percent protein, more than almost any other seed or nut—were consumed roasted or raw, hulled or unhulled, as is or ground up with flour. "Let no man make a jest at Pumpkins," warned one early settler, "for with this fruit the Lord was pleased to feed his people to their good content, till Corne and Cattell were raised."

The Pilgrims found a much greater range of colored squashes than we commonly see today, including blue, red, and gray varieties. Although unknown in the rest of the world, some of the more than twenty-five species of squash had been cultivated in the Americas for more than 9,000 years!

If a vote were taken to select the most unusual member of this large, ancient family, the winner might be the spaghetti squash, the only type that calls for its own distinct treatment for cooking purposes. But certainly everybody's favorite would be the one winter squash that people buy in great numbers but never eat, that they prepare not for the table but for the front porch, and that is served not with a sauce outside but with a candle inside. Named for the occasion, some of the current pumpkin types include Spooky, Triple Treat, and the miniature Jack Be Little, which fits neatly on the end of a witch's broomstick. No cooking required.

CONSUMER AND COOKING GUIDE: Winter Squash

Market Selection: Sweet varieties include acorn, butternut, hubbard, delicata, kabocha, and sweet dumpling. Pumpkin, banana, and golden acorn squash are more fibrous in texture and milder in flavor. Spaghetti squash differs from the others in that the flesh separates into strands when cooked (hence its name). Select firm, thick-shelled squash. If you plan to cook pumpkins, select small ones.
Availability: Peak season—September through March
Storage: Whole squash may be stored in a cool, dry place for up to 2 months. Cut squash should be wrapped in plastic and stored in the refrigerator for up to 1 week.
Flavor Enhancers: Nutmeg, allspice, cinnamon, cloves, curry powder
Nutritional Value: Good source of vitamin A

   80 calories per cup
Cooking and Handling Notes: To make squash puree, cut the squash in half and bake, cut-side down, in a preheated 400°F oven for about 45 minutes, or until tender. Remove the skin and seeds, scoop out the flesh, and puree the flesh in a food processor.

To bake spaghetti squash, leave the squash whole and pierce it in several places. Bake in a preheated 400°F oven for about 45 minutes, or until tender. Allow to cool before handling. Cut in half, remove seeds, and scoop out strands.

Butternut Squash Soup with Tomatoes and Corn

3 tablespoons oil
1 leek, white part only,
  sliced
1 cup chopped tomato
½ teaspoon dried thyme
4 cups chicken stock
  (page 343)
1 butternut squash, peeled,
  seeded, and diced
½ cup cream
  Salt and pepper
1 cup corn kernels
1 tomato, seeded and diced
½ cup chopped fresh chives

In a large pot, heat the oil. Sauté the leek, chopped tomato, and thyme for about 5 minutes. Add the stock and bring to a boil. Add the squash, lower the heat, and cook for about 30 minutes, or until tender.

Puree the mixture with the cream. Season with salt and pepper and return to the pan. Add the corn and diced tomato and cook on low heat for 5 minutes. Garnish with chopped chives.

SERVES 6

Sautéed Winter Squash with Shiitake Mushrooms and Rosemary

2 tablespoons butter
2 tablespoons oil
1 tablespoon brown sugar
1 medium squash
  (butternut, delicata, or
  acorn), peeled and diced
½ pound shiitake
  mushrooms, stems
  removed and caps sliced
½ teaspoon dried rosemary
  Salt and pepper

In a large skillet, cook the butter, oil, and brown sugar until the sugar melts. Add the squash and mushrooms; sauté for about 10 minutes, or until tender. Stir in the rosemary and season with salt and pepper.

SERVES 6

Spaghetti Squash Salad with Olives and Sun-Dried Tomatoes

1 large spaghetti squash
baked (see Cooking Notes,
page 195), seeds discarded
and flesh reserved

1 cup Kalamata olives,
pitted and halved

½ cup sun-dried tomatoes
packed in oil, cut into
strips

1 cup diced smoked
mozzarella cheese

1 cup chopped fresh parsley

DRESSING

1 clove garlic, minced

3 tablespoons red-wine
vinegar

1 tablespoon fresh lemon
juice

¾ cup olive oil
Salt and pepper

SERVES 6

Combine the flesh from the spaghetti squash with the olives, sun-dried tomato, cheese, and parsley.

Whisk the dressing ingredients until smooth. Toss with the spaghetti-squash mixture and season with salt and pepper.

Winter Squash and Green Bean Ragoût with Pancetta

2 tablespoons oil
¼ pound pancetta, diced
1 small red onion, diced
1 squash (butternut,
  delicata, or sweet
  dumpling), peeled and
  diced (about 2 cups)
1 cup chopped tomato
½ cup chicken stock (page
  343) or water
½ teaspoon dried oregano
1 pound green beans,
  trimmed and cut into
  1-inch pieces
Salt and pepper

SERVES 6 TO 8

In a sauté pan or skillet, heat the oil. Add the pancetta and onion and cook for about 3 minutes. Add the squash and cook for 8 minutes. Stir in the tomato, stock, and oregano and bring to a boil. Lower the heat and simmer for about 3 minutes, or until the squash is almost tender. Add the green beans and cook for another 4 minutes. Season with salt and pepper.

Pumpkin Pot de Crème

2 cups pumpkin puree (see
  Cooking Notes, page 195)
5 egg yolks
⅔ cup sugar
1 tablespoon vanilla
½ teaspoon ground
  cinnamon
½ teaspoon ground nutmeg
½ teaspoon ground ginger
3 cups heavy cream
  Whipped cream for
  garnish (optional)

SERVES 8

Preheat the oven to 325°F.
Whisk the pumpkin and egg yolks until smooth. Add the sugar, vanilla, cinnamon, nutmeg, and ginger and whisk again until well combined. Bring the cream to a simmer and beat it into the pumpkin mixture.

Divide the mixture among eight 6-ounce ramekins. Place the ramekins in a shallow baking pan. Add enough boiling water to come halfway up the sides of the ramekins. Bake for 25 minutes. (The custards may not appear firm.)

Remove from the water bath and let cool at room temperature. (The custard will thicken as it cools.) Cover with plastic wrap and refrigerate. Serve cold, with a dollop of whipped cream if desired.

Spaghetti Squash with Turkey Meatballs

MEATBALLS

1 pound ground turkey or a
  mixture of other ground
  meats
2 tablespoons bread crumbs
1 egg, lightly beaten
1 shallot, minced
1 tablespoon prepared
  mustard
½ teaspoon dried oregano
½ teaspoon salt
¼ teaspoon pepper

3 tablespoons oil
2 cloves garlic, minced
¼ cup red wine
  One 28-ounce can
  tomatoes, drained and
  chopped
2 tablespoons tomato paste
  Salt and pepper
1 spaghetti squash
1 cup grated Parmesan

SERVES 4 TO 6

Combine the ground meat with the bread crumbs, egg, shallot, mustard, oregano, salt, and pepper. Form into walnut-sized balls.

In a large sauté pan, heat the oil with the garlic. Add the meatballs and brown on all sides. Add the wine and bring to a boil. Add the chopped tomato and tomato paste. Reduce the heat and simmer for about 45 minutes. Season with salt and pepper.

Preheat the oven to 350°F.

Meanwhile, pierce the squash in several places. Place it in a rimmed baking pan and bake for about 1 hour, or until the shell yields to pressure.

Cut the squash in half and remove the seeds. Scoop the flesh into a bowl; it will separate into strands. Toss with some of sauce and top with the remaining sauce and meatballs. Sprinkle with cheese if desired.

Curried Pork and Pumpkin Stew

2 pounds boneless pork butt
    or shoulder, cut into cubes
    Salt and pepper
    Flour for dredging
4 tablespoons oil
1 large onion, diced
3 cloves garlic, minced
1 small piece fresh ginger,
    peeled and grated
½ teaspoon cayenne
2 teaspoons ground cumin
1 teaspoon ground turmeric
1 teaspoon salt
2 cups peeled and diced
    pumpkin
2 medium potatoes, peeled
    and diced
2 cups chicken or beef stock
    (pages 343 and 344)
2 carrots, peeled and sliced
2 zucchini, sliced
    Fresh cilantro for garnish

SERVES 8

Sprinkle the pork with salt and pepper and dredge in flour. Heat the oil in a large shallow pan. Brown the pork on all sides; remove and reserve.

In the same pan, cook the onion until soft. Stir in the garlic, ginger, cayenne, cumin, turmeric, and salt, and cook for about 5 minutes. Add the pumpkin, potato, and reserved pork and cook, stirring, until the pork is coated with the onion mixture. Add the stock and bring to a boil. Lower the heat and simmer for 15 minutes.

Add the carrot and zucchini and simmer for another 5 minutes. Taste for salt and serve garnished with cilantro sprigs.

TOMATOES

CHERRY TOMATOES are popular at cocktail parties for the same reason that pitted olives and roasted almonds are: there are no telltale pits left behind to count up and feel guilty about. Some people also eat them because they like the taste, which sometimes, though not always, resembles that of a tomato.

Tomatoes are possibly the major casualty of modern produce-handling techniques, which include picking tomatoes prematurely and gassing them to desired redness (but not ripeness) in transit. The result is a general and justifiable suspicion by Americans of all tomatoes, especially the most beautiful.

Another recent tomato trend is more positive. Tomato growers, from professional producers to home gardeners, are seeking out tasty old varieties in all shapes, colors, and sizes. At produce stands, farmers' markets, and even corner grocery stores, more of them are showing up every day. This means choice: tiny persimmon-colored "currant" tomatoes, yellow and red pear-shaped miniatures; flavorful multicolored jewels called Pixies, Tiny Tims, and Golden Pygmies. Equally succulent are the larger specimens: the surprisingly cream-colored White Beauties, the yellow and red Striped Caravans, the large Oxhearts, the yellow Lemon Boys, and the two meaty, pink, enigmatically named oddities, Stump of the World and Mortgage Lifter. The most important question in getting to know tomatoes, however, is not: What is your name? It is, rather: Were you ripened on the vine?

Even major supermarket chains are beginning to realize that their customers have little taste for ethylene. This is especially true for tomatoes because they are so often eaten raw. In salads, salsas, and cold soups, tomatoes act as both central ingredient and main condiment. In cooked dishes, tomatoes enhance the ingredients they accompany. Tomatoes are popular from the Sahara Desert, where they are baked into bread, to the Catalan region of Spain, where they are rubbed into sliced bread to become the ubiquitously popular *pa amb tomaquet*, to San Francisco, where the famous fish dish cioppino gets its distinction from the tomato.

The Latin binomial for tomato, *Lycopersicon esculentum*, has a strange translation: "edible wolf's peach." Perhaps this ominous designation reflects the awe that greeted the vegetable when it was first brought to Europe from the New World. Native Americans, however, made much use of it, even devising techniques for sun-drying tomatoes on slanted boards. This they taught to Cortez, who reportedly passed it on to his countrymen. Ironically, when the newly discovered vegetable was reintroduced back to the Americas, it met with varying degrees of success. In Salem, Massachusetts, for example, a determined Italian painter brought tomatoes to town in the early 1800s, only to have them summarily rejected. Yet, a quarter of a century later, tomatoes were extolled by a visitor as the "great luxury of the American table."

Serious tomato discussions eventually get around to the recurring debate about whether tomatoes are a fruit or a vegetable. By some definitions, the tomato is not only a fruit (because it consists of an ovary and its seeds), it is also a berry because it contains more than one seed. This sort of debate might have remained forever insoluble had it not become a matter of economics. When an importer argued that no duty had to be paid on his tomatoes because, at the time, they fell under the duty-free category of fruit, the controversy reached the attention of the Supreme Court. In its ruling, presumably issued after some judicious meal planning, the judges contended that tomatoes are indeed a vegetable because they are "usually served at dinner, in, with, or after the soup, fish, or meat, which constitute the principal part of the repast, and not, like fruits, generally as dessert." And that's the law.

CONSUMER AND COOKING GUIDE: Tomatoes

Market Selection: Red and yellow round; red and yellow cherry; red and yellow Roma (plum-shaped); beefsteak; saladette (in between a Roma and a red round); zebra (red and yellow or green and yellow striped); grape (cherry tomato-sized, green in color). All types should be smooth, firm, and intense in color.

Availability: Year-round; peak—July through September

Storage: Store unwashed, at room temperature. Avoid refrigeration unless tomatoes become very soft.

Flavor Enhancers: Parsley, basil, tarragon, dill

Equivalents: 1 large tomato = 1 cup, coarsely chopped

Nutritional Value: Potassium, good source of vitamins A and C
          40 calories per cup

Cooking and Handling Notes: To peel tomatoes, submerge them in boiling water for about 30 seconds. Plunge them into cold water and slip the skins off. To seed, cut them in half crosswise and gently squeeze out seeds.

Basic Cooking Methods: See individual recipes.

Summer Tomato Soup

16 tomatoes (yellow or red
   Romas), halved and seeded
¼ sweet onion
1 teaspoon salt
½ teaspoon freshly ground
   pepper
1 tablespoon honey
   Juice of 1 lemon
½ cup heavy cream
½ cup plain yogurt
1 cucumber, peeled, seeded,
   and diced
½ cup chopped fresh chives

SERVES 6

In the bowl of a food processor, combine the tomatoes, onion, salt, pepper, honey, and lemon juice. Process until pureed; add the cream and yogurt. Process just until blended. Stir in the cucumber and chives. Chill about 2 hours and serve.

Tomato and Two-Bean Soup

2 tablespoons butter
2 tablespoons oil
2 large sweet onions,
   chopped
12 large beefsteak tomatoes,
   coarsely chopped
1 cup chicken stock
   (page 343)
1 pound green beans, cut
   into 1-inch pieces
1 can cannellini (white
   kidney beans), drained
4 sage leaves, chopped
   Salt and pepper
½ cup grated Parmesan

SERVES 6 TO 8

In a large saucepan, heat the butter and oil. Sauté the onion until very soft, about 10 minutes. Add the tomato and cook for about 20 minutes.

Puree the mixture in a food processor; then pass through a food mill to remove seeds and skin.

Bring to a boil with the stock. Add the beans and sage and simmer for 10 minutes. Season with salt and pepper. Serve hot, garnished with a sprinkling of cheese.

Red and Yellow Cherry Tomato Bruschetta

12 ½-inch slices good crusty
    bread
    About 2 tablespoons olive
    oil
1 large cut clove garlic
4 red cherry tomatoes, finely
    chopped
4 yellow cherry tomatoes,
    finely chopped
1 teaspoon balsamic vinegar
6 basil leaves, chopped
½ teaspoon salt
½ teaspoon freshly ground
    pepper

SERVES 6 AS AN
APPETIZER

Brush both sides of the bread with the olive oil. Grill or broil the bread on both sides until it just begins to color. Rub one side with the cut clove of garlic. Combine the remaining ingredients and spread on the bread. Serve as soon as possible.

Minted Summer Garden Salad with Cumin Vinaigrette

4 large tomatoes, cut into 6
   wedges, then each wedge
   cut in half, crosswise
2 small zucchini, thinly
   sliced
1 red or yellow bell pepper,
   diced
1 bunch green onions, sliced
½ cup imported black olives,
   pitted and halved
2 tablespoons chopped fresh
   parsley
2 tablespoons chopped fresh
   mint

DRESSING

1 teaspoon cumin seed,
   toasted (page 347) and
   crushed
1 clove garlic, minced
¼ cup fresh lemon juice
   Pinch sugar
6 tablespoons olive oil

SERVES 8

Combine the vegetables in a large bowl. Mix the dressing ingredients until thoroughly combined. Toss with the vegetables; marinate, covered, in the refrigerator for about 2 hours before serving.

Rigatoni with Prawns, Tomatoes, and Fennel

3 tablespoons olive oil

1 tablespoon fennel seed, crushed

2 cloves garlic, minced

½ pound prawns, shelled and deveined

1 large fennel bulb, thinly sliced

6 large ripe Roma tomatoes, seeded and coarsely chopped

2 tablespoons tomato paste

Salt and pepper

1 pound rigatoni, cooked and drained

SERVES 4 TO 6 AS A MAIN COURSE; 8 AS A FIRST COURSE

In a skillet, heat the oil. Cook the fennel seed and garlic for about 1 minute, or until fragrant. Add the prawns and cook, stirring, just until they turn pink. Remove and reserve.

To the same skillet, add the fennel. Cook until it is slightly soft, about 4 minutes. Add the tomato and tomato paste and cook until thickened, about 10 minutes.

Return the prawns to the sauce and cook at a bare simmer for about 3 minutes. Salt and pepper to taste. Toss with rigatoni and serve.

FRUITS

APPLES

THE APPLES of Halloween: they were our favorites, as children. These were the devil-costume-red apples that came with dimes stuck in their sides. They were around for only one day a year and were served—if you can call it that—in a metal wash bucket full of water. No utensils were required, or even permitted, for this special preparation, just a willingness to stick our faces deep underwater and snare an apple with our bare mouths. We sputtered and choked, we surfaced for air and squeezed the water from our eyes, but we kept at it: we wanted our ten cents. For the rest of the year, we ate apples assiduously, hoping that at least one of them would hatch a dime, like the apples of Halloween.

Most of the time, however, we ate everyday apples: slippery McIntoshes, sugary red Delicious, sour green ones from the neighbor's tree. Apples were apples; there were millions of them and they were everywhere, or so it always seemed, once upon a time when we dwelled in apple-innocence. Now we know otherwise. Now we know there are apple "museums" like the one in North Grafton, Massachusetts, or the Sonoma Antique Apple Nursery in Healdsburg, California, which cultivate endangered apple species in order to keep them in existence. These include the Roxbury Russet, the Duchess of Oldenburg, the White Astrachan, and many others that have been forsaken by growers because they don't conform to modern requirements of commercial production, harvesting, and transportation. In fact, of the more than 7,000 apple varieties, this country cultivates only about 20, of which the Red Delicious comprises 25 percent.

Even stranger for a fruit that, in all probability, dates from Neolithic times is the fact that most varieties were developed over the past few hundred years. The ubiquitous Red Delicious, for example, has been with us for a mere century since it won first prize in an 1893 fruit fair in Louisiana, Missouri. Though called "Hawkeyes" by their Iowa developer, Jesse Hiatt, the apples were proclaimed "delicious" at the fair. Rome Beauties date from the 1830s and get their name from Rome Township, Ohio, where they were first produced by Alanson Gilett. The all-American-sounding Granny Smiths hail from mid-nineteenth-century Australia and did not even reach this country until the 1940s. The apple with the longest history, the Api, dates from the ancient world, where it was cultivated by the Etruscan horticulturalist for whom it is named. It is also known as lady apple.

The English have a strong tradition of respect and love for apples, as any reader of Edward Bunyard's lyrical *Anatomy of Dessert* knows. He remarks: "No fruit is more to our English taste than the Apple [which keeps] alive for us in winter, in its sun-stained flush and rustic russet, the memory of golden autumnal days." In the opposite corner, American writer Bertha Damon makes her case in *A Sense of Humus:* "Every New Englander believes the apple is supreme among all created fruits." There is a continuity here since, after all, it was the early English colonists who scattered the seeds of this devotion, both literally and figuratively. Once in bloom, the apple tree often served as staff of life. Crèvecoeur, in the late 1700s, reported: "My wife's and my supper half the year consists of apple-pie and milk." Apples were units of currency; one recorded transaction in Plymouth Colony in 1649 shows that 500 apple trees bought 200 acres of land. Until the 1850s, when the paring machine was invented, apple "bees" were a common social gathering for women, who would get together to peel, slice, and string apples and dry them for winter use.

Apples in colonial times were consumed in the form of drinks like apple brandy—an early New England nip—apple juice, and fermented apple cider. Apple-cider perfectionists blended their brews from different types of apples with the fastidiousness of wine makers. Apple desserts had homey names like apple slump, pippin' pudding, apple brown betty, and apple pandowdy. Through it all apple pie remained everybody's first preference. When fresh apples were not available, pies were made with applesauce or even dried apples, although this was not the poet's favorite:

> *I loathe, abhor, despise,*
> *Abominate dried apple pies . . .*
> *But of all poor grub beneath the skies,*
> *The poorest is dried apple pies . . .*
> *Tread on my corns, or tell me lies,*
> *But don't pass me dried apple pies.*
>
> —*Anonymous*

Apples were also included in many savory combinations, like cabbage-sausage casseroles, duck and pork dishes, and the old New England Feast Day dish of sweet potatoes and apples. American cookbook writers were proprietary and unswerving in apple matters: witness Eliza Leslie's mid-nineteenth-century instructions that roast pork should *always* be served with applesauce. Equally strict apple etiquette is decreed in Mrs. Rorer's 1886 cookbook, which admonishes, "Use only a silver knife in cutting."

Professional pomophiles enjoy debates about how each particular apple received its name. Some propose that the Westfield "Seek-No-Further" can be traced to a merchant vessel of that name, which supposedly delivered a sapling to this country in 1665. Other experts claim it originated in Hanover, New Hampshire, the home of Dartmouth College. From there we also get the Dartmouth Crab, "named in honor of some professor, maybe," according to one historian. It is certain that the Newtown pippin, a green apple grown in the 1700s in Newtown, New York, has nothing to do with Sir Isaac Newton. Likewise, the Summer Rambo, a favorite of John Chapman (a.k.a. Johnny Appleseed), has nothing to do with Sylvester Stallone.

Apple preferences differ, of course, but writer A. J. Liebling has made possibly the most straightforward pronouncement on the matter. People, he says, "have made a triumph of the Delicious apple because it doesn't taste like an apple, and of the Golden Delicious because it doesn't taste like anything."

Market Selection: Red Delicious, Golden Delicious, Granny Smith, Rome Beauty, Winesap, Newtown pippin, Cortland, McIntosh, Jonathan, Baldwin, Gravenstein, Empire, and Northern Spy are common varieties. Select firm apples that are blemish-free.

Availability: While most varieties of apples are available year-round, autumn has the largest harvest

Storage: Store in a plastic bag in the refrigerator, up to 2 weeks.

Flavor Enhancers: Cinnamon, nutmeg, curry, cardamom, fennel seed

Equivalents: 3 medium apples = 1 pound

  1 pound apples, cored and sliced = approximately 4½ cups

  1 large apple, grated or minced = 1 cup

Nutritional Value: Good source of fiber and minerals

  125 calories per large apple

Apple, Cabbage, and Leek Soup

3 tablespoons oil
1 bunch leeks, white part
  only, sliced
1 large green cabbage,
  shredded
4 apples (Granny Smith,
  pippin, or Northern Spy),
  peeled and thinly sliced
1 tablespoon crushed fennel
  seed
2 tablespoons brown sugar
2 tablespoons balsamic
  vinegar
5 cups chicken broth
  (page 343)
1 medium baking potato,
  peeled and diced
  Salt and pepper

SERVES 6

In a large saucepan, heat the oil. Sauté the leek, cabbage, and apple until tender, about 8 minutes. Stir in the fennel seed, sugar, and vinegar and cook for 2 minutes. Add the broth, bring to a boil, and add the potato. Lower the heat and simmer, partially covered, for 20 minutes.

In a food processor, puree one-third of the soup mixture; return it to the pot. Season with salt and pepper and reheat.

Apple-Cheddar Whole-Wheat Popovers

2 apples (pippin, Granny
  Smith, or Gravenstein),
  peeled and chopped
½ cup shredded cheddar
  cheese
¾ cup all-purpose flour
¼ cup whole-wheat flour
1 cup milk
1 tablespoon butter, melted
  Pinch of salt
2 eggs, beaten

MAKES 8 POPOVERS

Preheat the oven to 450°F. Grease 8 popover cups.

Place a tablespoon each of chopped apple and cheese in the bottom of each cup. Beat the flours, milk, butter, and salt just until smooth. Add the eggs and whisk just until well combined. Do not overbeat. Fill the cups two-thirds full with batter. Bake for 15 minutes; reduce the heat to 350°F and bake for another 20 minutes until puffed and golden brown. Let cool at least 15 minutes, then remove from pan.

Halibut with Apple Curry Salsa

4 tablespoons oil or butter
4 halibut steaks, about
    ¾ inch thick
    Salt and pepper
1 small onion, chopped
1 stalk celery, chopped
1 large apple (McIntosh,
    Jonathan, or Red
    Delicious), cored and
    chopped
1 small tomato, seeded and
    chopped
1 tablespoon curry powder
¼ teaspoon ground coriander
¼ teaspoon ground turmeric
2 tablespoons flour
1 cup chicken broth
    (page 343)
1 tablespoon sour cream
    Fresh cilantro leaves for
    garnish

SERVES 4

In a large skillet, heat 2 tablespoons of the oil. Sprinkle the fish with salt and pepper and cook for 3 minutes on each side. Remove to a plate, cover with foil, and keep warm.

Add the remaining 2 tablespoons of oil to the same skillet and heat. Sauté the onion, celery, and apple until tender, about 5 minutes. Stir in the tomato, curry powder, coriander, turmeric, and flour. Cook for 2 minutes. Add the chicken stock; bring to a boil, lower the heat, and simmer until thickened. Stir in the sour cream.

Return the fish to the pan and cook over low heat for about 4 minutes. Serve garnished with cilantro.

Creamy Rice Pudding on a Bed of Apples

4 tablespoons (½ stick)
  butter
4 tablespoons plus ½ cup
  sugar
4 Golden Delicious apples,
  peeled, cored, and cut into
  thin wedges
½ cup raw rice
1 quart milk, heated
¼ cup chopped walnuts
½ teaspoon ground
  cinnamon
  Pinch salt

SERVES 6

In a large skillet, heat the butter and 4 tablespoons sugar until the mixture turns golden. Add the apple wedges and cook for about 8 minutes, tossing gently.

Preheat the oven to 325°F. Spread the apple mixture on the bottom of a shallow 2-quart baking dish.

In a medium bowl, combine the rice, milk, walnuts, cinnamon, and a pinch of salt with the ½ cup sugar. Pour over the apples and bake, covered, for about 1½ hours. Remove the cover and continue to bake for about 20 minutes, or until the top is lightly browned. May be served warm or at room temperature.

Baked Apples in White Zinfandel

6 large Rome Beauty apples
2 teaspoons fresh lemon
  juice
3 tablespoons melted butter
  or margarine
½ cup chopped walnuts
¼ cup currants
2 tablespoons sugar
½ teaspoon ground
  cinnamon
  About 1 cup white
  Zinfandel
  Plain yogurt sweetened
  with honey (optional)

SERVES 6

Preheat the oven to 375°F.

Core the apples and pare the peels one-third of the way down from the stem ends. Sprinkle the exposed apple flesh with lemon juice. Combine the butter, walnuts, currants, sugar, and cinnamon. Fill the apple cavities with this mixture.

Place the apples in a shallow baking dish and pour in enough wine to reach about 1 inch up the apples. Cover the baking dish with foil and bake for about 1 hour, basting with wine every 20 minutes. Remove the foil and bake for another 15 minutes. Serve with a dollop of sweetened yogurt, if desired. May be served hot, cold, or at room temperature.

AVOCADOS

AVOCADOS ARE a demanding lot. They insist on being picked from their trees—handpicked in most cases—before they will even consider beginning the ripening process. They shirk excessive cold and, unlike many other more agreeable fruits and vegetables, will not abide refrigeration until they are completely ripe. Even then, their conditions are strict: not too cold nor for very long, thank you. Put into a plastic bag, they suddenly stop ripening altogether and, when released from this oxygenless environment, they simply rot. For the valiant avocado lover who coddles an avocado through these initial stages, there is the final insult. Once the peeled avocado enters the light of day, it begins to darken into an unappetizing dull gray.

"Why do avocados do these things to us? What can they be thinking," we ask, exasperated at tossing out yet another muddy, half-eaten bowl of guacamole.

The answer, strangely enough, seems to be love: avocados simply love to be loved. Theirs is not to sit around in graceful green slices or mashed up as dips or soups. Theirs is to be eaten and enjoyed immediately, as soon as they're ready: not a moment before, nor for many moments after. "Eat me," they command as they slip out of their skins, "or else."

The creamy texture and nutty flavor of the avocado have lured many of us into helpless compliance with its terms. For years, we have buried avocado pits in our guacamole, in the undemonstrable but hopeful belief that the pit would magically keep everything bright and green indefinitely, contrary to the fruit's obvious wishes. The pit was the avocado's Achilles' heel, or so many people hoped. In fact, as Harold McGee reports in his charming debunker, *The Curious Cook,* the pit does very little. After numerous pit-burying experiments, McGee discovered that only the guacamole directly beneath the pit, where it was not exposed to the air, was saved from discoloration. Much more effective, he found, is oxygen-impermeable plastic wrap pressed tightly against the guacamole. When sliced or cut-up avocados are mixed with acidic foods, like tomatoes or citrus fruits, browning is also somewhat diminished. But the best remedy is to consume the avocado preparation as soon as it's ready.

There are quite a few ways to get it ready, from fluffing it into avocado butters to stuffing avocado halves with baby shrimp or chicken salad. There are mousses, soups, both cold and hot, and all sorts of sauces and spreads. Avocado ice cream, a concoction that Somerset Maugham claimed to have created, is interesting for its literary associations, though perhaps for little else.

Brazilians treat avocado as the fruit that it technically is and make a dessert of its mashed flesh mixed with sugar. Even the leaves of the fruit are used in some Latin countries, where tortilla fillings are spiked with a sprinkling of toasted crushed avocado leaves, said to add a flavor like anise.

Guacamole has any number of variations, which is not surprising, given that it was first eaten by the Aztecs long before the arrival of the Spanish. In fact, the avocado is a New World fruit—its name comes from the Nahuatl *ahuacatl* ("testicle")—that has been cultivated for 7,000 years.

A relative of a subtropical tree in the laurel family, the avocado has more than one hundred varieties. They range in size from hefty 5-pounders down to the dimensions of a chicken egg. The two varieties most commonly available are the rough-skinned Haas, a dark green-to-black type of Guatemalan origin, and the lighter green, smooth-skinned Fuerte, a Guatemalan-Mexican hybrid. Of the 300 million pounds annually marketed in this country, domestic production is centered in California, which provides 80 percent, and Florida, which makes up the other 20.

Also known as alligator pears, avocados have been called "poor man's butter" because of their exceptionally high fat content, which can reach 20 percent. Unlike butter, however, they have no cholesterol.

CONSUMER AND COOKING GUIDE: Avocados

Market Selection: Haas and Fuerte are the most common varieties of California-grown avocados. They are richer in flavor than the Bacon, Zutano, Floridian Booth 7, and Lula varieties. Select avocados that yield to gentle pressure, with unspotted and undented skins.
Availability: Year-round; peak—April through August
Storage: To ripen a hard avocado, store it in a loosely closed paper bag at room temperature. Refrigerate cut avocados, wrapped in plastic wrap, for up to 3 days.
Flavor Enhancers: Cilantro, citrus juices, cumin, oregano
Equivalents: 1 large avocado = 1 cup, mashed
Nutritional Value: Good source of vitamins A, C, and E
      360 calories per avocado
Cooking and Handling Notes: If cooking with avocado, add it at the last minute. Extensive cooking destroys the flavor and often turns avocados bitter. Best eaten uncooked.

Best, Basic Guacamole

2 large avocados
1 small tomato, seeded and
    coarsely chopped
1 jalapeño pepper, seeded,
    deveined, and minced
1 clove garlic, minced
2 green onions, chopped
¼ cup fresh cilantro leaves,
    coarsely chopped
1 tablespoon fresh lime or
    lemon juice
    Salt and pepper

MAKES ABOUT 2 CUPS

SERVE AS A TOPPING, spread, dip, or with any recipe that calls for guacamole.

Split the avocados in half, remove the seeds, and place the flesh in a medium bowl. Mash it coarsely with the back of a spoon or fork. (It should not be smooth.) Stir in the remaining ingredients until well mixed.

Avocado-Shrimp Mousse

1 envelope unflavored
    gelatin
3 medium avocados, mashed
1 tablespoon fresh lemon
    juice
1 teaspoon dried oregano
½ teaspoon cayenne
½ teaspoon dried cumin
2 cups sour cream or plain
    yogurt
¼ cup fresh cilantro leaves
6 ounces cooked bay shrimp
1 cup black olives, pitted
    and chopped
    Crackers or tortilla wedges

SERVES 12

Grease a fluted 10-inch quiche pan.

In a small saucepan, sprinkle the gelatin over ¼ cup cold water. Let stand for 5 minutes to soften. Cook over medium heat just until the water is boiling and the gelatin has dissolved.

In a food processor, combine the avocado, lemon juice, herbs and spices, sour cream, cilantro, and gelatin. Process until smooth. Pour the mixture into the prepared pan. Cover with plastic wrap and refrigerate until firm, about 6 hours.

To unmold, run the tip of a sharp knife around the edges of the pan and invert the pan on a flat platter. Arrange the shrimp and black olives in concentric circles on top. Serve with crackers or tortilla wedges.

Guacamole and Pinto Bean Torte

2 tablespoons oil or lard
1 clove garlic, minced
¼ cup chopped onion
1 16-ounce can pinto beans,
    drained
    Salt and pepper
2 cups Best, Basic
    Guacamole (see page 195)
½ cup sour cream
½ cup plain yogurt
1 tablespoon fresh lime juice
1 large tomato, seeded and
    chopped
1½ cups shredded sharp
    cheddar cheese
½ cup fresh cilantro leaves
    Warm tortillas

SERVES 10 AS AN
APPETIZER

In a skillet, heat the oil. Add the garlic and onion and cook until soft. Stir in the beans, salt, and pepper and with a potato masher or heavy-duty fork, mash the beans as they cook. Cook for about 5 minutes and let cool.

Spread the bean mixture in a 10-inch ceramic pie or quiche plate. Top with the guacamole. Combine the sour cream, yogurt, and lime juice. Spread this mixture over the guacamole. Starting from the outer edge, make concentric circles of chopped tomato, cheese, and cilantro. Serve with warm tortillas.

Avocado and Chicken Soup

2 tablespoons butter or oil
½ medium red onion, diced
½ jalapeño pepper, seeded, deveined, and diced
½ red bell pepper, seeded and diced
1 whole skinless, boneless chicken breast, cut into 1-inch pieces
6 cups chicken stock
Salt and pepper
1 large avocado, peeled and cut into 1-inch cubes

SERVES 6

In a large saucepan, heat the butter. Cook the onion, jalapeño, and bell pepper until soft, about 5 minutes. Stir in the chicken and cook for another 3 minutes, or until the chicken turns white. Add the stock; bring to a boil, lower heat, and simmer for 10 minutes. Season with salt and pepper. Stir in the avocado and serve.

Avocado-Orange Bisque

2 large avocados
1½ cups plain yogurt
½ cup fresh orange juice
1¾ cups chicken stock (page 343)
¼ teaspoon cayenne
¼ teaspoon ground cumin
1 teaspoon fresh oregano or ½ teaspoon dried
Salt and pepper
Chopped fresh chives

SERVES 4

Peel and seed the avocados. Cut them into chunks and place in the bowl of a food processor with 1 cup yogurt, juice, stock, cayenne, cumin, and oregano. Process until smooth. Chill; season with salt and pepper just before serving. Serve with a dollop of the remaining yogurt and a sprinkling of chives.

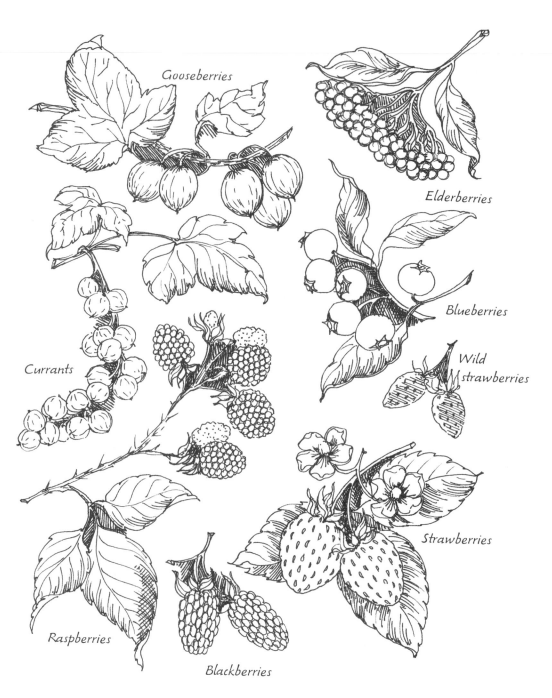

Gooseberries

Elderberries

Blueberries

Currants

Wild strawberries

Strawberries

Raspberries

Blackberries

BERRIES

HENRY THOREAU had high standards for his huckleberries: "The fruits do not yield their true flavor to the purchaser of them, nor to him who raises them for the market. . . . If you would know the flavor of huckleberries, ask the cow-boy or the partridge. It is a vulgar error to suppose that you have tasted huckleberries who never plucked them."

Even the most urban among us feels something of that pull to pure beginnings, that desire to breathe in the sun-warm smell of ripe berries and to taste them the very next moment. And we know by an instinct that prevails, through all the detours of civilization, which is better: to select for the shopping cart a cardboard carton of blueberries suffocating neatly under a piece of rubber-banded cellophane or to dine among the brambles on berries that fall off their vines into our hands.

The only problem is getting there; but thanks to patient berry growers and "U-pick" berry farms, it is still sometimes possible to gather a precious basketful of ollalieberries, or golden cap raspberries, or any of hundreds of other varieties. These include such members of the rose family as raspberries (black, red, and golden); blackberries; loganberries (a blackberry-raspberry hybrid, tasting more like the latter, developed by twentieth-century horticulturalist James Logan); marionberries (a hybrid of the previous three); boysenberries (a blackberry-loganberry hybrid named earlier this century for botanist Rudolph Boysen); and kotata berries (similar to boysenberries). There are also tayberries (which taste like a cross between blackberries and raspberries), nectarberries (resembling boysenberries), salmonberries, thimbleberries, and dewberries. And let us not leave out lingonberries, cloudberries, currants, gooseberries, or the New England wood mulberry. Even tomatoes are berries, since they are technically fruits bearing more than one seed.

Of them all, perhaps blueberries have the biggest family, with cousins and distant relatives sporting names like whortleberry, bilberry, hurtleberry, saskatoon, huckleberry, and even cranberry. The latter, named for its blossom's resemblance to the head of a crane, has a special kinship to the blueberry. In the beginning of this century, a New Jersey cranberry producer teamed up with a USDA researcher to develop several cranberry varieties suitable for cultivation. American natives, wild blueberries and their descendants hold an intrinsic fascination for us, much as they once did for the colonists who first bought them by the bushelful from Native Americans. From them they learned to sun-dry the berries, using them as a substitute for their accustomed but absent currants and raisins. By contrast, blackberry bushes were ripped from the soil with equal fervor wherever they grew, being considered a tenacious and useless weed. In fact, their only use was in a syruplike medicine for "summer complaint."

True berry cravers can practically taste each one of the summer's procession of berries just by pronouncing their names. Others are galvanized into culinary action by a desire for the homey-sounding desserts these berries so easily can become. These include buckles, flummeries, and slumps; grunts, shrubs, mushes, and plate cakes dribbled over with any kind of berry. Most berries can be used interchangeably in recipes for muffins, pies, pancakes, salads, fruit shakes, dressings, sauces, salsas, and vinaigrettes.

CONSUMER AND COOKING GUIDE: Berries

Market Selection: raspberries; boysenberries; ollalieberries; blackberries; blueberries; currants. All types should appear plump and smooth-skinned and have good color.
Availability: May through July
Storage: Use within 2 days of purchase, as deterioration is quick. To store, place berries, unwashed, in one layer in a paper towel–lined tray, covered with paper towel and plastic wrap. Refrigerate for up to 2 days.
Equivalents: 1 pound = 4 cups
Nutritional Value: Substantial Vitamin C
    Approximately 45 calories per cup
Cooking and Handling Notes: To seed berries for a smoother sauce, force them through a fine-meshed strainer.

Berry-Peach Ratafia

1 cup sugar
½ cup light brown sugar,
   tightly packed
2 tablespoons fresh lemon
   juice
2½ cups sliced, peeled peaches
1½ cup berries (blackberries,
   raspberries, or
   boysenberries)
½ teaspoon ground
   cinnamon
1 quart good-quality brandy

MAKES ABOUT 6 CUPS

SPECTACULAR *over ice cream, pound cake, or any dessert.*

Combine the sugars, ½ cup water, and lemon juice in a saucepan. Bring to a boil and boil rapidly, uncovered, for about 3 minutes. Let cool.

Place the sliced peaches and berries in a 2-quart glass jar with a cover. Add the cinnamon and brandy to the cooled syrup and stir well. Pour the mixture over the fruit and stir again.

Cover airtight and let sit in a cool place for at least a month, shaking the jar occasionally. When ready to use, strain the liquid, which may be served as a cordial, and refrigerate the fruit.

Blueberry Hots

1 cup sour cream
1 cup cottage cheese
2 tablespoons sugar
1½ cups flour
¼ teaspoon ground
   cinnamon
1 teaspoon baking soda
4 eggs
1 cup blueberries
   Shortening for skillet

SERVES 4 TO 6

Beat all the ingredients except the blueberries and shortening until smooth. Stir in the blueberries. Grease the skillet and heat. For each pancake pour about ¼ cup batter into the skillet. Cook over medium heat. When bubbles appear, turn the pancakes and cook them for 3 more minutes. Serve with blackberry syrup or butter.

Chicken with Raspberry Vinegar and Fresh Raspberries

2 tablespoons butter

2 tablespoons oil

8 skinless, boneless chicken-breast halves, lightly pounded

1 medium tomato, seeded and coarsely chopped

2 cloves garlic, minced

1 cup beef stock (page 344)

½ cup raspberry vinegar

¼ cup red-wine vinegar

1 tablespoon chopped fresh tarragon

2 tablespoons chopped fresh parsley

Salt and pepper

1 cup fresh raspberries for garnish

SERVES 8

In a large skillet, heat the butter and oil. Sauté the chicken breasts for about 5 minutes per side. Remove and keep warm.

Add the tomato and garlic to the same skillet and cook for about 3 minutes. Stir in the stock and vinegars and bring to a boil. Lower the heat and simmer until thickened, about 10 minutes. Stir in the tarragon and parsley and season with salt and pepper.

Return the chicken to the sauce and cook for another 5 minutes. Serve each chicken-breast half topped with sauce and fresh raspberries.

Berry-Cornmeal Scones

1½ cups flour
½ cup yellow cornmeal
¼ cup confectioners' sugar
1 tablespoon baking powder
6 tablespoons (¾ stick) butter
1 large egg
½ cup milk or cream
1 cup berries (currants, raspberries, or blackberries)

MAKES 12 SCONES

Preheat the oven to 450°F. Grease a cookie sheet.

In a bowl, mix the dry ingredients. Cut the butter into the mixture until it reaches a fine crumb consistency. Mix the egg and milk; stir the egg mixture into the flour mixture, along with the berries, just until moistened.

Knead the dough on a floured surface just until it holds together. Pat it into a 6 x 8-inch rectangle and cut into six squares; cut each square in half diagonally. Place on the greased cookie sheet and bake for about 13 minutes, or until golden-brown.

Berry Ice Cream

2 pints berries (raspberries, blackberries, ollalieberries, or blueberries)
1 tablespoon fresh lemon juice
3 cups half-and-half
½ cup sugar

MAKES ABOUT 1 QUART

Puree the berries with the lemon juice and pass through a food mill or strainer to remove the seeds. Mix with the half-and-half and sugar until well blended and pour into ice-cream maker. Freeze according to the manufacturer's directions.

Summer Currant Pudding

2 quarts black or red
  currants
¾ cup sugar
  About 2 tablespoons
  butter, at room
  temperature
6 slices firm-textured white
  bread, crusts removed
  Whipped cream for
  garnish

SERVES 6

In a medium saucepan, combine the currants, 2 tablespoons water, and sugar. Bring to a boil; lower the heat and simmer for about 10 minutes, or until the fruit begins to break down. Remove from the heat and let cool.

Meanwhile, butter a 4-cup soufflé dish. Line the bottom and sides with bread slices, cutting them to fit. (You should have some bread left over.) Pour the fruit mixture into the lined mold. Dip the remaining bread into the fruit mixture and place it on top of the fruit. Place a weighted plate on top and refrigerate overnight.

Remove from the refrigerator 1 hour before serving and let stand at room temperature. Invert the pudding onto a serving dish. Serve with whipped cream.

Currant Vinegar

6 cups black or red currants,
  coarsely chopped
5 cups white-wine vinegar
1 cup balsamic vinegar
5 tablespoons sugar

MAKES 4 CUPS

USE IN fruit salads, vinaigrettes, and sauces.

Combine the currants and vinegars in a 2-quart jar and stir well. Cover the jar and set aside for 10 days, stirring daily.

Strain the mixture into a noncorrosive saucepan, extracting as much juice from the currants as possible. Add the sugar and bring to a boil. Simmer for 3 minutes and let cool completely. Pour into sterilized containers and cork or cover. Store in a cool dry place.

Cranberries

THE CRANBERRY is such a sourpuss, it's a wonder it even exists. Taken straight from the vine, the cranberry is so astringent it does not lead to additional samplings; in fact, the fruit is edible only when mixed with extraordinary quantities of sugar. And yet, the annual consumption of cranberries is at least one pound per person in this country. There can be only one explanation: Thanksgiving. If it weren't for Thanksgiving, cranberries might not have survived the past few centuries.

This makes the news from the Plimouth Plantation in Massachusetts—a modern-day re-creation of New England's first successful English colony—all the more interesting. Apparently, there was no cranberry sauce at the first Thanksgiving dinner, the Plimouth historians have recently announced. Not only that, there were no cranberries either. Somehow, the ninety Indians and fifty Pilgrims managed to consume their "birds," which included swans, deer, and sea bass as well as turkey, sans sauce.

Cranberries, which are highly acidic, didn't really become popular until the availability of sugar. However, they were consumed raw by Native Americans who also sweetened them with maple syrup, thus creating, in effect, the first cranberry sauce. They also used the berries to make pemmican, a form of preserved dried meat.

By 1639 John Josselyn reported seeing cranberries in New England, where the fruit's high vitamin C content helped prevent scurvy. In the 1700s laws were passed regulating times permissible for their harvest and punishing those who picked them prematurely. Unknown abroad, cranberries were the first native fruits sent back to Europe, where they became popular in Great Britain, Scandinavia, and Germany.

Massachusetts, which today produces half this country's annual crop, has cultivated this crimson-colored cousin of the blueberry since 1840. New Jersey, Oregon, Washington, and Wisconsin also do their part in contributing to the pound-a-year average, most of which is turned into commercial cranberry sauce. In fact, the current demand for cranberries is so high, the fruit has won the nickname "red gold." Cranberries make delicious pies, salads, breads, muffins, relishes, puddings, coffee cakes, stuffings, and pancakes. They gel easily when cooked with sugar because of their high pectin content. Cranberries bounce like miniature rubber balls, although no one has harnessed that property to any culinary advantage.

Some claim that the cranberry got its name from the fact that its flower resembles the crane, a bird that frequents the coastal areas where the fruit grows. A member of the same family as rhododendron and heather, the cranberry thrives in bogs and moorlands. The different varieties vary in color and shape, from the dark red, large Cherry cranberry, to the elongated dark pink Bugle, to the coral-colored Bell. Because of the astringent nature of cranberries, they are not interchangeable with other berries. They do best in recipes like the following, which take advantage of their distinctive character.

CONSUMER AND COOKING GUIDE: Cranberries

Market Selection: Common varieties include Early Black, Howe, Searles, and McFarlin. Most commercial growers package cranberries in 1-pound plastic bags so the consumer does not have the opportunity to handpick them. Berries should be vivid in color and firm. Reject bags that have moisture buildup in them.
Availability: September through November
Storage: Refrigerate berries in plastic bags for up to 1 month. Freeze in plastic bags for up to 6 months.
Flavor Enhancers: Orange juice or zest, cinnamon, ginger
Equivalents: 1 pound = 4 cups
Nutritional Value: High in vitamins A and C
　　　　44 calories per cup

Cranberry Sauce

1 pound cranberries
½ cup sugar

MAKES ABOUT 3 CUPS

Combine the cranberries, sugar, and ½ cup water. Bring to a boil, lower the heat, and simmer for about 10 minutes, or until the cranberries begin to pop and the sauce is slightly thick. Serve warm, cold, or at room temperature.

Variations:
   Cook the mixture with 2 sticks of cinnamon; remove before serving.
   Cook the mixture with 3 strips of orange zest. Remove before serving.
   Stir in peeled and pithed tangerine sections after cooking.
   Stir in 2 tablespoons chopped candied ginger while the sauce is cooling.
   Substitute apple cider and/or orange juice for water.

Game Hens Glazed with Spiced Cranberry Sauce

2 medium game hens, split
   in halves, each half
   pounded flat
   Salt and pepper
1 cup Cranberry Sauce
   (see above)
1 jalapeño pepper, seeded
   and minced
1 clove garlic, minced
2 tablespoons orange
   marmalade
2 tablespoons brandy
1 tablespoon vegetable oil

SERVES 4

Preheat the oven to 425°F.
   Wash the hens and pat them dry. Sprinkle them with salt and pepper and place them on a roasting rack, skin side down. Bake for 5 minutes on each side.
   Meanwhile, combine the remaining ingredients to make a glaze.
   Remove the hens from the oven and reduce the heat to 375°F. Return the hens to a skin-side-down position and brush them with half the cranberry glaze. Bake for 15 minutes. Turn the hens over and brush them with the remaining glaze. Bake for another 10 minutes, basting with pan juices every so often. Let cool slightly before serving.

Cranberry-Walnut Cheesecake

CRUST

2 tablespoons confectioners'
  sugar
½ teaspoon ground
  cinnamon
1½ cups ground walnuts
3 tablespoons melted butter

TOPPING

½ cup sugar
2½ cups cranberries
1 tablespoon orange zest
12 walnut halves, for garnish

FILLING

1 pound cream cheese
1 pound cottage cheese
½ cup sugar
5 eggs
1 tablespoon orange juice

SERVES 12

Preheat the oven to 400°F.

In a medium bowl, combine the crust ingredients until evenly moistened. Press into the bottom of a 9-inch springform pan. Bake for about 8 minutes. Let cool on a wire rack. Lower the oven temperature to 350°F.

To make the topping: In a medium saucepan combine ⅓ cup water and the sugar; boil for 1 minute. Stir in 2 cups of cranberries and the orange zest. Cover and cook for about 5 minutes, or until the berries have popped and the sauce is thick. Force the sauce through a strainer and let cool. Stir the remaining cranberries into the topping. Set aside.

To make the filling: Beat the filling ingredients until smooth. Pour into the baked crust and bake for about 45 minutes, or until a toothpick inserted in the center comes out clean. Let the cake cool in the turned-off oven for about 2 hours. Spread the topping over the cake and chill 2 hours or overnight. Garnish with walnut halves. Serve cold or at room temperature.

Cranberry-Cornmeal Biscotti

1 cup all-purpose flour
1 cup yellow cornmeal
¾ cup sugar
1 teaspoon baking powder
1 teaspoon baking soda
½ cup cranberries, coarsely
  chopped
1 cup almonds, coarsely
  chopped
3 eggs
4 tablespoons (½ stick)
  butter, melted

MAKES ABOUT 36 BISCOTTI

Preheat the oven to 325°F. Line a baking sheet with parchment paper.

In a large bowl, combine the dry ingredients with the cranberries and almonds. In a small bowl, beat the eggs with the melted butter. Combine the egg mixture with the flour mixture until a soft dough forms.

Knead the dough briefly on a lightly floured surface. Form into two flattened logs about 2½ inches wide and place them on the prepared baking sheet. Bake for 40 minutes.

Remove the pan from the oven. Cut on the diagonal into 1-inch slices and bake, cut side down, for another 30 minutes. Let cool completely; store in an airtight container.

Strawberries

Curly-locks, Curly-locks
Wilt thou be mine?
Thou shalt not wash dishes
Nor yet feed the swine.
But sit on a cushion
And sew a fine seam,
And feed upon strawberries,
Sugar and cream.

—Anonymous

Apples are for teachers, but strawberries are for childhood. A strawberry is the first fruit we can deal with, whole and entire, without worrying about peels and pits and sharp-edged cores. We eat our strawberries in innocence, free from the cottony fuzz of peaches, the infinite interruptions of watermelon seeds, or the sudden, surprising bitterness of plums. As children, we receive a slice of apple, a segment of orange, a half a peach; but strawberries we are given undivided. The only thing we want when we finish one strawberry is another.

So it comes as a shock, when we reach a certain age, to read in Harold McGee's *Of Food and Cooking* that the strawberry is a " 'false fruit,' derived from the base of the flower rather than the ovary." And yet despite this breach of botanical semantics, we stand ready to forgive a fruit, however false, that came to us initially in the form of jellies and jams, shortcake and ice cream. And Jell-O: Jell-O is strawberry, strawberry is Jell-O, as any child well knows.

But what are we to think of John Gerard, who, in his highly respected *Herball* (1597), says nothing about the lush, thick taste of this member of the rose family, concentrating instead on its medicinal advantages. He informs us that strawberry leaves make a great poultice but ignores all of the sensual charms of the berry about which Izaak Walton, quoting William Butler, wrote, "Doubtless God could have made a better berry, but doubtless God never did." Even the usually reserved Samuel Johnson was once moved to call out, "*Toujours* strawberries and cream."

Actually, to be fair, Gerard did not know the strawberry as we know it today because it did not exist. The modern-day strawberry began with the discovery of two New World strawberries. The first was the delicate and flavorful scarlet woodland strawberry, found in Virginia. Like peas and corn —and almost everything else, for that matter—this highly perishable berry was best eaten on the spot where it grew. Then, in the early eighteenth century, a French naval officer named Frezier (incredibly, his name in French, *frasier*, means "strawberry plant") came across the Chilean strawberry on the west coast of South America. Hardy, fat, and sometimes as large as an apple, this variety had very little taste.

The crossing of these two varieties produced a less-perishable, sweet, plump red berry that gained immediate popularity all over the world. For his work on strawberries, the nineteenth-century English gardener Michael Keens was awarded the silver cup by the Royal Horticultural Society.

By the 1850s this country was caught up in what was known as "strawberry fever," with people throwing strawberry parties, horticultural societies sponsoring strawberry exhibits, and whole towns, like Belmont, Massachusetts, holding the first strawberry festivals. In Philadelphia, the fashionable crowd made the rounds of strawberry gardens, where they could taste the fruit at its peak. Recipes began to appear for everything from the sublime-sounding Sister Abigail's Strawberry Flummery to strawberry soups, fruit leather, mousse frappés, wine, and even a strawberry concoction to bathe in. Popular preparations like strawberries Romanoff gave rise to the usual disputes over authorship. Some contend that this recipe originated with Chef Arbogast in San Francisco's Palace Hotel; others give credit to Hollywood's Mike Romanoff. Many insist it was Antonin Carême, chef to Czar Alexander I of Russia, who created the dish, but James Beard argued that "it was an Englishman, Cardinal Wolsey, who started the fad of eating strawberries with cream. Mother was deeply indebted to him . . ." As was her appreciative son. From somewhere the word *fragariaphobia,* or "fear of strawberries," emerged, though no one has ever seemed to suffer from such a malady.

California produces more than 70 percent of the nation's crop, including hundreds of varieties the names of which—Douglas, Pajaro, Chandler, and Selva—are largely unknown to the consumer. Most, if not all, of these are red, but reports of delicious creamy-white strawberries have been reported from such distant points as Hawaii and Turkey, and green strawberries are also a rare but extant possibility.

In this country every state produces strawberries. This somehow seems appropriate in a country that once looked, at first sight, like an endless field of strawberries. On Saturday, June 12, 1630, John Winthrop wrote of the land on which he was to found the colony of Massachusetts Bay: "Most of our people went on shore upon the land of Cape Ann, which lay very near us, and gathered store of fine strawberries." What he was seeing, lyrically if eurocentrically, was a new land, a new beginning, a second childhood for a weary, aging Europe. And its symbol, at least for the moment, was the strawberry.

CONSUMER AND COOKING GUIDE: Strawberries

Market Selection: Chandler, Douglas, Pajaro (large, red); *fraises de bois* (very tiny, red and white); long-stem (any variety picked with stem). Select berries that are firm and uniform in color. Avoid berries with white "shoulders" (stem ends).
Availability: Year-round; peak—May through September
Storage: Refrigerate, unwashed, in a bowl covered with plastic wrap pierced in several places, for up to 2 days.
Flavor Enhancers: Cinnamon, mint
Nutritional Value: Good source of vitamin C
        55 calories per cup
Cooking and Handling Notes: Use a tweezer to pull hulls from berries.

Sparkling Strawberry Spritzer

1 cup strawberries, pureed
   in blender or food
   processor
½ cup dry white wine
½ cup club soda
2 tablespoons honey
4 whole strawberries for
   garnish

SERVES 2

Combine the strawberry puree, wine, club soda, and honey. Pour into two chilled glasses and top each with two strawberries.

Sautéed Shrimp with Warm Strawberry Vinaigrette

5 tablespoons olive oil
2 cloves garlic, minced
1 pound medium shrimp,
   peeled and deveined
2 tablespoons balsamic
   vinegar
1 tablespoon freshly ground
   pepper
1 tablespoon honey
1 cup sliced strawberries
4 cups mixed greens

SERVES 4

In a large skillet, heat 3 tablespoons of the olive oil. Cook half the garlic until fragrant; add the shrimp. Sauté until the shrimp turn pink all over, about 4 minutes. Remove and keep warm.

Add the remaining oil and garlic to the same skillet. Heat for about 30 seconds; add the vinegar, pepper, and honey. Cook for about 1 minute. Add the strawberries and cook just long enough to warm through. Pour over the shrimp and serve on a bed of mixed greens.

Tropical Fruit Medley with Strawberry-Balsamic Puree

1 banana, sliced
1 mango, cubed
1 papaya, sliced
½ pineapple, peeled, cored,
    and sliced
1 pint strawberries, hulled
2 tablespoons strawberry
    jam
2 tablespoons balsamic
    vinegar
3 tablespoons confectioners'
    sugar
Mint leaves for garnish

SERVES 6 TO 8

Arrange the fruit, except the strawberries, on a serving platter. Puree the strawberries, jam, vinegar, and sugar in a food processor until smooth. Strain to remove seeds. Pour over the fruit and garnish with mint.

Strawberry-Cinnamon Compote

1 cup red wine
¼ cup sugar
2 teaspoons ground
   cinnamon
3 tablespoons fresh lemon
   juice
6 cups small strawberries,
   hulled

MAKES ABOUT 2 CUPS

In a medium saucepan, combine all of the ingredients, except the strawberries, with 1 cup water. Bring to a boil and cook until the liquid is reduced to about 1¼ cups. Gently stir the berries into the hot syrup and let cool. Serve alone or over vanilla ice cream.

Strawberry-Hazelnut Bread

4 eggs
1 cup vegetable oil
1¼ cups sugar
1 pint strawberries, sliced
3 cups flour
1 tablespoon ground
   cinnamon
1 teaspoon baking soda
1 teaspoon salt
1½ cups toasted hazelnuts (see
   page 347), coarsely
   chopped

MAKES 2 LOAVES

Preheat the oven to 350°F. Butter and flour two 8 x 5 x 3-inch loaf pans.

In a large bowl, beat the eggs until fluffy. Add the oil, sugar, and strawberries and mix well. In a separate bowl, combine the flour, cinnamon, baking soda, and salt. Add to the strawberry mixture and mix just until combined. Stir in the nuts. Pour the batter into the prepared pans.

Bake for about 1 hour, or until a toothpick inserted in the middle comes out clean. Cool in pans for about 10 minutes before turning out. Slice and serve.

CHERRIES

EVERYBODY KNOWS, on the happiest days, what life is just a bowl of. Of all summer's reassurances, cherries always seem the bounciest, the plumpest, the most bursting with flavor. Cherries are candy, the bonbons of summer produce. Sibling rivalry wouldn't be the same without cherries: fighting over whose fruit salad has the most cherries in it; or who gets the double cherry, the one magically joined at the stem; or who stole from the box of assorted chocolates the one with the gooey cherry center.

The tragicomedies of cherries are not limited to childhood. It is said that the great epicure Lucullus, who is credited with having introduced the cherry to Europe around 70 B.C., took his life on the day he realized he had only a few thousand cherries left. Possibly to avoid a similar fate, King Charles V of France planted, not a mere 1,000 cherries, but more than 1,000 cherry *trees* in his gardens at St. Paul and Tournelle in the mid-1300s. And when it comes to moral allegories, what could be more poignant as a lesson in honesty than having someone admit that he chopped down a cherry tree?

The Romans knew three kinds of cherries, and even today, we know what they called them. Bright red sweets were Apronians, the blunted rounds were Caecilian, and the darkest were Lutatians. For practical purposes, we have two categories: sour or tart cherries, used for pies and cooked desserts; and sweet cherries, for eating fresh. The former are small and round, ranging in color from yellow and green, to pink and red. They include chokecherries, sand cherries, and ground cherries (also called cape gooseberries). Most are only available canned or frozen. In addition to the deep maroon Bings and Lamberts, sweet-cherry varieties include Vans, Chapmans, Burlats, Deacons, Chinooks, Black Tartarians, Rainiers, and Republicans.

Cherries make excellent liqueurs and brandies, most notably Danish Cherry Herring and the *eau de vie* called kirsch or *kirschwasser*. Early New Englanders developed their own contender in this category, giving it the particularly American-sounding name Cherry Bounce.

Members of the rose family, known as drupes or stone fruits, cherries can be sun-dried and kept for up to a year. Dried cherries make a delicious addition to waffle batter, scones, and other baked goods, and brighten up a mouthful of any miscellaneous mix of dried fruits. They even taste pretty good by themselves. But they don't taste much like cherries. Ask a kid, any kid.

Market Selection: Sweet-cherry varieties include Bing, Burlat, Lambert, and Chapman, all of which have deep red skins and flesh. Lighter-colored sweet varieties include Royal Ann and Rainier. Montmorency is the most common variety of tart or sour cherries, sometimes known as "pie cherries." All types should be blemish free and firm to the touch.

Availability: Peak season—June

Storage: Store cherries, unwashed, in paper towel–lined shallow bowls in one layer, covered with paper towels. They will keep this way in the refrigerator for up to 4 days.

Flavor Enhancers: Cinnamon, nutmeg, mint

Equivalents: 1 pound = 2 cups pitted cherries

Nutritional Value: Good source of vitamin A

65 calories per cup

Cooking and Handling Notes: Cherries are easily pitted with an inexpensive gadget called a cherry (or olive) pitter, available at good cookware stores.

Chilled Cherry, Sherry, and Mint Soup

½ pound sour cherries, pitted
  (see page 244)
½ pound Bing cherries, pitted
½ cup dry sherry
 2 tablespoons fresh lemon
  juice
¼ cup sugar
¼ teaspoon ground
  cinnamon
 6 mint leaves, julienned
 1 cup sour cream
 1 cup plain yogurt
 6 Bing cherries for garnish

SERVES 6

Place the cherries, 2 cups water, sherry, lemon juice, sugar, and cinnamon in a medium saucepan. Bring to a boil and let simmer, uncovered, for 20 minutes, or until the liquid has thickened. Puree in a food processor and stir in the mint by hand.

Chill the mixture and stir in the yogurt and sour cream. Serve cold, garnished with a cherry.

Chicken with Cherries

 3 whole skinless, boneless
  chicken breasts, split
  Salt and pepper
½ cup flour for dredging
 2 tablespoons butter
 2 tablespoons oil
 2 tablespoons chopped
  shallot
½ pound Bing cherries,
  pitted (see page 244) and
  coarsely chopped
¼ cup cherry brandy
½ cup white wine
¾ cup chicken stock (page 343)
 1 bay leaf
12 whole cherries for garnish

SERVES 6

Sprinkle the chicken with salt and pepper and dredge in flour. In a large skillet, heat the butter and oil. Cook the chicken breasts for 6 minutes per side, or until golden; remove and reserve.

In the same skillet, cook the shallot until soft. Add the cherries and cook for another 2 minutes. Add the cherry brandy and wine and cook over high heat until reduced by half. Add the chicken stock and bay leaf and bring to a boil. Cook for 10 minutes, or until the sauce is thick.

Return the chicken to the pan and cook over low heat for 5 minutes. Serve chicken with cherry sauce and garnish with fresh cherries.

Cherry-Almond Tart

1 *recipe* Pâte Brisée
(*see page 344*)

FILLING

⅔ *cup almonds*
⅓ *cup sugar*
5 *tablespoons butter, at*
room temperature
1 *egg, at room temperature*
1 *tablespoon flour*
1 *tablespoon kirsch (cherry*
liqueur)
1 *pound large sweet*
cherries, pitted
(*see page 244*)

GLAZE

¼ *cup red currant jelly*
1 *tablespoon kirsch*

SERVES 8

Preheat the oven to 400°F.

Make the *pâte brisée;* roll out the dough to fit a 9- or 10-inch tart pan with a removable bottom. Fit the dough into the pan. Place in the refrigerator while preparing the filling.

Place the almonds and sugar in the bowl of a food processor; process until fine. Add the butter, egg, flour, and kirsch; process until smooth. Remove the tart shell from the refrigerator and spread the almond filling on the bottom. Place the cherries evenly over the filling. Bake for 40 minutes until bubbly. Let cool on a cake rack.

Meanwhile, prepare the glaze: Melt the jelly in a small saucepan and stir in the kirsch. Brush the glaze over the cooled cherries in the tart. Serve at room temperature.

Dried Cherry and Chocolate Rugalach

DOUGH

4 ounces cream cheese, at
room temperature
4 ounces (1 stick) butter, at
room temperature
1 tablespoon sour cream or
plain yogurt
1¼ cups flour
¼ teaspoon salt

FILLING

3 ounces pitted dried
cherries
1 cup walnuts
3 tablespoons sugar
½ teaspoon ground
cinnamon
1 ounce bittersweet
chocolate, cut into small
pieces
4 teaspoons cherry jam

Confectioners' sugar

MAKES 2 DOZEN
RUGALACH

Preheat the oven to 375°F. Line 2 cookie sheets with parchment paper.

In a food processor or with a hand-held electric mixer, combine the cream cheese, butter, and sour cream until smooth. Add the flour and salt and process until a dough forms. Divide the dough in half and form two 5-inch disks. Wrap them in plastic and refrigerate while making the filling.

Place all of the filling ingredients except the jam in a food processor and process until finely chopped. (The mixture will form a paste.) Remove the dough from the refrigerator. On a floured surface, roll each disk into a 9-inch circle. Spread each circle with 2 teaspoons of jam. Pat half the cherry mixture onto each circle. With a pastry wheel or pizza cutter, cut each circle into twelve wedges. Starting at the wide end, roll each wedge up and place it, point-side down, on a cookie sheet.

Bake for 30 minutes, or until lightly browned. Cool on a cake rack and dust with confectioners' sugar.

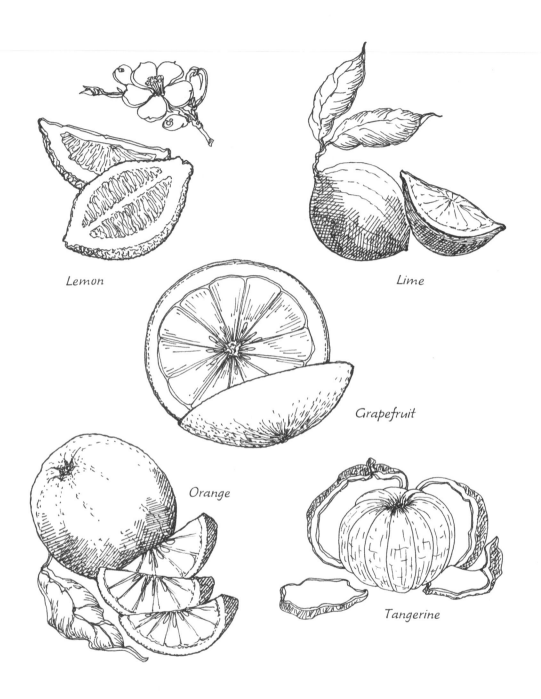

Lemon

Lime

Grapefruit

Orange

Tangerine

CITRUS FRUITS

WITH ONE EXCEPTION—the grapefruit—all citrus fruits are millions of years old. First cultivated in India, Japan, and China, they are semitropical plants native to Southeast Asia. By the twelfth century A.D., the Moors in Spain had planted citrus trees from Seville to Granada, but these citrus varieties were bitter and served mainly medicinal or ornamental purposes. The demand for oranges increased dramatically in the 1500s, after the Portuguese brought back the first sweet oranges from India and China. In the New World, citrus fruits did not exist until the Spanish explorers planted seeds in the fifteenth century. Such distinguished fellows as Ponce de León and Hernando de Soto have been credited with the first plantings, but in fact, every America-bound sailor was given 100 seeds to sow. It wasn't long before Europe would be importing the fruits of these labors by the bushelful.

Although all types of citrus—with that one unexpected exception—have a venerable culinary history, each one has its own juicy past.

Oranges

THE SANSKRIT NAME for this 20-million-year-old fruit is *nagrunga,* meaning "fruit favored by the elephants." One can only surmise that oranges must have tasted quite different in those days, since elephants seldom leap to mind when one contemplates the flavor of oranges. Navel oranges, which comprise 10 percent of the U.S. crop, are the seedless, big, sometimes bumpy globes usually eaten out of hand. Most of the navel varieties available today— Golden Nugget, Thompson, Golden Buckeye—stem from Brazilian plantings only a century ago. Valencias, or juice oranges, which make up half the U.S. crop, are also useful in baking cakes and pies. Seville or bitter oranges are best for marmalade as well as liqueurs like curaçao. Blood oranges, available in such varieties as Moro, Tarocco, and Sanguinello, are a popular novelty because of their bright color and full flavor. Temple oranges are a cross between mandarins and oranges.

American cookbooks from less frantic times contain directions for making orange "baskets" by meticulously slicing around and under the orange skin, carefully removing the sections, filling the cavity with fruit, and performing various other acts of prestidigitation. These days, most people usually use a bowl.

Lemons

LEMONS COME IN SO MANY SIZES, shapes, and shades of yellow-green that they may resemble everything from a big grandfather grapefruit to a baby green lime. Lemons may even have been confused with apples, at least according to some recent research which looks askance at all the tales about golden apples. If the day comes when the old mythologies are updated for botanical accuracy, we may be reading that the Trojan War began when Paris presented Aphrodite with the Golden Lemon of Discord and that, at her marriage to Zeus, Helen received a gift of the Golden Lemons of the Hesperides. But somehow, the stories don't have the same ring to them.

Not that lemons aren't wonderful in their way. From juice to rind, they serve as the essence of the Greek soup *avgolemono* and of the seasoning mix *gremolata*; of marinades, dressings, sauces, and souring agents. It may seem ironic that such a tart, astringent fruit can metamorphose into beloved desserts like lemon custard pie (said to be Calvin Coolidge's favorite) and the classic lemon meringue pie, whose fame can be traced to Boston's Parker House.

Some old cookbooks include lemons in their "sick room receipts," where, in the form of Irish-moss lemonade or flax-seed lemonade, they are recommended as "excellent for feverish colds and all pulmonary troubles."

Limes

POSSIBLY THE WORLD'S LEAST complicated recipe direction, and the most important in terms of enhancing flavor, is the one that suggests, ever so offhandedly, "a squeeze of lime." And yet, this squeeze is the tangy squirt that can transform the simple into the complex, the flat into the three-dimensional. Limes strike the exotic note in highly spiced dressings and spreads, in ceviches, gazpachos, and even desserts.

The seedless Californians called Bears, and Florida's acidic Persians and Tahitis, are the most common. Key limes, which food writer Raymond Sokolov says "[have] more personality" than any other, are not widely produced or marketed. They make an unforgettable Key lime pie and a traditional Key West sauce called Old Sour, a concoction of lime-drenched pickled peppers. As with most lime recipes, lemons may be substituted, though the taste will obviously not be the same.

Mandarins/Tangerines

THOUGH THE TWO NAMES are often used interchangeably, tangerines are technically a North African (Tangiers) variety of mandarin. The species also includes tangelos, a cross between tangerines and grapefruits, and clementines, a type of seedless Algerian tangerine now being grown more widely in California. The Chinese and Japanese cultivated these fruits for millennia before they were discovered by the West only about a century ago. Their loose-fitting peels make them convenient for eating out of hand and for adding to salads and fruit compotes.

Grapefruits

IN THE CITRUS COMMUNITY, the grapefruit is indisputably the new kid on the block. Unlike its million-year-old cousins, the grapefruit has been around for only a few centuries, and its very origins remain a mystery. It probably developed as a sport, or mutation, somewhere in the West Indies, where various citrus varieties had been growing for a few hundred years. The grapefruit is a cross between the orange and the pomelo, the latter being a yellowish bowling-ball-sized citrus fruit, which, if nothing else, explains where the French got their word for grapefruit, *pamplemousse.*

The pink grapefruit is also a quirk of nature and can be traced to a McAllen, Texas, farm where it was discovered in 1929. The Star Ruby and Marsh Ruby are its popular pink descendants, most of which still originate in Texas. White varieties, such as Indian River, Orchid Isle, and White Marsh, come from Florida, which provides 70 percent of the world's supply, as well as from Arizona and California. Half a grapefruit remains a favorite breakfast fruit which, for the purposes of maintaining morning good humor, should always be accompanied by one of those special, serrated grapefruit knives.

CONSUMER AND COOKING GUIDE: Citrus Fruits

Market Selection: Orange varieties include Hamlin, pineapple, and Valencia, which are considered juice oranges; navel, California, Valencia, and blood oranges, which are eating oranges. The main commercial varieties of lemons are the large Eureka and the smoother-skinned Lisbon. Meyer lemons are gaining popularity but are most often grown in home gardens or found at small farmers' markets. Persian (or Tahiti) limes are the most common variety. Dancy, Satsuma, Kinnow, Fairchild, and the hybrid tangelo are some of the more common mandarins or tangerines. Grapefruit varieties include the White Marsh, Marsh Ruby, and Star Ruby, also known as Ruby Red.

Availability: Year-round; peak season—November through April

Storage: May be stored at room temperature for 1 week or in the refrigerator (uncovered) for up to 2 weeks.

Equivalents: 3 oranges = 1 pound

   1 orange = ½ cup juice

   ½ orange = 1 tablespoon grated zest

   1 lemon or lime = about 3 tablespoons juice

   1 lemon or lime = 1 tablespoon grated zest

Nutritional Value: Excellent source of vitamin C

   70 calories per orange

   100 calories per grapefruit

   30 calories per lemon

   70 calories per tangerine

   30 calories per lime

Cooking and Handling Notes: The *zest* is the outer colored skin of the citrus fruit. The white layer underneath is the *pith* and is very bitter. To "zest" a citrus fruit, use a vegetable peeler or a special tool called a *zester*.

Savory Avocado-Orange Cheesecake

8 ounces wheatmeal or other
  wheat-type crackers,
  crushed
¼ cup melted butter
3 navel oranges
1 large avocado
2 tablespoons fresh lemon
  juice
4 ounces cream cheese
2 eggs, separated
½ cup sour cream or plain
  yogurt
1 envelope unflavored
  gelatin
2 tablespoons sugar
½ teaspoon cayenne
Salt

MAKES 12 APPETIZER
SERVINGS

Combine the crushed crackers and butter; press the mixture into the bottom of an 8-inch springform pan.

Grate the rind of one orange; peel it and trim the segments. Squeeze the juice from the other two.

Peel and slice the avocado and sprinkle it with lemon juice. Puree the avocado with the cream cheese, egg yolks, sour cream, orange zest, and juice. Dissolve the gelatin in a little water and add to the avocado mixture.

Beat the egg whites with the sugar until stiff and fold into the avocado mixture with the cayenne. Taste for salt and pour into the prepared pan. Chill until firm, about 4 hours. Cut in wedges, garnish with orange slices, and serve as an unusual first course.

NOTE: This recipe contains raw eggs, which can contain salmonella bacteria.

Spicy Olive and Lemon Caponata

8 ounces pitted green olives
8 ounces pitted black olives
2 tomatoes, seeded and
  chopped
¼ cup oil
6 cloves garlic, minced
1 tablespoon tomato paste
  Three ¼-inch-thick slices
  lemon
1 teaspoon chili powder
½ teaspoon cayenne
  Salt

MAKES 2 CUPS

A WONDERFUL ADDITION to an antipasto tray.

In a medium saucepan, combine the olives with the tomato, oil, garlic, and tomato paste. Simmer for 8 minutes. Add the lemon, chili powder, pepper, and ¼ cup water. Simmer until the water is absorbed. Let cool and taste for salt.

Lemon-Walnut Bread

2 tablespoons dry yeast
1 tablespoon honey
1½ cups warm water (about
  110°F)
1 cup whole-wheat flour
3 cups all-purpose flour
2 teaspoons salt
1 egg, lightly beaten
  Juice and zest of ½ lemon
1 cup coarsely chopped
  walnuts, lightly toasted
  (see page 347)

MAKES 2 LOAVES

In a large bowl, combine the yeast with the honey and water. Let stand for about 5 minutes to proof (see page 349). Stir in the flours, salt, egg, juice, and zest. Mix until you have a smooth dough. Knead in the walnuts; continue to knead for about 8 minutes. Place the dough in large greased bowl, cover, and let rise in a warm spot until doubled in bulk, about 1 hour.

Punch the dough down and grease two 8 x 5-inch loaf pans. Divide the dough in half and shape into loaves. Place in the prepared pans and let rise again until doubled.

Preheat the oven to 375°F. Bake the loaves for 50 minutes, until brown and crusty. Remove the loaves from the pans and let cool on racks.

Pan-fried Snapper with Tarragon and Lime

6 snapper fillets
   Salt and pepper
1 cup dry bread crumbs
2 tablespoons fresh minced
   tarragon or 1 tablespoon
   dried
   Flour for dredging
2 egg whites, beaten
5 tablespoons butter
1 tablespoon oil
1 tablespoon honey
2 tablespoons fresh lime
   juice
1 lime, cut into thin wedges

SERVES 6

Sprinkle the snapper with salt and pepper. Combine the bread crumbs with the tarragon and set aside. Dredge the snapper in flour, dip in egg white, and coat on both sides with the bread-crumb mixture.

In a large skillet, heat 3 tablespoons of the butter and the oil. Cook the fillets for about 3 minutes per side, or until golden-brown. Remove and reserve.

Add the remaining 2 tablespoons butter, honey, and lime juice to the skillet and cook until the sugar dissolves. Pour over the fish and garnish with lime wedges.

Lemon-Lime Icebox Cookies

1½ cups (3 sticks) butter, at
    room temperature
1 cup sugar
1 teaspoon vanilla
1 tablespoon grated lime zest
1 tablespoon grated lemon
    zest
2 tablespoons fresh lime
    juice
2 tablespoons fresh lemon
    juice
1½ cups flour
1 teaspoon baking powder
½ teaspoon baking soda
¼ teaspoon salt
Confectioners' sugar for
    garnish

MAKES ABOUT 4 DOZEN
COOKIES

With an electric mixer, cream the butter and sugar until light in color. Add the vanilla, zests, and juices and beat until the mixture is smooth. Combine the flour with the baking powder, soda, and salt; beat into the butter mixture.

On a piece of waxed paper, form the dough into a log 1½ inches in diameter. Wrap and chill for 2 hours. (The dough may be frozen, wrapped in foil, for up to 2 months.)

Preheat the oven to 350°F.

Cut the log into ⅛-inch-thick slices; place them about 1½ inches apart on an ungreased cookie sheet. Bake for 8 to 10 minutes, or until the edges are golden. Cool on wire racks, then dust with confectioners' sugar.

Turkey Cutlets with Tangerines and Olives

1 pound turkey cutlets,
  ¼ inch thick
Salt and pepper
Flour for dredging
4 tablespoons oil
1 cup Niçoise olives, pitted
  and halved
3 cloves garlic, minced
1 celery stalk, chopped
2 tomatoes, seeded and
  chopped
½ teaspoon dried rosemary
½ cup white wine
2 tangerines, peeled and
  sectioned, white pith
  removed
2 tablespoons brandy or
  cognac
Salt and pepper

SERVES 6

Sprinkle the turkey with salt and pepper and dredge in flour. In a large skillet, heat the oil. Cook the turkey for 2 minutes per side; remove and keep warm.

To the same pan, add the olives, garlic, celery, tomato, rosemary, and wine. Bring to a boil, lower heat, and simmer for 15 minutes.

Add the tangerines and cognac and return to a boil. Cook for 2 minutes. Season sauce with salt and pepper and pour over turkey cutlets.

Grapefruit Marmalade

2 small white grapefruits
2¼ cups sugar

MAKES ABOUT 3 CUPS

Cut a ½-inch slice from the end of each grapefruit. Cut the grapefruits in half lengthwise. With the cut sides down, slice the grapefruits crosswise as thinly as possible. Collect the juice and the slices; discard the seeds.

In a heavy nonreactive 4-quart pan, bring the grapefruits, juice, and 5 cups water to a boil. Boil gently for ½ hour. Add the sugar and boil until a candy thermometer registers 220°F. Test the marmalade by putting a spoonful on a saucer. If the marmalade does not run when tipped, it is done. Pour into sterilized jars; let cool and cover. Refrigerate. Will keep for about 3 months.

Spinach and Pink Grapefruit Salad with Sautéed Scallops

1 bunch fresh spinach,
  stemmed, leaves torn into
  bite-size pieces
2 small pink grapefruits
2 tablespoons butter
3 tablespoons oil
1 pound sea scallops, halved
  into 2 disks
1 tablespoon honey
2 tablespoons balsamic
  vinegar
1 teaspoon mustard
  Salt and pepper
½ cup chopped fresh chives

SERVES 6

On a shallow platter, make a bed of spinach leaves. Section 1½ grapefruits; squeeze the juice from the remaining half and reserve. Remove the white membranes from the grapefruit and arrange the sections over the spinach.

In a medium skillet, heat the butter and oil. Sauté the scallops until golden. Remove and keep warm. To the same skillet, add the grapefruit juice, honey, and vinegar. Bring to a boil and stir in the mustard. Season with salt and pepper.

Sprinkle half the dressing on the spinach-grapefruit mixture and toss the scallops in the remaining dressing. Arrange the scallops in the center of the platter. Garnish with chives.

Candied Citrus Peel

4 lemons or 3 oranges or
  2 grapefruits
1 cup sugar

MAKES 2 CUPS

Scrub the skin of the fruit with hot water and kitchen soap. Rinse well and dry. Using a sharp peeler, pare the outer skin (the zest) from the fruit. Remove the pith (the white part) from the peelings. Cut the peel into 2- to 3-inch lengths.

In a large saucepan, combine the sugar with 1 cup water; bring to a boil. Add the peel, lower the heat, and cook at a bare simmer for 15 minutes. Set aside to cool for 10 minutes; drain the syrup from the peel.

Preheat the oven to 275°F. Spread the peel on a lightly greased cookie sheet and bake for 15 minutes. Let cool; store in an airtight container. May be used in recipes calling for candied citrus peel or as a decoration on other desserts. Also delicious as is.

For chocolate-covered candied peel, melt 8 ounces bittersweet chocolate; dip candied peel in the chocolate and let it dry on a cooling rack.

FIGS

BEFORE DETERIORATING into its current disreputable state, the smuggling profession was a more wholesome, and occasionally nutritious, pastime. In ancient Greece, an entire segment of enterprising smugglers was able to live by figs alone, delivering the fruits to their figless clients and possibly nibbling a few in transit. These scoundrels had to be constantly on the lookout, however, because informing on fig smugglers was also a highly paid activity. These informers were called "sycophants," from the Greek words *sukon* ("figs") and *phantēs* ("accuser").

There are some who wonder why anyone would ever have risked life and limb for a fig. There are some who could never understand, no matter how many times their mothers tucked a dried fig into their lunch boxes, why they had to eat such a chewy, gritty-tasting item. There are some who, when they think of figs, are reminded of leathery pouches for odd coins or miniature thick-skinned elephant ears. There are some who would gobble down any kind of cookie any time, so long as it wasn't a Fig Newton. But fortunately for smugglers, there are obviously many others who feel quite different about figs.

Scientists tell us, in fact, that for the young, figs are one of the almost-irresistibles. That is because they are intrinsically sweet, the taste that all newborns innately prefer. Figs are 55 percent sugar, the highest sugar content of any common fruit. In fact, a syrup made from figs was used as a sweetener by the Assyrians in 3000 B.C., a practice that continued into the Middle Ages. When sugar became scarce during the American Civil War, fig syrup came back into vogue. Scientists also insist that the fig is, from a botanical perspective, an inside-out strawberry. Its seedlike fruit is surrounded by thick flesh, just the opposite construction of the strawberry. Figs also share a trait with pineapples and papaya leaves: they contain an enzyme that digests proteins and can therefore be used to tenderize meats.

Figs, which originated in Asia Minor, have been cultivated for 6,000 years. They have the dubious distinction of being the first fruit in history selected for artificial ripening, which was accomplished as early as the fourth century B.C. by rubbing them with oil. During the Renaissance, figs were brought to England from Italy, but they were not cultivated in this country until the eighteenth century when Franciscan friars had them planted at the California missions.

That was the origin of the Mission fig, the purple-to-black, fairly large variety, sold both fresh and dried. Calimyrna is also a California variety, a variation on the ancient Smyrna fig, which is lighter in color. Both are delicious dried. Smaller and less sweet, but similar in appearance, is the Adriatic, sold fresh and dried. The Kadota is thick-skinned and is available fresh or canned.

Those who know only dried or canned figs are always amazed at the fresh fruit, from its delicate flesh, smooth as a baby's cheek, to its deep, heady, purple-smelling perfume. Once peeled, a fig can disappear in a few succulent, appreciative bites; but it can also be wrapped with prosciutto, roasted on a skewer, or served with port, cream, or almost any kind of cheese. Dried figs, which should be slightly moist, lend themselves to stuffing, stewing, chopping into muffins and turnovers, frying, or soaking in brandy. They can be pickled or made into a steamed pudding with ginger and molasses. Fig paste, a specialty of some Mediterranean countries, is used in many confections and baked goods. But it is Turkey that has come up with the world's most unusual fig preparation: there they dry the figs, string them together, and wear them as necklaces.

CONSUMER AND COOKING GUIDE: Figs

Market Selection: Mission, Brunswick, Brown Turkey, and Calimyrna are black-skinned with pinkish flesh. These are sweeter than the green-skinned, violet-fleshed Kadota. All figs should be soft to the touch. The skins should be free of blemishes and should not be split.
Availability: July through September
Storage: Use figs as soon as possible. They may be stored, wrapped airtight, in the refrigerator for up to 3 days.
Equivalents: 1 pound = 8 large or 15 small figs
Nutritional Value: Good source of natural sugar and iron
      50 calories per fig

Fig and Cheese Crostini

12 slices Italian bread, lightly
   toasted
1 garlic clove, cut in half
12 slices scamorza cheese or
   smoked mozzarella
3 fresh figs, each cut into
   four slices

MAKES 12 *CROSTINI*

Rub each slice of toast with the cut edge of the garlic. Place a piece of cheese, topped with a fig slice, on each toast. Place under the broiler or in a 450°F. oven until the cheese is melted and bubbly. Serve immediately.

Rice Pilaf with Figs and Prosciutto

2 tablespoons butter
2 tablespoons oil
1 small onion, chopped
1 clove garlic, chopped
¼ pound prosciutto, diced
6 fresh figs (preferably
   Kadota), diced
3 fresh sage leaves, minced,
   or 1 teaspoon dried
1½ cups long-grain rice
3 cups chicken stock
   (page 343)
3 tablespoons minced fresh
   parsley
   Salt and pepper

SERVES 6

In a medium saucepan, heat the butter and oil. Sauté the onion, garlic, and prosciutto for about 10 minutes. Stir in the figs, sage, and rice. Cook, stirring, for 3 minutes, making sure that the rice grains are coated with butter and oil. Add the stock and bring to a boil. Reduce the heat, cover, and simmer for 18 minutes.

Remove from the heat, place a tea towel under the cover, and let stand for about 10 minutes. Stir in the parsley and season with salt and pepper.

Fresh Fig and Toasted Almond Ice Cream

2 cups ripe figs, pureed in
    food processor or blender
1 tablespoon fresh lemon
    juice
2 cups milk
1 cup heavy cream or
    half-and-half
½ cup sugar
1 teaspoon almond extract
1 cup toasted almond pieces

In a food processor, combine all of the ingredients
except the almonds until smooth. (Process in batches if
necessary.) Freeze in an ice-cream maker according to
the manufacturer's directions. Stir in almonds at the
end.

MAKES ABOUT 1 QUART

Fresh Figs in Yogurt

12 fresh figs, coarsely
    chopped
1 tablespoon fresh lime juice
2 tablespoons chopped fresh
    mint
1 cup plain yogurt

*WONDERFUL as a breakfast fruit course, as a soothing
relish for spicy dishes, or as a topping for toasted pound cake.*

Combine all of the ingredients and let marinate in the
refrigerator for at least 3 hours before serving.

MAKES 1½ CUPS

Fig and Walnut Focaccia

1 package dry yeast
1 teaspoon honey
¾ cup warm (110°F) water
2 cups all-purpose flour
½ cup whole-wheat flour
½ teaspoon salt
3 tablespoons olive oil
3 tablespoons cornmeal
1 cup toasted walnut pieces
   (page 347)
10 fresh or dried Mission
   figs, coarsely chopped

MAKES ONE 10 x 15-INCH
FOCACCIA

Combine the yeast and honey with the water and let stand for about 5 minutes to proof (see page 349). In a separate bowl, mix the flours with salt. Stir in the yeast and 1 tablespoon of olive oil and mix until a dough forms. Knead briefly on a floured surface, form into a ball, and place in an oiled bowl. Cover with plastic wrap, place in a warm spot, and let rise until doubled in bulk, about 45 minutes.

Preheat the oven to 450°F. Punch the dough down and knead it briefly. Cover the dough and let it rest for about 10 minutes. Roll the dough out into a 10 x 15-inch rectangle and place on a baking sheet dusted with cornmeal. Sprinkle the surface with walnut and fig pieces and press into the dough. Brush the surface with the remaining 2 tablespoons of olive oil. Let rise for 10 minutes; bake for 15 minutes until golden brown. To serve, cut into squares.

GRAPES

THE TASTE of grapes varies greatly, depending on where you eat them. The grapes eaten on a picnic blanket in the Bois de Boulogne, and the grapes served complete with little silver scissors at someone's boss's annual banquet, and the grapes from the bottom of the soggy paper bag at the baseball game, and the grapes placed poetically though unreachably in the center of cheese platters at book-signing parties, and the grapes you steal surreptitiously from your own shopping cart as you stand in eternal lines at produce markets—all these grapes have a succulence and satisfaction just slightly less magnificent than the grapes you eat in bed, the bunch propped on your chest as you read the Sunday paper, prematurely delivered on Saturday night.

There is also the question of how to eat grapes: popped onto the tongue one by one, discretely conveyed by means of thumb and index finger; or crowded into the mouth, a handful at a time; or sucked directly from the stem of a delicately small cluster which, when stripped clean, is replaced by yet another delicately small cluster. And if the grapes have seeds, well that's another question.

The problem of whether to eat upwards or downwards is a concern to some grape lovers, most of whom are content with their favorite fruit in its more or less natural state. Nevertheless, some people have decided to do things to grapes, everything from cooking them with guinea fowl (an old Russian technique), to stuffing them into roasting chickens, to sautéing them with fish (sole *à la* Véronique). They also contribute mightily to fruit salads, casseroles, curries, sauces, and desserts. And, of course, they are made into wine.

In all these transformations, they remain one of the world's favorite fruits, a position they have enjoyed since several thousand years B.C., when Egyptians painted them on their tombs and native American Indians scattered grape seeds around their dwellings. At one time, southern Italy was called Oenotria, or "land of grapes." In France, Richard the Lion-Hearted let his enthusiasm run away with him on occasion when he sentenced those who stole grapes to the loss of an ear. In eighteenth-century Virginia, Thomas Jefferson covered Monticello, almost literally, with grape vines.

Were we to categorize grapes by color, we would have the Lights: Thompson seedless, Niagara whites, Finger grapes, and Perlettes, just to name a few; and the Darks: purple to black Concords, Red Emperors, Malagas, Muscats, Flame Tokays, and Ribiers. The taste of the Strawberry grape, a variety known in the 1920s that has since seemed to disappear, has been described as a cross between a black currant and a Tom Cat. According to one British observer, "If, as some think, [the Strawberry grape] is of American origin, it may well explain certain recent developments in that country."

Market Selection: Seedless varieties include the green Perlette, the Thompson, and the Red Flame. Other common table grapes (with seeds) are the Almeria, Black Ribier, Red Emperor, Flame Tokay, and Exotic. Black Corinths look like baby grapes and are used for dried currants. All varieties should have good color and smooth, unblemished skins.

Availability: Year-round; peak season—June through December

Storage: Refrigerate, unwashed, in a paper or plastic bag for up to 5 days.

Equivalents: 1 pound = 3 cups

Nutritional Value: Good source of potassium and vitamins A and C

70 calories per cup

Pickled Grapes

4 cups grapes, halved and
  seeded
2 tablespoons sugar
¼ teaspoon ground
  cinnamon
2 teaspoons balsamic vinegar
3 cups dry sparkling white
  wine

Place the grapes in a bowl and sprinkle them with
sugar and cinnamon. Let them stand at room
temperature for about 1 hour, tossing every so often.
Sprinkle with vinegar, toss, and refrigerate, covered,
until ready to serve.

Divide the grapes among six individual bowls or
goblets. Pour about ½ cup wine into each and serve.

SERVES 6 AS A RELISH

Sweet-and-Sour Grape Chutney

1 onion, chopped
1 pippin apple, peeled,
  cored, and chopped
1 pound green seedless
  grapes
¼ cup red-wine vinegar
¼ cup brown sugar
1 tablespoon chopped fresh
  ginger
1 teaspoon grated lemon zest
¼ cup golden raisins

Combine all of the ingredients in a medium saucepan
and bring to a boil. Lower the heat and simmer,
stirring occasionally, until thick, about 45 minutes.
Cool to room temperature and store, covered, in the
refrigerator. Will keep for about 2 months. Great with
poultry and pork.

MAKES 2 CUPS

Chicken Salad with Grapes and Toasted Almonds

4 cups cooked, diced chicken
1 small bulb fennel, diced
1 bunch green onions, thinly
    sliced
2 cups seedless green grapes,
    halved
1 cup slivered almonds,
    toasted

DRESSING

1 cup mayonnaise
½ cup plain yogurt
2 tablespoons fruit chutney
1 tablespoon strong mustard
2 tablespoons chopped fresh
    parsley
2 tablespoons fresh lemon
    juice
    Salt and pepper

Watercress for garnish

SERVES 8

In a large bowl, combine the chicken, fennel, onion, grapes, and almonds. Mix the dressing ingredients until well combined and toss with the chicken mixture. Season with salt and pepper. Mound on individual plates and garnish with watercress.

Grape and Garlic Risotto

2 tablespoons butter
3 tablespoons olive oil
4 cloves garlic, minced
1 small onion, chopped
2 cups Arborio rice
½ cup white wine
6 to 7 cups simmering
  chicken stock (page 343)
2 cups Red Flame grapes,
  halved
½ cup grated Parmesan
  Salt and pepper
  Additional butter
  (optional)

SERVES 6

In a large sauté pan, heat the butter and oil. Cook the garlic and onion just until wilted. Do not let the garlic brown. Stir in the rice and cook for about 2 minutes, or until the grains are coated with the butter mixture. Add the wine and simmer until it evaporates.

Ladle the stock into the rice mixture, cooking and stirring until the stock is absorbed. When half the stock has been used, stir in the grapes gently. Continue to add stock until almost all of it has been added and cook, stirring, until the rice is just tender. This should take about 18 minutes.

Stir in the cheese and season with salt and pepper. Add additional butter for an even creamier texture.

Shrimp and Grapes with Curried Ginger Sauce

3 tablespoons butter

1½ pounds medium shrimp, shelled and deveined

1 small onion, chopped

1 small tomato, seeded and chopped

2 slices candied ginger, chopped

2 teaspoons curry powder

1 tablespoon flour

1 cup fish or chicken stock (page 343)

¼ cup heavy cream

1 tablespoon fresh lime or lemon juice

½ pound Black Ribier or red grapes, halved and seeded

SERVES 4

In a skillet, heat the butter. Cook the shrimp just until they turn pink. Remove to a bowl and reserve.

In the same pan, cook the onion, tomato, and ginger for about 4 minutes. Stir in the curry powder and flour and cook for another 2 minutes. Add the stock, bring to a boil, and cook for about 3 minutes, or until thick. Stir in the cream and lime juice and season with salt and pepper.

Return the shrimp and accumulated juices to the pan, along with the grapes. Heat through for about 1 minute. Serve with rice pilaf.

Grape-Ricotta Tart

1 *recipe* Pâte Brisée
(*page 344*)

FILLING

1½ *cups ricotta cheese*
⅔ *cup sugar*
½ *cup sour cream*
3 *eggs, separated*
1 *tablespoon grated lemon*
zest
Pinch salt

¾ *cup grape jelly*
1 *tablespoon fresh lemon*
juice
2 *cups red seedless grapes*

SERVES 8

Preheat the oven to 400°F.

Roll out the pastry and fit it into a 9-inch tart pan with a removable bottom. Prick the dough with a fork, line with foil, and fill with weights (rice or beans). Bake for 10 minutes, remove foil and weights, and return to the oven for another 10 minutes, or until the dough is lightly colored and appears dry. Remove from the oven and prepare the filling.

Beat the ricotta with ⅓ cup of the sugar, the sour cream, egg yolks, and lemon zest. In another bowl, beat the egg whites with salt until soft peaks form. Then beat in the remaining ⅓ cup sugar until stiff. Fold the whites into the ricotta mixture and pour into the tart shell. Bake for about 30 minutes, or until puffed and golden. Cool to room temperature.

Boil the jelly with the lemon juice for about 2 minutes to make the glaze. Spread ¾ of the glaze on the cooled tart in a thin layer. Place the grapes on the glaze and brush grapes with the remaining glaze.

KIWI

IF FRUITS and vegetables were fairy-tale characters, the kiwi would be Sleeping Beauty. Under its original name, *yang tao*, the oblong brown fruit once lived very happily in its native home in China's Yangtze Valley. Then one day, at the beginning of this century, a handsome prince came along—actually he is more commonly described as a British botanist—gathered up some samples, and planted them in the West. New Zealanders soon became enamored with the *yang tao*'s hidden charms, began cultivating the fruit, and anglicized its name, calling it the Chinese gooseberry. The French also appreciated the ''new'' fruit and didn't mind eating it, even though the name they gave it, *souris végétales*, or "vegetable mice," sounds less than appetizing (except, perhaps, to a vegetable cat).

But when it came to exporting the fruit for American consumption, none of these names had the kind of panache necessary for success in the international produce market. Its botanical name, *Actinidia chinensis*, specifically identified the fruit, which is actually a berry of a woody vine, but most people didn't find the Latin nomenclature particularly catchy. Besides, New Zealanders wished to avoid confusing their fruit with gooseberries, Chinese or otherwise, and wanted to associate the fruit with their homeland. What better way than to use the name of one of their national symbols, the kiwi bird.

This unique bird (it cannot fly) is as unusual as the fruit named in its honor, which it resembles both in its oblong shape and in its bristly appearance. But despite an unpromising exterior, kiwi fruit attained culinary stardom a few years ago, possibly because of its beautiful emerald color and fresh, just-tart-enough taste. As a garnish it was novel and trendy, and as an edible, the possibilities seemed limitless. It can be pureed as an instant sauce for both savory dishes and sweet desserts and is delicious in puddings and fruit salads; it may be included in vegetable dishes; and it becomes a distinctive appetizer with cheeses, prosciutto, and jícama. It is also completely edible, from skin to seeds, although most people prefer to strip off the fuzzy skin with a potato peeler. For a while, at least, kiwi had evolved, as Elizabeth Schneider puts it, into the *"enfant terrible* of nouvelle cuisine."

The success of kiwi stimulated interest in other subtropical fruits and encouraged growers and importers to make a wider variety available to the general public in this country. Spurred by its popularity, California growers began to cultivate the odd-looking fruit. The California season (November through April) complements that of New Zealand (May through October), assuring fresh fruit in season all year round.

The flavor of a kiwi challenges the most wily and discerning tongue. Some find a hint of honeydew, others are reminded of strawberries, or an exotic citrus fruit, or the American gooseberry. The fact that its flavor is so elusive may account for some of its appeal. It's all part of the mystery, as any true beauty knows.

Market Selection: Choose kiwis that yield to the touch but have no very soft spots. The skin should be free of mold.

Availability: Year-round

Storage: If kiwis are firm, ripen them at room temperature, uncovered. When ripe, store in the refrigerator in a paper bag for up to 4 days.

Flavor enhancers: Walnuts, currants, cinnamon

Equivalents: 1 kiwi = ½ cup sliced fruit

Nutritional Value: Good source of vitamin C

     40 calories per kiwi

Kiwi and Fennel Salad

2 medium fennel bulbs,
  sliced very thin
3 kiwis, peeled, halved
  vertically, and thinly
  sliced
1 small red onion, thinly
  sliced
2 cups arugula

DRESSING

1 teaspoon mustard
½ teaspoon crushed fennel
  seed
4 tablespoons raspberry
  vinegar
½ cup olive oil
  Salt and pepper

SERVES 6

Toss the fennel with the kiwi, onion, and arugula. Mix the dressing ingredients until smooth and combine with the kiwi mixture.

Winter Fruit Salad with Kiwi Sauce

2 bananas, sliced

3 tangerines, sectioned,
white pith removed

2 cups red seedless grapes

1 large Red Delicious apple,
diced

2 kiwis, peeled and sliced

2 teaspoons fresh lemon
juice

1 tablespoon brown sugar

SAUCE

3 kiwis, peeled and sliced

1 tablespoon honey

2 tablespoons sour cream or
plain yogurt

SERVES 6

Combine the fruit with the lemon juice and sugar. To make the sauce, puree the kiwi with the honey and stir in the sour cream. Spoon the fruit into individual serving dishes and top with a dollop of sauce.

Kiwi and Berry Crumble

1½ cups chopped walnuts
1 cup flour
1 cup granulated sugar
¼ cup brown sugar
½ cup (1 stick) butter, at room temperature
6 kiwis, peeled and diced
4 cups berries (blueberries, strawberries, raspberries)
2 tablespoons fresh lemon or lime juice
Lightly sweetened whipped cream (optional)

SERVES 6 TO 8

Preheat the oven to 350°F. Grease a shallow 3-quart baking dish.

Combine 1 cup of walnuts with the flour, ¾ cup granulated sugar, and the brown sugar. With your fingertips, work the butter into the mixture until it forms coarse crumbs. In another bowl, combine the kiwi with the berries, remaining ½ cup walnuts and ¼ cup sugar, and the lemon juice. Place the fruit in the baking dish and sprinkle the crumb mixture over all.

Bake for 45 minutes, or until the top is golden-brown. Serve warm, with a dollop of whipped cream if desired.

MELONS

WHEN PEOPLE STAND around melon counters, they can't help revealing something essential about their upbringing. There they are, melons in hand, thumping, sniffing, shaking, slapping, and listening.

"My grandfather always said that watermelons must sound hollow," says one.

"No, no. Dull and muffled, never hollow," contends another.

"Casabas have no aroma," insists one casaba lover to another, whose horrified response—"The aroma is subtle; but it's there"—briefly threatens the tranquillity of the produce department.

If asked, practically no one hesitates to reveal his or her family wisdom about how to select the sweetest melon from among surrounding lookalikes. These tricks and hints are part of people's heritage, exchanged between generations at long summertime, corn-and-watermelon dinner tables.

Whether or not they are "true," whether or not they work every time, is not important. The giving of melon information is the passing on of lore, a revelation about the color, shape, and flavor of one's family. It is what people say to each other: great-aunts to nieces, big cousins to little, uncles to everyone. Perhaps, in the long run, people eat sweeter melons because of it, but certainly they eat them more contentedly.

Hegemony among melons transcends family alliances to become regional and even national in proportion. The Crane melon, for example, is the pride of northern California, where a single family has produced it for generations, along with scientifically measured testimony about the melon's superior sweetness. There are even rumors that if anyone outside the family tries to grow this special melon, they will get warts, their soil will turn to sand, or both. The taste of the orange-fleshed French Charentais melon—pale, lime-green, and smooth-skinned—is said to haunt forever anyone who dares to savor it even once. The Ogen melon, a greenish-yellow cantaloupe, has tantalized many melon-sampling tourists in its native Israel.

It is difficult to be definitive about melons because there are so many of them. At a melon-tasting held in 1987 as part of northern California's annual Tasting of Summer Produce, growers presented more than 100 samples of melon varieties, beginning with Ambrosia, Ananas, and Angelina and proceeding through Jubilee, Kharbooseh, and Marble White on down to Sharlynn, Tender Gold, and Yellow Doll. There is even a Santa Claus melon —so named because it ripens in December—and a Snap Melon that snaps open when ripe.

Of the entire showing, the most startling were the watermelons. Perhaps nothing is so shocking as learning that not all watermelons are red. But proof positive lies in such varieties and hybrids as the apricot-fleshed Sweet Siberian, yellow-fleshed Gold Baby, and white-fleshed Crystal. Watermelons may also be small or round or splotched with starlike patterns. Similarly, purists would have us believe that even our beloved, practically all-American cantaloupes are not "true" cantaloupes but rather muskmelons. To add to the confusion, bitter melons and winter melons are really vegetables, and carambolas, also known as tree melons, can be used exactly like legitimate melons. But none of these last three belongs to the official melon family. Eating, as always, is believing.

And that is probably the best thing to do with a ripe, sweet melon, though, of course, it can also be cut into chunks or sliced and wrapped with a sliver of prosciutto or fussed up into balls for a fruit salad, or pureed for a fruit soup.

The seeds can be dried and eaten as snacks, and the rind of watermelons even makes a delicious pickle. Melon flesh can be dried and stored, like fruit leather, and can be reconstituted.

Melons have been around for thousands of years, judging from ancient Egyptian paintings and from the dating of melon seeds. Claims for their specific birthplace include Africa, Persia (Iran), and India (there is a Sanskrit word for "melon"). The Romans enjoyed melons, which were only about the size of an orange at the time. Most of Europe came to know melons through the Spanish Moors.

Melons arrived in America with the slave trade, although the first melon seeds were said to have been planted by the Columbus expedition in 1494. Apparently, it took another 400 years for anyone to plant them again on a large scale in this country, which has only cultivated melons commercially for the last century. Today, the country's major producers include Florida, Texas, Georgia, and California.

CONSUMER AND COOKING GUIDE: Melons

Market Selection: Green- and orange-fleshed honeydew, Persian, Canari, cantaloupe, Crenshaw, casaba, Sharlynn, Calsweet watermelon, and Yellow Doll watermelon. Except for watermelons, blossom ends should yield to gentle pressure and melons should be aromatic. Good, tasty watermelons can be recognized more easily because they are generally precut. Flesh should be vividly colored, and very little underside should be visible.
Availability: Depending on variety, sporadically all year
Storage: Unripe whole melons may be kept in a paper bag at room temperature for 2 to 3 days. Ripe melons should be wrapped in plastic wrap and refrigerated for up to 5 days.
Flavor Enhancers: Mint, lemon juice
Equivalents: 1 pound of melon = 1 cup, cubed
Nutritional Value: Most melons are a good source of vitamin C.
      Melons with deep orange or red flesh are rich in vitamin A.
      80 calories per ½ cantaloupe
      50 calories per wedge of honeydew
      110 calories per 1-inch slice of watermelon

Melon and Currant Chutney

2 medium onions, chopped
1 cup currants
2 cups tightly packed brown
    sugar
2 cups cider vinegar
1 teaspoon pickling spice
2 tablespoons grated lemon
    zest
1 teaspoon grated fresh
    ginger
1 teaspoon salt
1 teaspoon freshly ground
    pepper
4 cups cubed melon flesh
    (cantaloupe or Persian)

MAKES ABOUT 6 CUPS

Place all the ingredients except the melon in a medium saucepan. Bring to a boil, lower the heat, simmer for about 1 hour, or until thick. Stir in the melon and cook for another half hour. Let cool; store in an airtight container in the refrigerator for up to 3 months.

Grilled Melon Wrapped in Pancetta

12 melon wedges (cantaloupe,
    Persian, or honeydew),
    1½ inches thick, peeled
2 teaspoons dried thyme
12 thin slices pancetta

SERVES 6 AS A FIRST
COURSE

Preheat the grill.

Sprinkle the melon with the thyme and wrap each wedge in a slice of pancetta. Place a skewer through each wrapped melon wedge to secure and to facilitate turning.

Place on a hot grill and cook on both sides, until the pancetta is golden-brown. Serve hot or warm.

Mixed Melon and Shrimp Cocktail

DRESSING

⅓ cup olive oil
2 tablespoons chopped fresh
    mint leaves
2 tablespoons chopped
    cilantro leaves
1 teaspoon crushed red
    pepper flakes
1 tablespoon honey
2 tablespoons fresh lime
    juice
1 tablespoon white-wine
    vinegar

3 cups assorted melon balls
24 large prawns, cooked and
    shelled

SERVES 6

Combine the dressing ingredients until smooth. In separate bowls, toss half the dressing with melon and half with shrimp. Let marinate for 30 minutes to 1 hour.

Divide the melon among six goblets and place four shrimp in each, with tails overhanging the edge.

PEARS

PEARS ARE WORSE than fingerprints: even on the same tree, you can't find two that are identical. One has a whimsical crook in its neck, another has a blush as round and red as a circus clown's, while a third has a squat bottom designed for sitting lazily in a fruit bowl. And though the whole treeful has the same general taste, unique to its type, each pear differs ever so slightly in perfume and juiciness and in just how quickly it melts on the tongue.

But it is this very elusiveness that makes them so irresistible, not only to ordinary eaters but to botanists and growers as well. For thousands of years, pear-minded horticulturists have been experimenting with the fruit's various desirable qualities, attempting to roll everything they wanted into one perfect genetic scheme. Considering the fact that pears are one of the two dozen plants that have been under cultivation for more than 4,000 years, this has been going on for quite a while. The Romans especially loved pears, according to Pliny, who, two millennia ago, was able to enumerate more than forty varieties.

The development of a new pear has often been greeted with a certain fame and fanfare. Witness the debut of the late-season, apple-shaped variety that Olivier de Serres—known as the Father of French Agriculture—brought forth on his experimental farm in seventeenth-century France. In the French town of Angers, a commemorative plaque celebrating the introduction of the Comice in 1849 still graces the town's old stone wall. Closer to home, we have the story of Farmer Seckel, whose name was given to the diminutive variety, said to be Walt Whitman's favorite, that he grew on his Philadelphia farm just after the Revolutionary War. At that time, the first cookbook tailored to the newly independent nation warned its citizens about the independent nature of pears: "There are many different kinds; but . . . in the same town they differ essentially."

And yet the new country was already fond of pears and had been using them in many different ways. One of the earliest reports tells of the Virginia farm of Mr. Richard Kenisman in the year 1648, where the autumn harvest yielded no less than "50 butts of Perry," also called pear cider. Butts—or casks—of perry were also popular in New England, especially because the pear varieties from that area were often somewhat bitter when raw, though they cooked into delicious compotes, pastries, and drinks.

In California, where the weather was kinder, the Mission friars cultivated the pear to perfection. In 1879 a somewhat official count published by the American Pomological Society described 115 varieties. There are now several thousand, most of them introduced in the last 300 years. It is small wonder that confusion reigns in the pear section of the produce department, where Bartlett, Comice, Winter Nelis, Anjou, and Bosc vie for attention, with occasional competition from a stray Seckel or a rare Red Bartlett.

Some have divided pears into two simple categories: the European soft, buttery types and the crisper Asian specimens, also called sand pears. This sort of distinction is meaningless to pear addicts like Edward Bunyard, who insists, in his book *The Anatomy of Dessert*, that "it is, in my view, the duty of an apple to be crisp and crunchable, [but] a pear should have such a texture as leads to silent consumption." Less enthusiastic commentators have noted that, in their opinion, the two types of pears can be described as those that resemble the tase of shampoo and those that don't.

Pears can be included in any course, from salads and starters to an after-dinner sip of Poire William. According to an old Korean proverb, they may even have a practical application. "Eating pears," so the ancient maxim goes, "cleans the teeth."

CONSUMER AND COOKING GUIDE: Pears

Market Selection: Bartlett, Anjou, Bosc, and Comice are the most common European pears found in the marketplace. They are buttery in texture and quite juicy when ripe. Most pears are sold while the skin is still green. For a ripe, ready-to-eat pear, look for a russet-hued skin. New on the scene is the Asian pear or sand pear, whose texture is crisp, like that of an apple. For this reason, it is sometimes called apple-pear. It is not generally used in cooking. Asian pears are generally sold ripe. Depending on the variety, skin color should be either golden-brown or yellow-green.

Availability: European pears are available year-round; peak season—August through December. Asian pears are available August through December.

Storage: Unripe pears should be placed in a paper bag at room temperature until ripe. Ripe pears should be refrigerated, unwashed, for up to 3 days.

Flavor Enhancers: Cinnamon, nutmeg, cloves, blue cheese

Equivalents: 1 pound = 3 medium pears
　　　　　1 pound = 2 cups, sliced

Nutritional Value: Pears provide small amounts of phosphorus, potassium, and vitamin C.
　　　　　100 calories per pear

Cooking and Handling Notes: To core a halved pear, use a melon baller.

Pear-Potato Bisque

4 tablespoons (½ stick)
  butter
4 medium potatoes, peeled
  and diced
4 pears (Anjou, Bartlett, or
  Comice), peeled, cored,
  and diced
1 shallot, chopped
4 cups chicken stock
  (page 343)
½ cup heavy cream
  Chopped fresh chives for
  garnish

SERVES 6 TO 8

In a large saucepan, heat the butter. Sauté the potato, pear, and shallot for about 5 minutes. Add the chicken stock; bring to a boil, reduce the heat, cover, and simmer for about 15 minutes.

Puree with the cream in a food processor or blender. Reheat and serve with a sprinkling of chives.

Pear, Watercress, and Endive Salad with Sweet Gorgonzola

2 heads Belgian endive, cut
  into julienne
2 bunches watercress, coarse
  stems removed
2 ripe pears, cored and
  cubed
¼ cup white-wine vinegar
1 teaspoon prepared mustard
1 tablespoon minced fresh
  parsley
½ cup olive oil
¼ pound crumbled sweet
  (young) Gorgonzola cheese

SERVES 6

In a salad bowl, combine the endive, watercress, and pears. In another bowl, whisk the vinegar, mustard, parsley, and olive oil until blended. Toss the salad with the dressing and sprinkle with Gorgonzola.

Puffed Pear Pancake

4 tablespoons (½ stick)
  butter
2 pears (Bosc or Comice),
  peeled, cored, and sliced
2 tablespoons sugar
3 eggs
½ cup milk
½ cup flour
4 tablespoons melted butter
2 tablespoons brown sugar
½ teaspoon ground
  cinnamon

SERVES 6

Preheat the oven to 475°F.

In a 10-inch ovenproof skillet, heat the butter. Add the pears and sugar. Cook over high heat until the pears soften and the sugar turns golden. Meanwhile, beat the eggs with the milk and flour until smooth; pour over the pears.

Place the skillet in the oven and bake for about 12 minutes, or until the pancake is puffed and golden brown. Pour the melted butter over the pancake and sprinkle with brown sugar and cinnamon. Return it to the oven for another 5 minutes. Serve warm, cut into wedges.

Chicken Sauté with Pears and Pine Nuts

One 3-pound chicken,
  cut into serving pieces
Salt and pepper
Flour for dredging
2 tablespoons butter
2 tablespoons oil
1 leek, white part only,
  thinly sliced
3 tablespoons currants
2 firm pears (Bartlett or
  Comice), peeled, cored,
  and sliced into wedges
¼ cup balsamic vinegar
1 cup chicken stock
  (page 343)
¼ cup toasted pine nuts
  (page 347)

SERVES 4

Sprinkle the chicken with salt and pepper and dredge in the flour, shaking off any excess. In a large skillet, heat the butter and oil. Cook the chicken on all sides until golden. Remove and reserve.

Add the leek and currants to the same skillet and cook for about 5 minutes. Add the pears and cook for about 1 minute. Stir in the vinegar and cook for 1 minute; add the stock. Bring to a boil, lower the heat, and return the chicken to the pan.

Simmer, partially covered, for 20 minutes. Season with salt and pepper. Serve sprinkled with pine nuts.

Pear Tart with Pinot Noir Glaze

1 recipe Pâte Sucrée
  (page 345)
½ cup finely ground almonds
3 large pears (Bosc or
  Comice), peeled, cored,
  and sliced
2 tablespoons butter

GLAZE

¼ cup Pinot Noir
2 tablespoons fresh lemon
  juice
¼ cup currant jelly

SERVES 8

Preheat the oven to 375°F. Roll out the *pâte sucrée* dough to fit a 9-inch tart pan with a removable bottom. Fit the dough into the pan and sprinkle with almonds. Place the pear slices over the almonds, with the most attractive slices on the top layer. Dot with butter and bake for about 50 minutes, or until the edges of the tart are golden-brown. Remove from the oven and prepare the glaze.

In a small saucepan, cook the Pinot Noir and lemon juice until reduced to about 3 tablespoons. Stir in the jelly and cook until melted. Spoon the glaze over the tart and let cool.

PERSIMMONS

No one who has ever seen it can forget the sight of a persimmon tree in late December. Its stark, leafless form looks like a series of bony antlers randomly stuck with bright orange globes, the color of tropical sunsets. The contrast of the dry skeletal branches with their summery-looking fruit has, over the centuries, inspired Chinese dramatists, Japanese legend makers, and American folksingers. In fact, the persimmon has probably been responsible for more poetry than recipes. And for good reason.

The persimmon is not what it seems. It is a shameless flirt, decked out in the come-hither colors of ripeness and topped with a green and frilly coquettish collar. But though its firm, plummy flesh promises imminent pleasure, the eager eater soon tastes a disappointment that may not be bitter but is certainly astringent. For persimmons are tricksters. When they seem succulent and ready, they are all but inedible, turning the mouth and tongue furry and dry. True persimmon lovers learn to wait past the guises of ripeness until the fruit seems much too soft, almost semi-liquid. Only then is it ready to be, in its simplest and most obvious preparation, spooned from its skin like a ready-made, instant sherbet.

Its taste? Like mangoes and papayas, say some. Apricotish, according to others. Or like an apple and an orange put together, according to one child, leading us to wonder if there is an age beyond which one can no longer imagine such happy anomalies. Because of the limited availability of persimmons, few people have had the opportunity to make up their minds, at least until now.

Persimmons are principally an Asian delight, originating in northern China but widely popular in Japan as well. In fact, it is the large, juicy-looking Japanese fruit that is cultivated most extensively in this country, even though there is a smaller, walnut-sized North American native, found mostly in the Midwest. (Raymond Sokolov, in his delicious book, *Fading Feasts*, devotes a chapter to his determination to enjoy the ones he searched out in Gnaw Bone, Indiana.) The slightly oval Hachiya, the flatter, crisper-textured Fuyu, and the Tanenashi are the most likely Japanese persimmons to be encountered, though no one should shun the rare opportunity to taste the Sharon fruit, a nonastringent variety from Israel's Sharon Valley. Other names, fortunate and otherwise, that signify persimmons include the date plum, monkey guava, bush kaki, keg-fig, apple of the Orient, Chinese fig, and, last but least enticing, swamp ebony. The last nickname is due to the persimmon's membership in the ebony family, whose wood is used for everything from golf clubs to shoe lasts. Persimmon leaves can be dried and steeped for a tea that tastes like sassafras.

In his informative and fascinating book *The Curious Cook,* Harold McGee recounts the saga of his experiments with persimmons to reduce their astringency and render them edible, sooner. In the course of this pursuit, he also learned quite a bit about the comparative virtues of various plastic wraps, which can help ripen the fruit. He obtained the best results by swathing a persimmon in three layers of plastic wrap, then leaving it in a 100°F environment for twelve hours and at room temperature for an equal amount of time.

Although some Native Americans took advantage of the natural astringency of persimmons, a result of the presence of tannins, and used the fruit for medicinal purposes, this attribute is far from a gustatory delight. "Harsh and choakie" was the reaction of William Strachey, author of *Historie of Travell into Virginia Britania* (1612), and probably one of the first men to taste a persimmon in the newly explored southern territory. Early settlers used it to make wines, brandies, and beer; no record is left of any complaints about these endeavors.

Recipes that feature persimmons include puddings, breads, ice creams, cakes, sherbets, purees, jams, and stewed fruits. The French, who call the fruit *kaki,* after its Japanese name, enjoy a dessert of the scooped-out fruit filled with kirsch. The Chinese dry the fruit for candy or sometimes let it freeze on the tree. The pulp freezes well and keeps a long time. About the only no-no, once the fruit is ripe, is this fourteenth-century Chinese dictum: "Dried persimmons must not be eaten with turtle."

CONSUMER AND COOKING GUIDE: Persimmons

Market Selection: There are two basic persimmon varieties. The Fuyu, a tomato-shaped persimmon, is eaten while the fruit is firm. The pointy Hachiya must ripen to the "mush" stage. Touch is the best barometer of ripeness. The skins turn bright orange long before the fruit is ripe.
Availability: Mid-October through December
Storage: Ripen persimmons at room temperature in a paper bag. Refrigerate ripe fruit in a plastic bag up to 1 week.
Flavor Enhancers: Cinnamon, nutmeg, allspice, cloves
Equivalents: 1 large Hachiya = 1 cup puree
      1 large Fuyu = 1 cup sliced or diced fruit
Nutritional Value: Good source of vitamins A and C, phosphorus, and
      potassium
      80 calories per persimmon

Persimmon and Spinach Salad with Cilantro-Mint Dressing

1 bunch spinach leaves, torn
    into bite-size pieces
3 Fuyu persimmons, sliced
1 small red onion, thinly
    sliced

DRESSING

2 tablespoons fresh cilantro
    leaves
5 fresh mint leaves
½ teaspoon ground cumin
½ teaspoon ground coriander
⅛ teaspoon cayenne
4 tablespoons fresh lemon
    juice
½ cup oil
    Salt and pepper

1 cup toasted sunflower
    seeds (page 347) for
    garnish

In a large bowl, combine the spinach, persimmon, and red onion. Puree the dressing ingredients in a food processor. Toss the persimmon mixture with the dressing and sprinkle with sunflower seeds.

SERVES 6

Persimmon-Ginger Fool

2 large Hachiya persimmons
1 cup sugar
1 teaspoon fresh lemon juice
½ teaspoon ground ginger
2 cups heavy cream,
    whipped
2 tablespoons candied
    ginger, diced

Remove the pulp from the persimmons and puree with the sugar, the lemon juice, and the ground ginger. Fold into the whipped cream with the candied ginger and spoon into goblets or parfait glasses. Chill before serving.

SERVES 8

Persimmon-Pecan Brownies

½ cup (1 stick) butter, cut
    into small pieces
2 ounces bittersweet
    chocolate
½ cup sugar
1 egg, at room temperature
1 teaspoon almond extract
1 cup flour
¾ cup Hachiya persimmon
    puree
1 teaspoon baking powder
½ teaspoon baking soda
½ cup coarsely chopped
    pecans
    Confectioners' sugar for
    dusting

MAKES 12 BROWNIES

Preheat the oven to 350°F. Grease an 8-inch square baking pan.

In a medium saucepan, melt the butter. Remove from the heat and stir in the chocolate and the sugar until the mixture is smooth. Let cool for about 8 minutes. Whisk in the egg and almond extract. Stir in the flour, persimmon puree, baking powder, baking soda, and pecans just until blended.

Spread the batter in the prepared pan and bake for about 25 minutes, or until a toothpick inserted in the center comes out clean. Cool on a wire rack and dust with confectioners' sugar. Cut into squares.

Persimmon-Banana Crisp

3 Fuyu persimmons, sliced
2 bananas, sliced
¾ cup brown sugar
½ teaspoon ground nutmeg
1 tablespoon fresh lemon
    juice
1 cup rolled oats
⅓ cup flour
    Pinch salt
5 tablespoons melted butter

SERVES 6

Preheat the oven to 350°F. Butter a shallow 1½-quart baking dish.

Combine the persimmon, banana, ¼ cup sugar, and nutmeg. Arrange in the prepared baking dish and sprinkle with the lemon juice. In a small bowl, combine the oats, flour, remaining ½ cup sugar, salt, and butter. Mix just until crumbly and spread over the fruit.

Bake for about 30 minutes, or until the top is brown and crisp. Serve warm, with whipped cream or ice cream.

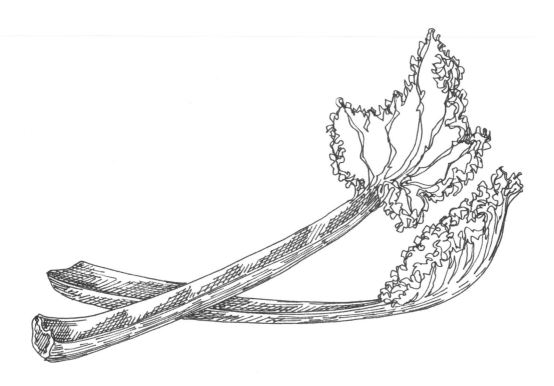

RHUBARB

IT'S TOO BAD they decided to call rhubarb "rhubarb." It doesn't have the sound of a big happy fruit, like honeydew or mango. In fact, it sounds a bit forbidding, which is perhaps as it should be, considering that both the leaves and roots are deadly poisonous. Nor is it particularly appetizing to know that cooking rhubarb in your pots is a wonderful way to clean out stains. Connoisseurs of Alaskan cuisine may be excited by the fact that Eskimos enjoy eating rhubarb raw, but for most people, rhubarb tartare remains a fairly exotic first course (or possibly last course, depending on its level of toxicity).

All this seems a bit unfair to a plant whose past extends back to the time of the Greeks, who named it after the barbarians with whom they associated the plant—*Rha barbaron,* or "barbarians from the Rha (Volga) river." The barbarians were obviously not put off by the fact that rhubarb is botanically a relative of dock, a common weed, which grows to heights of 3 to 5 feet.

Eventually, rhubarb's popularity spread to Holland, Scandinavia, northern Germany, and Afghanistan, never having lost its favored status in Siberia. It was cooked as a vegetable and used in omelets, soups, and stews. In one Persian recipe, *khoresh,* it is simmered in cinnamon and lemon and used as a sauce for rice. But because of its high acid content, which could be offset with honey or sugar, rhubarb became most popular as a dessert. It was transformed into delicious compotes, jams, cobblers, ice cream sauces, and even wine. In this country, with its traditional sweet tooth, cooks welcomed the challenge of transforming it into typical American desserts. They folded the cooked fruit into whipped cream to make rhubarb fool; they baked it with oranges for a rhubarb betty; they contrived many a pudding pie, rhubarb crisp, and rhubarb crumble. The Pennsylvania Dutch used the productive plant in their jellies, marmalades, and whips.

Rhubarb's nickname—the pie plant—reveals its most common usage. In cold climates rhubarb is welcomed enthusiastically as the first sign of spring. After a pie-sparse winter, rhubarb is often the first choice because it is the only choice.

In today's markets, rhubarb selection will range from young pink stalks to green, red, or red-streaked varieties. The dangerous leaves and roots have already been removed, but it's a good idea to check. Rhubarb may not be the most romantic-looking edible on earth, but it's a welcome sight, in early spring, when everyone's fancy turns to thoughts of pie.

Market Selection: Two types of rhubarb are available: field-grown (large, dark red- and green-streaked stalks with a very tart flavor) and the less-tart hothouse rhubarb (small, light pink, and almost stringless). Both types should be firm and crisp. We prefer the field-grown variety for its intense flavor and rosy red color.

Availability: March through June; peak—May

Storage: Refrigerate in plastic wrap, unwashed, for up to 1 week.

Nutritional Value: Good source of calcium and potassium

      20 calories per cup

Flavor Enhancers: Cinnamon, nutmeg, berries, apples, pears

Equivalents: 1 pound = about 3 cups, sliced

Cooking and Handling Notes: All leaves should be removed from rhubarb, as they are poisonous. Strings should not be removed, as they contain most of the rhubarb's color. Strings will break down during cooking.

Grilled Chicken with Rhubarb Relish

RHUBARB RELISH

3 cups diced rhubarb
¾ cup sugar
1 tablespoon grated orange
   zest
1 cup orange juice
1 or 2 jalapeño peppers,
   seeded and chopped
2 shallots, minced

6 skinless, boneless chicken-
   breast halves
   Salt and pepper
1 tablespoon fresh lemon
   juice
   Olive oil

SERVES 6

Place all of the relish ingredients in a saucepan. Bring to a boil; reduce the heat and simmer, stirring every so often, for about 10 minutes, or until the mixture thickens. Cool.

Preheat the grill.

Sprinkle the chicken with salt and pepper. Brush with lemon juice and oil. Grill for about 6 minutes per side. Serve with rhubarb relish.

Rhubarb-Apple Strudel

FILLING

2 cups sliced rhubarb
3 Red Delicious apples,
  diced
½ cup sugar
2 tablespoons grated orange
  zest
3 tablespoons golden raisins
2 tablespoons tapioca

12 sheets phyllo dough
½ cup melted butter or
  shortening
½ cup finely chopped
  walnuts

SERVES 12

Combine the filling ingredients, except the tapioca, with ½ cup water in a medium saucepan; bring to a boil. Lower the heat and simmer for about 12 minutes. Stir in the tapioca and let cool. Set aside.

Preheat the oven to 375°F.

Using six sheets of phyllo for each strudel, spread each sheet with butter, sprinkle with nuts, and stack.

Spoon half of the rhubarb mixture along the long edge of each stack of phyllo sheets. Fold the edges over to enclose the filling and roll up, jelly-roll fashion. Place on a greased baking sheet. Brush the tops with butter; with a sharp knife, cut four slits in each. Bake for about 25 minutes, or until golden-brown. Let cool for at least 10 minutes before slicing.

Rhubarb-Raspberry Gratin with Brown-Sugar Meringue

¼ cup red wine
½ cup sugar
1 teaspoon ground
  cinnamon
3 cups sliced rhubarb
1 pint raspberries
3 egg whites
¼ cup brown sugar, ground
  fine in a food processor
¼ cup white sugar

SERVES 6

In medium saucepan, combine the wine, sugar, cinnamon, and rhubarb with ¼ cup water. Bring to a boil, lower the heat, and simmer, partially covered, for about 10 minutes. Remove from the heat and stir in the berries. Cool slightly.

Preheat the oven to 375°F.

Pour the rhubarb mixture into a shallow 9 x 13-inch baking pan. Beat the egg whites until they hold a shape. Gradually add the sugars and beat until stiff and shiny. Spread over the rhubarb mixture and bake for about 10 minutes, until golden-brown.

Flo Braker's Rhubarb Rolls

FILLING

2 cups sliced rhubarb
¾ cup sugar
5 tablespoons butter
⅔ cup light brown sugar

DOUGH

2 cups flour
2 tablespoons sugar
1 tablespoon baking powder
½ teaspoon salt
⅓ cup shortening
1 egg
½ cup milk

MAKES 8 ROLLS

FLO BRAKER IS a nationally renowned baker and teacher. Her reputation for exquisitely delicious pastries and desserts is reflected in these brunch or teatime coffee cakes.

Preheat the oven to 400°F.

In a large bowl, combine the rhubarb with the sugar and toss well. Set aside.

In a 9-inch round baking dish, melt 3 tablespoons of the butter and sprinkle with brown sugar. Set aside.

To make the dough, combine the flour, sugar, baking powder, and salt. Cut in the shortening until the mixture resembles cornmeal. Mix the egg with the milk and stir into the flour mixture until it forms a soft dough. Knead the dough lightly and roll it out to a 9 x 13-inch rectangle. Spread with the rhubarb mixture and dot with the remaining 2 tablespoons butter. Beginning with a long side, roll up, jelly-roll style. Pinch the edges to seal and cut into 1-inch slices.

Place the rolls closely together, cut side down, in the prepared pan. Bake for 30 minutes, or until golden-brown. Cool for 5 minutes, and invert on a serving plate. Serve hot, warm, or at room temperature.

Apricots

Peaches

Nectarines

Plums

STONE FRUITS

Apricots

IN THE HUNZA VALLEY in northern India, where people customarily live to be over one hundred and where diseases like cancer are scarce, there is one common denominator: apricots. Needless to say, this coincidence has stirred up quite a bit of interest in the little golden fruits. But if the health benefits of apricots depend on eating them at optimum ripeness, things can get pretty complicated. In fact, it takes some watchfulness to catch an apricot at its peak, which lasts only a day or two. It is even possible that only those who have pulled a ripe apricot from the tree can know the full intensity of its flavor. Most of us can only maintain vigilance during apricot season, select apricots with the fullest, most glowing color, and taste early and often.

Because of its ephemeral nature, the taste of apricots is the object of many culinary quests. To capture it, apricots are crystallized or preserved in syrup. Drying the fruit, whole or halved, is another way to take advantage of its rich aromas and complex flavors. The cut fruit is usually treated chemically, however, to prevent browning during the drying process. Many liqueurs are also made from apricots, including Apry, Apricotine, Capricot, apricot brandies, and barack—a Hungarian *eau de vie*. Even the pits are used for such liqueurs as *crème de noyaux* and amaretto and as a flavoring for the popular Italian macaroons called amaretti. Like those of peaches, plums, and other common fruits, the seeds of apricots contain cyanogens which can combine with certain enzymes to produce deadly cyanide. Although this is not a problem unless the seeds are consumed directly and in considerable quantity, it is advisable to avoid munching on the seeds.

Fresh and dried apricots are used in a wide range of preparations, from main-course lamb dishes, like Persian *mishmishaya*, to South African kebabs called *sassaties*, to a California rabbit dish called conejo casserole. Apricots are naturals for dessert in the form of ice cream, sherbet, soufflées, bavarians, jams, and sauces, plus a noteworthy Austrian dumpling called *Marillenknödel*, to which Tom Stobart (*The Cook's Encyclopedia*) ascribes a certain "diet-shattering splendor."

A native of China, the ancient apricot has been cultivated for 4,000 years. The Romans called it the "tree of Armenia" when it arrived in the Mediterranean in the first century A.D. Its Latin name, *proecocia*, or "precocious," is a reference to the fact that it is one of the earliest-ripening fruits of summer.

Of the many varieties, which differ in size, texture, firmness, and even color, the most generally available include the Tilton, Moorpark, Rival, Royal, and Blenheim.

For all its exotic history and connotations, today's apricot is most likely grown in this country, since the United States produces 90 percent of the world's supply, most of which is dried.

CONSUMER AND COOKING GUIDE: Apricots

Market Selection: The different varieties, such as Royal, Blenheim, Castlebrite, and Katy, are similar in size and color. Color should be orange and intense and texture not too firm.
Availability: June through August
Storage: Soft apricots should be used immediately or refrigerated in a plastic bag for up to 2 days. Firm apricots should be ripened at room temperature.
Flavor Enhancers: Cinnamon, nutmeg
Equivalents: 1 pound = approximately 10 apricots
        10 apricots = 2 cups, halved or sliced
Nutritional Value: Vitamins A and C
        20 calories per apricot

Walnut and Gorgonzola–Stuffed Apricots

¼ pound sweet Gorgonzola
  cheese
2 ounces cream cheese
¼ cup ground walnuts
12 apricots, halved, pitted,
  and brushed with lemon
  juice
24 walnut halves

MAKES 2 DOZEN CANAPÉS

Cream the cheeses with the ground walnuts until smooth. Pipe the cheese mixture with a pastry bag into the cavities in the apricot halves. Top each with a walnut half. Arrange, walnut-side up, on a serving platter.

Arugula-Apricot Salad with Prosciutto

DRESSING

1 tablespoon fruit chutney
1 teaspoon Dijon mustard
2 tablespoons fresh lemon
  juice
2 tablespoons red-wine
  vinegar
½ cup olive oil

1 pound arugula leaves
5 ripe apricots, halved and
  thinly sliced
½ small red onion, thinly
  sliced
¼ pound prosciutto, thinly
  sliced and cut into thin
  strips

SERVES 6

Mix the dressing ingredients until well combined. In a salad bowl, combine the remaining ingredients. Toss with the dressing and serve.

Apricot-Almond Chutney

2 pounds ripe apricots,
  pitted and diced
2 medium onions, chopped
1 cup raisins
1½ cups granulated sugar
½ cup light brown sugar,
  tightly packed
4 cloves garlic, minced
2 tablespoons minced fresh
  ginger
1 tablespoon salt
2 teaspoons mustard seed
1 teaspoon ground ginger
1 teaspoon ground
  cinnamon
½ teaspoon crushed red-
  pepper flakes
2 cups cider vinegar
2 cups blanched almonds,
  toasted (page 347) and
  coarsely chopped

MAKES ABOUT 6 CUPS

In a large pot, combine all of the ingredients except the vinegar and almonds. Mix well and bring to a boil. Lower the heat and simmer, partially covered, for about 30 minutes, stirring occasionally. Add the vinegar and cook, stirring frequently, for 20 minutes. Add the almonds and cook for another 5 minutes.

Let cool and ladle into sterilized canning jars. Seal the jars according to the manufacturer's canning directions. (If refrigerating or freezing, the canning process is not necessary. Simply refrigerate or freeze in air-tight containers.) For best flavor, let the chutney mellow for about 3 weeks before using.

Fresh Apricot Mousse

2 pounds fresh ripe apricots,
    halved and pitted
1 cup orange juice
4 eggs
½ cup sugar
½ teaspoon vanilla
3 tablespoons Grand
    Marnier
2 cups heavy cream
½ cup confectioners' sugar
    Fresh mint leaves for
    garnish

SERVES 8

In a medium saucepan, simmer the apricots with the orange juice for about 15 minutes, or until very soft. Allow the apricots to cool; puree them with ½ cup of the cooking liquid in a food processor.

Beat the eggs with the sugar until very thick and pale in color, about 8 minutes. Fold in the pureed apricots with the vanilla and Grand Marnier. Beat the cream until soft peaks form, adding confectioners' sugar while beating. Fold into the apricot mixture and spoon into wine goblets. Chill for at least 4 hours and garnish with fresh mint.

NOTE: This recipe contains *raw eggs*, which can contain salmonella bacteria.

Apricots Poached in Blush Wine with Ricotta Cream

4 cups white Zinfandel
½ cup sugar
4 pounds ripe apricots,
    halved and pitted
1 cup ricotta cheese
2 tablespoons honey
2 tablespoons sour cream or
    plain yogurt

SERVES 8

In a large saucepan, boil the wine and sugar until the sugar dissolves. Add the apricots and cook for about 20 minutes. Remove the apricots with a slotted spoon and reserve.

Boil the cooking liquid until it is thick and syrupy, about 20 minutes. Pour the liquid over the apricots and let cool.

Meanwhile, puree the ricotta, honey, and sour cream in a food processor until very smooth. Arrange the apricots on individual plates and top with ricotta cream.

Peaches and Nectarines

WHEN THE POET Wallace Stevens writes: "With my whole body/I taste these peaches," we know what he means. Peaches have something for all the senses, from the enticing red-gold blush and soft down of their flesh, to their summer-warm smell and juice-dripping tart-sweetness. Even the ears are stirred when they receive the welcome news that peaches, in any form, are about to be served.

People have always appreciated the peach, from the ancient Chinese, who first cultivated the fruit and who believed that it assured the gods longevity, to Native Americans like the Creeks and Seminoles (the Natchez even named one of their months after the peach), to eighteenth-century Virginians, who, according to the wealthy planter, William Byrd, grew peaches in incredible numbers. They coped with the brief peach season by crushing the fruit to a paste and drying it so they could use it year-round in breads and cakes as well as in beer, brandy, and other spirits.

The fascination with the peach (whose Latin name, *Prunus persica*, means "plum of Persia") has literally filled volumes. U. P. Uedrich, in *The Peaches of New York*, identifies more than 2,000 varieties, while Edward Schafer, in *The Golden Peaches of Samarkand*, explores their importance in Chinese mythology. The stories of Marco Polo's travels in China include descriptions of peaches weighing several pounds apiece.

The peach has inspired homey recipes like peach crab lantern, an unmistakably American concoction of fried peach pie shaped like a half-moon, and peach Melba, an equally unmistakable French production created by Escoffier for Dame Nellie Melba, the great Australian soprano. In its original incarnation, peach Melba consisted of peaches and vanilla ice cream perched between the wings of a carved ice swan. Growers have been moved to name their varieties loftily after birds, kings, and presidents (Sea Eagle, Royal George, Madison), although at least one, Samuel Rumpf of Marshville, Georgia, immortalized his wife, Elberta, with the freestone he produced in 1870.

The two basic categories of peach are freestone (the flesh is easily separated from the pit) and cling (the flesh clings to the pit). Of the several thousand varieties now cultivated, the pale white Babcocks and Georgia Belles are often singled out for particular excellence. In this country thirty-five states provide us with peaches, though most of the crop comes from California, South Carolina, Pennsylvania, and Georgia. In these days of ethylene-gassed produce, a healthy-looking color may not assure the sweetest fruit. More important are ripeness when picked and treatment in transport; peaches do not sweeten after harvest, and cold storage results in a woolly texture.

Fresh peaches are always a good excuse for ice cream—and vice versa—and are sunny additions to morning cereal, blended yogurt drinks, and salads. They are delicious macerated briefly in champagne and/or served under a glistening veneer of pureed strawberries. Peaches can be cooked into cobblers, dumplings, puddings, mousses, and every kind of pastry. They can also be spiced, pickled, or dried. Slightly underripe peaches actually seem to develop in flavor when poached with their skins on in a small amount of sweetened liquid.

Some people think of the nectarine as a fuzzless variety of peach. Nectarine lovers, however, counter that it would be just as logical to call the peach a fuzzy type of nectarine. Biologically speaking, the gene for fuzziness is dominant, which means that nectarines are naturally the rarer of the two. Named for *nektar*, the Greek drink of the gods, nectarines are considered fuller and finer in flavor than their cousins, the peaches, although some favor the texture of the latter.

Like peaches, hundreds, if not thousands, of varieties of nectarines exist—from Fantasia and Flavortop to Goldmine and Desert Dawn—and like peaches, the whites are considered the best. "That happy freak, the Nectarine," as Edward Bunyard called it in his 1929 paean to fruit, *The Anatomy of Dessert*, can be used interchangeably with peaches in any recipe. But the best way to taste them is Wallace Stevens style: with the whole body.

CONSUMER AND COOKING GUIDE: Peaches and Nectarines

Market Selection: The best and most common varieties of peaches for eating and cooking include O'Henry, Fay Elberta, Elegant Lady, June Lady, Georgia Belle, and the white-fleshed Babcock. Nectarine varieties include Firebrite, May Grand, Flamekist, Spring Red, and Fantasia. Peaches should have a creamy or golden background color and yield to gentle pressure. Avoid green-hued, hard peaches. Nectarines should have an orange-red background color and should yield to gentle pressure but not be as soft as peaches.

Availability: Peaches: June through October; peak—August

Nectarines: June through September; peak—July

Storage: Peaches and nectarines may be kept for 2 to 3 days at room temperature to ripen. Ripe fruit should be refrigerated, covered in plastic wrap, for up to 1 week.

Flavor Enhancers: Cinnamon, nutmeg, ground coriander, mint

Equivalents: 1 pound nectarines or peaches = 3 medium

1 pound nectarines or peaches = 2 cups, sliced

Nutritional Value: Peaches and nectarines are good sources of vitamin A

50 calories per medium peach

85 calories per medium nectarine

Cooking and Handling Notes: To peel a peach or nectarine: Plunge the fruit into rapidly boiling water for 40 seconds. Remove and let sit until cool enough to handle. Skins should slip off.

Nectarine Butter

4 pounds nectarines, peeled,
   pitted, and sliced
2 tablespoons fresh lemon
   juice
¼ cup honey

MAKES ABOUT 2 CUPS

In a large pot, combine all of the ingredients with 2
cups water and cook over medium heat until the
nectarines are very tender, about 30 minutes. Puree
the mixture and return it to the pot.

Cook over low heat, partially covered, for about 2½
hours, or until very thick. Let cool and refrigerate in
airtight containers. Spread on toast or crackers.

Duck Breasts with Peaches, Peppers, and Port

4 skinless, boneless duck-
   breast halves
   Salt and pepper
   Flour for dredging
2 tablespoons oil or duck fat
2 tablespoons butter
1 tablespoon chopped shallot
1 bunch green onions, white
   parts only, thinly sliced
1 red or yellow bell pepper,
   diced
⅓ cup port
½ cup beef stock (page 344)
¼ cup soy sauce
2 tablespoons peach jam
2 freestone peaches, peeled
   and sliced into wedges
4 sage leaves

SERVES 4

Remove all of the excess fat from the duck breasts and
sprinkle them with salt and pepper. Dredge them in
flour and cook them in hot oil and butter for 5 minutes
per side. Remove and keep warm.

In the same pan, sauté the shallot, onion, and
pepper until very soft, about 12 minutes. Add the port,
stock, and soy sauce, scraping the bottom of the pan to
deglaze, and boil until syrupy, about 4 minutes. Stir in
the peach jam until melted; add the peaches and sage.
Cook for 3 minutes.

Meanwhile, slice the duck breast on the diagonal
and fan out on serving plates. Top with peaches and
sauce and serve.

Peach Pockets

FILLING

1 cup cottage cheese
3 ounces cream cheese
1 egg yolk
½ cup sugar
2 teaspoons grated lemon
   zest

2 peaches, peeled, pitted,
   and sliced in eighths
8 sheets phyllo dough
½ cup melted unsalted butter
½ cup ground almonds

MAKES 1 DOZEN

Prepare the filling by combining the cheeses with the egg yolk, sugar, and lemon zest until smooth. Set aside, along with the peaches.

Preheat the oven to 375°F. Line a baking sheet with parchment paper.

Place one sheet of phyllo lengthwise in front of you on a clean working surface. Keep the rest from drying out by covering them with a towel. Brush with melted butter and sprinkle with some almonds. Place a second sheet on top and brush again with butter. With a sharp knife or razor, cut into three equal strips lengthwise. On the left-hand corner of each strip, place 2 tablespoons of the cheese filling, followed by two peach slices. Fold down the corner as you would a flag; continue folding, flaglike, until you have a many-layered triangle.

Place it on the baking sheet and brush the top with butter. Continue in this manner with the remaining ingredients. You should have twelve pockets. Bake for 18 minutes, or until golden-brown and puffed. Let cool before serving.

Peach and Raspberry Cornmeal Cobbler

3 pounds peaches, peeled,
   pitted, and sliced
2 tablespoons fresh lemon
   juice
3 tablespoons brown sugar
½ teaspoon ground nutmeg
2 tablespoons flour
2 cups raspberries

TOPPING

½ cup all-purpose flour
¾ cup yellow cornmeal
¼ cup sugar
 2 teaspoons baking powder
   Pinch salt
   Pinch ground cinnamon
¼ cup (½ stick) butter
½ cup milk

SERVES 8 TO 10

Preheat the oven to 400°F. Butter a shallow 3-quart baking dish.

In a large bowl, combine the peaches with the lemon juice, sugar, nutmeg, and flour. Toss to combine and let stand for about 10 minutes. Pour into the prepared baking dish and top with raspberries.

To make the topping: mix the dry ingredients together. Cut in the butter until the mixture is crumbly; stir in the milk just until blended. Drop by tablespoonfuls over the peach mixture and bake for about 30 minutes, or until well browned and bubbly. Serve warm or at room temperature.

Plums

THERE IS POETRY in plums, as we may hear in the words of Edward Bunyard's *The Anatomy of Dessert*. For him, the mere memory of plums affords a "careless rapture" as he contemplates their taste like "ineffable nectar" which is "drunk rather than eaten." Even the late-season plum has its particular virtue, a "gracious richness of harvest under its golden coat."

He is not alone in his romance with the plum, the ancient egg-shaped member of the rose family. There are some who nearly swoon at the mention of the mirabelle, the yellow-green gem from Alsace and Lorraine. Its pleasures are equally tempting in the form of thick preserves or as the *eau de vie* of the same name. From the plum of Damascus known as damson, to the *reine-claude*, named for the young queen of François I who died at age twenty-five, plums have a certain mystique. Their classically elegant shapes, their regal gold-to-purple colors, their complex and sophisticated perfume all coexist with a primal wildness that makes them a hands-on fruit, invitingly tactile, intoxicating. Plums have intrigued people for thousands of years, judging from their presence in the Hanging Gardens of Babylon and, more recently and probably more metaphorically, in the plum pie of Little Jack Horner. (According to those who make it their business to demystify children's fairy tales, it wasn't a real pie that Jack stuck his thumb into but a pile of deeds; the word *plum* designated the "best of the lot.")

Although there are thousands of varieties—Pliny refers to an "enormous crowd of plums" or, as he put it, *"ingens turba prunorum"*—a simple two-category system satisfies our purposes. There are the Fresh and the Cookable.

In the first group, experts generally agree that the world's superlative plums—such as *reine-claude*, or greengages, and Coe's Golden Drop—are those with yellow to green flesh. But, as with all food preferences, there is always room for disagreement from those of us who grew up equating the word "plum" with the color purple.

Recipes for fresh, uncooked plums ranging from salads to desserts have a venerable antecedent in the ancient Assyrian *Herbal*, which advises eating them with honey and butter. Even the petals of plum blossoms have inspired chefs to include them in salads, sorbets, and ice creams and use them as garnishes. Cooked plums make stuffings, jams, chutneys, tarts, cakes, sauces, and soups. In old Rome plums were preserved in vinegar, as they are in modern-day Japan, where the salt plum—*umeboshi*—is used as a substitute for vinegar. Quetsch is a plum *eau de vie,* and sloe gin fizzes refer not to the speed of the gin but to a kind of wild plum that flavors it. Some sources contend that the plum evolved from a hybrid of two wild varieties, the sloe and the cherry plum, both of which grow in Asia. Most plums can be dried to make prunes, but certain varieties are cultivated for that purpose. For all purposes, freestone plums are, of course, easier to pit than clingstones.

In addition to indigenous American wild plums, like the Chickasaw, the Texan, and the Oregon, this country features numerous varieties of cultivated plums. These include Friars, Empresses, Yakimas, and Casselmans. The Jefferson may be our most patriotically named plum; it was also appreciated by the poetic Mr. Bunyard as "a little tough in fibre, a virtue in Presidents and quite pardonable when accompanied with real merit." The Santa Rosa plum, developed by Luther Burbank in the city for which it is named, accounts for 35 percent of the California harvest, which constitutes 90 percent of the country's crop. Antarctica is the only continent where plums are not cultivated.

Those who do not grow their own plums are advised to live next door to people who do, especially if the branches of their trees hang over the fence. Since many of these overhanging plums will fall naturally when ripe, it is wise to provide a suitable landing pad for them. Such inadvertent "plum traps" might be simple strips of cheesecloth stretched in gravity's path. If the plums do not drop in sufficient quantities, the best time for picking is when the neighbors are not at home. As might be suspected, personal experience has prompted this suggestion.

Market Selection: The most common yellow-fleshed varieties include Santa Rosa, Black Amber, Nubiana, Laroda, El Dorado, Kelsey, and Friar. Red-fleshed varieties are less numerous and include Elephant Heart and Black Beauty. Freestone, green-fleshed plums include Italian and Standard, both of which are used for prunes. Choose plums that are full colored for their variety. Avoid fruit with blemished and broken skin.

Availability: June through October; peak—August

Storage: Plums may be kept for 2 days at room temperature to ripen. Ripe fruit may be refrigerated for up to 3 days.

Flavor Enhancers: Cinnamon, cardamom, nutmeg

Equivalents: Red- and yellow-fleshed

> 1 pound = 4 to 5 plums
> 1 pound = 2 cups, sliced
> Green-fleshed
> 1 pound = approximately 14 plums
> 1 pound = 2 cups, sliced

Nutritional Value: Good source of vitamin A

> 30 to 60 calories per plum

Plum, Prosciutto, and Arugula Salad

6 cups arugula or other fresh
   greens with a zesty bite,
   torn into bite-size pieces
4 ripe plums, pitted and
   thinly sliced
1 small red onion, thinly
   sliced
⅓ cup olive oil
3 ounces prosciutto, cut into
   thin strips
¼ cup balsamic vinegar
   Salt and pepper

SERVES 6

Combine the arugula, plum, and onion with the olive oil and toss well. In a small skillet, preferably nonstick, cook the prosciutto for about 1 minute. Add the vinegar and cook over medium-high heat until syrupy and reduced. Pour the mixture over the greens, toss well, and serve.

Plums in Port

2 pounds assorted red and
   black plums, pitted and
   sliced
¼ cup port wine
1 teaspoon ground
   cinnamon
½ cup sugar
1 teaspoon crushed anise
   seed
2 tablespoons orange zest

SERVES 6

FOR AN ELEGANT DESSERT, serve in champagne goblets topped with lightly sweetened whipped cream.

Place all of the ingredients in a medium saucepan with ¼ cup water. Bring to a boil; lower the heat, cover, and simmer for 15 minutes. Let cool and refrigerate.

Turkey Cutlets in Plum-Mustard Sauce

6 turkey cutlets, lightly
  pounded
  Salt and pepper
  Flour for dredging
2 tablespoons oil
2 tablespoons butter
2 tablespoons chopped
  shallot
1 tablespoon grated fresh
  ginger
1 jalapeño pepper, seeded
  and chopped
4 plums, pitted and chopped
2 tablespoons brown sugar
½ cup beef stock (page 344)
⅓ cup white wine
2 tablespoons soy sauce
2 tablespoons prepared
  mustard
  Chopped fresh parsley or
  cilantro for garnish

SERVES 6

Sprinkle the turkey with salt and pepper and dredge in flour. In a large skillet, heat the oil and butter. Sauté the turkey for about 5 minutes per side. Remove and reserve.

In the same skillet, cook the shallot, ginger, and jalapeño for about 1 minute. Add the plums and sugar and cook for another 2 minutes. Stir in the stock, wine, and soy sauce and cook over medium-high heat until the sauce thickens. Stir in the mustard over low heat and cook for another minute. Return the turkey to the sauce and heat through. Sprinkle with parsley and serve.

Plum-Pepper Catsup

4 pounds Italian or
   Standard (prune) plums,
   pitted and sliced
2 large onions, chopped
1 large red bell pepper,
   seeded and chopped
1 clove garlic, minced
1 tablespoon salt
1 cup cider vinegar
1 tablespoon mustard seed
1 tablespoon ground ginger
1 teaspoon ground
   cinnamon
1 teaspoon ground coriander
½ teaspoon crushed red
   pepper flakes
¼ cup dark brown sugar
¼ cup granulated sugar

MAKES 4 CUPS

In a large pot, combine all of the ingredients and bring to a boil. Lower the heat and simmer for about 30 minutes, stirring often. Raise the heat and cook for another 5 to 10 minutes, or until the mixture thickens.

Pour through a strainer or pass through a food mill. Taste and add more sugar if desired. Ladle into sterilized jars, cover, and allow to mellow in the refrigerator for 2 to 3 weeks before using.

Plum Summer Pudding

1½ pounds Italian (prune)
   plums, pitted and sliced
¼ cup sugar
1 tablespoon grated lemon
   zest
8 slices day-old white bread,
   crusts removed
1 tablespoon butter
   Whipped cream or plain
   yogurt (optional)

SERVES 6

In a medium saucepan, cook the plums over low heat with the sugar until soft, about 10 minutes. Stir in the lemon zest. Drain the plums and reserve the syrup.

Cut the bread slices to fit a 4-cup soufflé dish or charlotte mold. Butter the mold. Dip the bread into the reserved syrup and line the bottom and sides of the mold, reserving some bread slices for the top. Fill with cooked plums and top with the remaining bread slices. Weight the top down with a saucer; refrigerate overnight.

To unmold, run a thin knife around the edge and invert on a serving dish. Serve with whipped cream.

Pineapple

Mango

Papaya

Bananas

TROPICAL FRUITS

Bananas

FOR MANY, the banana is a first-thing-in-the-morning food, as urgent in its way as orange juice or coffee. If it is not there to be sliced into corn flakes, or cut up into a breakfast fruit cup, or just peeled and nibbled slowly behind the comforting wall of the morning paper, a great grumpiness may result.

Of course, bananas can be eaten at other times of day as well. They are especially popular as desserts, in the form of fritters, dumplings, ice cream, cookies, breads, puddings, and of course banana cream pie. They may be grilled, fried whole or in slices, even cooked until creamy in their skins, from which they can be eaten with a spoon. Bananas can be minced in a bowl with yogurt and spices as a condiment, or whirled in a blender with yogurt and honey as a drink. In Mexico and India fibrous banana leaves are used to wrap food for cooking and to make thatched roofs, table mats, and rope. The dried cooking varieties yield a highly digestible banana flour. In Uganda, banana beer is popular, while elsewhere banana wines, jams, and liqueurs have their advocates.

At the morning marketplace in Bogotá, Colombia, or Bahia, Brazil, or anywhere in Central America, bananas are a photographer's delight. At one booth bunches of rust-red bananas poke out among clusters of thick yellow bananas piled as high as the banana seller's nose. Across the crowded passageway, another booth is framed by an arch made of long strings of tiny bananas, while the counter beneath offers every size of a tough-skinned, half-green specimen probably meant for cooking. On one mountain of bananas, the proprietor has slashed through several to show the black seeds, hard enough, it is said, to crush the teeth.

Here and there, a white cardboard sign is stuck among the bunches to identify the type. They might be dainty fig bananas, or the prickly perfumed dwarfs brought originally from the Canary Islands; there are plantains to be sliced and dried or to be fried into the crisp appetizers called *tostones;* there are the blunt-ended varieties we call Cavendish and the tapered Gros Michels. Many are members of the most common variety, *Musa sapientum,* or ''banana of the wise,'' so named because sages were said to lie in their shade and eat the fruit. In such a marketplace, it is easy to believe that there are hundreds of varieties of bananas, though we in America are familiar with only a few.

Banana eating is a tradition as old as recorded history. Originating in Southeast Asia, the banana was one of the first domesticated plants and has been cultivated for thousands of years. It seems strange that in this country, which consumes more than half of the world's production, the fruit was unknown until the Philadelphia Centennial Exposition in 1876, where Americans first bought them, foil-wrapped, for a dime apiece. Equally strange is the fact that no American cookbook even mentioned the fruit until the end of the century. Some books advised cutting the exotic fruit only with a silver knife, or cooking it as a starchy vegetable like potatoes, or serving a variety of three different bananas whole—"the large, red and lady fingers mixed."

Advancements in refrigerated shipping soon brought bananas everywhere, including Fulton, Kentucky, which calls itself both the Banana Capital of the World and the Banana Crossroads of the United States. Every August the town hosts a Banana Festival, complete with banana-eating contests, cook-offs, and a 2,000-pound banana pudding.

CONSUMER AND COOKING GUIDE: Bananas

Market Selection: In addition to the common, long, tapered yellow variety (Gros Michel), one can also find the more exotic, dark-red Cuban bananas, which are very creamy in texture. The short, stubby, golden-hued Finger bananas are more tart in taste. The plaintain, a banana lookalike, contains more starch and is eaten cooked as a vegetable.

Selection depends on individual taste. Green-tipped bananas will be firmer in texture and tart in taste. Brown-flecked bananas will be very soft and sweet. Plaintains should be green or yellow and firm.
Availability: Year-round
Storage: Keep bananas and plaintains at room temperature and use ripe fruit quickly.
Flavor Enhancers: Citrus juices, curry powder
Equivalents: 3 medium bananas = 1 pound
  1 pound = 1 cup, mashed
Nutritional Value: Good source of potassium
  100 calories per banana

Banana Cream Soup

3 tablespoons butter
1 small onion, chopped
1 or 2 jalapeño peppers,
  seeded, deveined, and
  minced
½ teaspoon ground coriander
2 tablespoons flour
1 cup chicken stock
  (page 343)
1 cup mashed ripe bananas
1 cup half-and-half
  Salt and pepper
  Fresh cilantro leaves for
  garnish

SERVES 4

In a medium saucepan, heat the butter. Cook the onion and jalapeño until soft, about 5 minutes. Stir in the coriander and flour and cook for another 3 minutes. Add the chicken stock and bring to a boil. Stir in the banana and half-and-half and heat through. Season with salt and pepper and sprinkle with fresh cilantro leaves.

Hot-Sweet Banana Relish

1 cup plain yogurt
  Pinch salt
1 jalapeño pepper, seeded,
  deveined, and finely
  minced
1 tablespoon brown sugar
½ teaspoon ground cumin
1 tablespoon chopped fresh
  mint
1 tablespoon chopped fresh
  cilantro
1 firm (not too ripe) banana,
  diced

MAKES ABOUT 2 CUPS

Combine all of the ingredients except the banana and gently whisk until well blended. Stir in the banana and refrigerate until ready to serve.

Plantain Chips

2 large green plantains
Vegetable or peanut oil for
   deep-frying
¼ teaspoon salt
¼ teaspoon ground turmeric
¼ teaspoon ground cumin

MAKES 4 CUPS

Peel the plantains and slice them wafer thin. Heat the oil in a deep pan or wok. When the oil is hot, put in as many slices as will fit in one layer. Fry until golden-brown; remove to paper toweling with a slotted spoon to drain.

In a small bowl, combine the salt, turmeric, and cumin. Sprinkle this mixture over the fried plantain chips. Store in an airtight container until ready to serve.

Sautéed Sole with Caramelized Bananas

4 sole fillets (1 pound, total)
Salt and pepper
1 cup flour for dredging
¼ teaspoon cayenne
2 tablespoons oil
2 tablespoons butter
¼ cup firmly packed dark
   brown sugar
2 tablespoons fresh lemon
   juice
2 tablespoons orange juice
2 tablespoons white wine
3 bananas, cut into ¼-inch
   slices
Watercress sprigs for
   garnish

SERVES 4

Blot the sole dry; sprinkle with salt and pepper. Combine the flour and cayenne. Dredge the sole in the flour mixture.

In a large skillet, heat the oil and butter. Cook the sole for about 4 minutes per side, or until golden-brown. Remove with a slotted spoon to a serving plate and keep warm.

To the same skillet, add the sugar, lemon and orange juices, and white wine. Cook, stirring, until the sugar has dissolved and the mixture is bubbly. Add the banana slices and cook, stirring gently, until they are hot and coated with syrup. Pour the banana mixture over the sole and serve, garnished with watercress.

Banana and Black Pepper Cookies

1 cup (2 sticks) butter, at
  room temperature
1 cup sugar
1 teaspoon orange zest
2 teaspoons fresh lemon
  juice
½ cup mashed ripe banana
1½ cups flour
½ cup whole-wheat flour
½ teaspoon baking soda
¼ teaspoon salt
½ cup chopped pecans
1½ tablespoons freshly ground
  black pepper

MAKES ABOUT 4 DOZEN

Preheat the oven to 400°F. Grease two cookie sheets.

In a large bowl, beat the butter with the sugar until light and fluffy. Add the orange zest, lemon juice, and banana and beat until well combined. In a smaller bowl, combine the flours, baking soda, and salt. Add to the banana mixture and beat until well blended. Stir in the pecans and black pepper.

Drop dough by rounded teaspoonfuls about 2 inches apart on the prepared cookie sheets. Flatten each mound slightly with moistened fingertips. Bake for 12 minutes, or until the edges are slightly browned.

Bittersweet Chocolate and Banana Torte

½ cup dry bread crumbs
½ cup finely ground walnuts
1 teaspoon baking powder
1 teaspoon baking soda
6 eggs, separated
  Pinch salt
1 cup sugar
3 tablespoons unsweetened
  cocoa
½ cup pureed or mashed ripe
  banana
2 teaspoons grated lemon
  zest

ICING

6 ounces bittersweet
  chocolate, chopped into
  small pieces
4 ounces heavy cream

TOPPING

1 large banana, sliced
½ cup apricot jam, heated

SERVES 10

Preheat the oven to 375°F. Grease a 10-inch round cake pan.

Combine the bread crumbs, walnuts, baking powder, and soda in a medium bowl; set aside. With an electric mixer, beat the egg yolks for 1 minute. Gradually add the sugar, beating at high speed, until thick and pale in color, about 5 minutes. On low speed, add the cocoa and banana. Add the bread-crumb mixture and lemon zest and beat just until blended. Set aside.

In a large bowl, beat the egg whites with salt until stiff but not dry. Fold one-third of the egg whites into the banana mixture. Gradually fold the banana mixture into the remaining whites until no whites show.

Pour into the prepared pan and bake for about 25 minutes, or until the torte starts to come away from the sides of the pan. Cool on a rack for about 5 minutes; invert the pan on the rack and remove the torte from the pan.

Combine the chocolate and cream in a small saucepan. Cook over low heat until the mixture is smooth. Allow the icing to cool and firm up a bit, until it is the consistency of heavy cream. Spread it over the cake and decorate with banana slices that have been dipped in apricot jam.

Mangoes

SOMEWHERE THERE ARE PEOPLE who do not always have to take a bath after they eat a mango. These are the people who know about the mango fork, a miraculous three-pronged device that pierces the mango pit and holds the fruit steady so that one can eat it like a lollipop. But perhaps there is no real market for the mango fork since for many mango lovers the messiness is half the fun.

The other half is the taste: slightly acidic, peachy sweet, lush, sensual, the essence of tropical. No wonder it has been cultivated for 6,000 years or more and that there are more than 1,000 existing varieties. Ranging in shape from round to oval, in color from green to red, and in size from 5 pounds down to the size of a plum, most mangoes have a custardy, pumpkin-orange flesh.

Originating in Southeast Asia, this member of the cashew and pistachio family has always been one of India's major crops. The Portuguese were responsible for bringing the fruit to Europe and then to the Americas, where, it is theorized, they exchanged it for the pineapple. Nobody lost out on that deal.

Exotic though the mango may be, its varietal names are fairly prosaic: Tommy Atkins, Haden, Keitt, and Palmer are those most commonly found in this country.

Some ardent mango fans believe that the best recipe for a mango is no recipe. For these purists, the only permissible transformations of a mango are sherbets, purees, ice creams, uncooked mousses, fresh fruit puddings, and fruit salads. But it must be admitted, in whispered tones perhaps, that mangoes are also excellent cooked: as chutneys, nut breads, tortes and tarts, savory spreads, and relishes. There is even a mango leather made from the juice itself. Well, maybe that is going a bit too far.

Market Selection: The most common varieties include the yellow-skinned Manila, the large red and green–skinned Tommy Atkins, the yellow and pink–skinned Haden, and the green-skinned Keitt. All varieties may be used interchangeably, the difference being the degree of juiciness and tartness. All types should yield to gentle pressure and have unblemished, smooth skins.

Availability: January through August

Storage: Ripen at room temperature, turning often. Refrigerate ripe fruit in a paper bag for up to 3 days.

Flavor Enhancers: Cinnamon, nutmeg, citrus juices

Equivalents: 1 pound mango = ¾ cup sliced or diced fruit

Nutritional Value: High in vitamins A and C

  150 calories per mango

Cooking and Handling Notes: An easy way to peel a mango: Hold the mango vertically, with the pointed end up. Slice through the skin from top to bottom as if quartering the mango. Peel it back as you would a banana.

Curried Turkey Salad with Mango and Cashews

4 cups cooked turkey, diced

2 tablespoons fresh lemon juice

2 mangoes, peeled, pitted, and cut into 1-inch cubes

2 stalks celery, chopped

4 green onions, thinly sliced

¼ cup mayonnaise

¼ cup plain yogurt

1½ teaspoons curry powder

½ teaspoon ground cumin

1 cup cashews, chopped

Lettuce leaves

2 tablespoons chopped fresh cilantro or parsley for garnish

SERVES 6

In a large bowl, toss the turkey, lemon juice, mango, celery, and green onion. In a small bowl, combine the mayonnaise, yogurt, curry, and cumin. Toss with the turkey mixture and cashews. Serve on lettuce leaves, garnished with fresh cilantro.

Grilled Swordfish with Mango-Mustard Sauce

SAUCE

2 tablespoons oil
1 clove garlic, minced
2 shallots, minced
½ cup dry vermouth
½ cup chicken stock
   (page 343)
1 large ripe mango, peeled,
   seeded, and pureed
2 tablespoons mild mustard
⅓ cup heavy cream or half-
   and-half
Salt and pepper

Four ¾-inch-thick
swordfish steaks (about
6 ounces each)
Salt and pepper
¼ cup olive oil
1 tablespoon mild mustard

SERVES 4

Preheat the grill.

In a medium saucepan, heat the oil. Cook the garlic and shallot for about 3 minutes over medium heat. Add the vermouth and chicken stock; boil until the liquid is reduced to about ¼ cup. Stir in the mango, mustard, and cream and cook for about 8 minutes, or until the sauce thickens. Season with salt and pepper; set aside and keep warm.

Blot the fish dry and sprinkle with salt and pepper. Combine the oil with the mustard and brush on both sides of the fish. Grill for about 4 minutes per side. Serve with mango sauce.

Mango-Peanut Mousse

4 medium mangoes, peeled,
   pitted, and sliced
¼ cup fresh lime juice
2 egg whites
   Pinch salt
⅓ cup sugar
½ cup heavy cream, whipped
1 cup unsalted dry-roasted
   peanuts, coarsely chopped

SERVES 8

Puree the mango with the lime juice. Beat the egg whites with the salt until foamy. Gradually beat in the sugar until the egg whites are firm. Fold the egg whites into the whipped cream; then fold the mango puree into the whites mixture with the crushed peanuts.

Spoon into eight individual dessert goblets and chill for at least 3 hours before serving.

NOTE: This recipe contains raw eggs, which can contain salmonella bacteria.

Papayas

A NATIVE of the American tropics, papaya has been called "the melon that grows on trees" and "the fruit of the angels." These nicknames indicate an appreciation for this versatile vegetable/fruit, which flaunts its natural charms raw or cooked. Like melon, it is delicious in fresh fruit salads, especially in combination with tropical neighbors like pineapple and banana. It makes sunny-colored purees, drinks, ice creams, dressings, and uncooked mousses.

Cooking does nothing to diminish papaya's flavor, making it an interesting and unusual candidate for baking in halves like squash, sautéing in slices, or simmering with any number of spices. As a dessert, papaya can become a richly textured tart or a pie as easily as a smooth custard or a pudding. The leaves may be included in salads or used as wrappers for meats. Papaya's tiny charcoal-gray seeds add a peppery bite to any dish.

Papayas come in many shapes, colors, and sizes, but in this country the most common is the yellow Hawaiian Solo variety, so named because it is just large enough for one person. The larger Mexican papaya, which may reach 8 or 9 pounds, can serve as a family-sized feast.

CONSUMER AND COOKING GUIDE: Papayas

Market Selection: The most common papaya is the pear-shaped, yellow-green–skinned Solo. The large (sometimes as big as 10 pounds) Mexican variety is usually found in Hispanic markets and is sold by the piece. Choose papayas that yield gently to pressure and have more yellow than green in the skin.
Availability: Year-round
Storage: Unripe papayas should be kept in an open paper bag at room temperature until soft. Refrigerate ripe fruit in a paper bag for up to 4 days.
Flavor Enhancers: Ginger, curry powder, citrus juices, chili peppers
Equivalents: 1 medium papaya = 1½ cups cubed fruit
Nutritional Value: Good source of vitamins A and C and potassium. Contains the enzyme papain, an ingredient in meat tenderizers and a digestive aid.
120 calories per papaya

Papaya-Tomato Salsa

1 ripe papaya, peeled,
   seeded, and diced
½ small red onion, diced
1 jalapeño pepper, seeded,
   deveined, and diced
1 clove garlic, minced
2 Roma tomatoes, seeded
   and chopped
1 tablespoon fresh tarragon,
   minced
2 tablespoons fresh cilantro
   leaves, chopped
½ teaspoon ground cumin
2 tablespoons fresh lime
   juice
1 tablespoon oil
   Salt and pepper

Combine all of the ingredients.

MAKES ABOUT 2 CUPS

Baked Papaya Stuffed with Coconut Cream

2 ripe papayas
2 teaspoons fresh lemon
   juice
1 cup ricotta cheese
2 tablespoons sour cream
2 tablespoons honey
1 egg yolk
2 teaspoons grated lemon
   zest
½ cup unsweetened grated
   coconut

Preheat the oven to 375°F.

Cut the papayas in half lengthwise and remove the seeds. Sprinkle them with lemon juice. Combine the ricotta, sour cream, honey, egg yolk, lemon zest, and half the coconut in a food processor or blender; process until very smooth.

Pour the mixture into the papaya halves and place them in a shallow baking dish. Sprinkle the cheese mixture with the remaining coconut. Bake for about 20 minutes, or until lightly browned.

SERVES 4 AS A FIRST
COURSE

Papaya-Prawn Salad with Hot-Sweet Dressing

2 tablespoons vegetable or
  peanut oil
1 clove garlic, minced
1 tablespoon fresh ginger,
  minced
1 pound medium prawns,
  shelled

DRESSING

3 tablespoons fresh lime
  juice
2 tablespoons honey
1 tablespoon soy sauce
1 teaspoon Chinese chili
  sauce
2 green onions, minced
2 tablespoons chopped fresh
  cilantro

1 large ripe papaya, peeled,
  seeded, and diced
1 small cucumber, seeded
  and diced
1 small red bell pepper,
  seeded and diced
1 large head romaine lettuce,
  thinly sliced
¾ cup pine nuts, toasted
  (page 347)

SERVES 6

In a skillet, heat the oil. Cook the garlic and ginger for 30 seconds; then add the prawns. Cook until the prawns turn pink. Remove and reserve.

Combine all of the dressing ingredients.

In a large bowl, combine the papaya, cucumber, red pepper, and reserved prawns. Toss with the dressing. Line plates with lettuce and spoon the salad on top. Garnish with pine nuts.

Pineapples

NOTHING TASTED quite like those perfectly circular, hole-in-the-middle, canned pineapple rings of childhood. No fresh fruit could match its sugar-soaked, toothsome, slurpy-wet virtues. Compared with those juicy, honey-yellow rounds, the first taste of fresh pineapple was a real disappointment. It seemed too dry, too formal, nowhere near as sweet as the syrup-drenched "authentics" from the can.

With practice, and the help of better-informed taste buds, the natural pineapple eventually seemed to improve in flavor and texture. Cut in chunks and eaten directly from the end of a thin wooden skewer, the fruit became exotic, worldly, pleasantly mysterious. It finally seemed plausible that George Washington might well have said, in comparing several tropical fruits he tasted on a trip to Barbados, "None pleases my taste as do's the pine."

The "pine," as he called it, got its name from its resemblance to the pine cone. The first Spaniards who saw it called it *piña de Indias*, but it also became known as "king of fruits." This was probably more a reference to the "crown" on its head, however, than to any horticultural hierarchy.

In its native habitat, the pineapple was a symbol of hospitality among the Carib Indians, who hung it as a welcome sign on their doorways. This custom was translated architecturally onto the gateposts and entranceways of Europe and New England as the popularity of the New World fruit spread. Although the pineapple is virtually synonymous with Hawaii, it was not introduced there until the late 1700s. The three most common types sold in this country are the Smooth Cayenne, the Sugar Loaf, and the Red Spanish.

A Hawaiian appetizer of bacon-wrapped pineapple has probably passed its heyday, but there are countless other possibilities for the raw and the cooked, from cool salads to hot sauces, from sherbets to shish kebabs. Because pineapple contains a natural enzyme, protease, which digests gelatin, it can be used in gelatin-containing desserts only if it is boiled first. Last but not least, it can be used in that traditional favorite, pineapple upside-down cake, as long as one heeds the words of Jane Grigson: you must "resist the temptation to stick glacé cherries into the holes of the pineapple slices."

CONSUMER AND COOKING GUIDE: Pineapples

Market Selection: Only one variety of pineapple is commonly found in markets and should have a label that assures the consumer it was jet-shipped to guarantee the freshness of the fruit. The color of the skin may vary from light brown to green. An easily released leaf does not guarantee ripeness or sweetness. Select large, chubby pineapples with bright-green leaves.
Availability: Year-round
Storage: Store at room temperature for up to 4 days. Cut pineapple may be stored in the refrigerator, covered with plastic wrap, for up to 3 days.
Flavor Enhancers: Cinnamon, brown sugar, mint, cloves, allspice
Equivalents: 1 medium pineapple = 3 pounds
      3 pounds = 3 cups cubed fruit
Nutritional Value: Good source of vitamin C
      52 calories per cup

Pineapple Relish with Mustard Seed

2 cups cubed pineapple
½ red bell pepper
½ small cucumber, peeled
  and seeded
2 green onions
1 jalapeño pepper, seeded
  and deveined
1 tablespoon chopped mint
1 tablespoon brown sugar
1 tablespoon balsamic
  vinegar
1 tablespoon oil
2 tablespoons mustard seed

In a food processor, combine all of the ingredients except the mustard seed until coarsely chopped. Stir in the mustard seed by hand. Let stand, covered, for about ½ hour for the flavors to develop. Goes well with poultry or fish.

MAKES ABOUT 2 CUPS

Pineapple and Strawberries with Pineapple Sauce

SAUCE

½ cup sugar
4 cups chopped fresh
  pineapple
¼ teaspoon ground
  cinnamon
¼ teaspoon ground allspice
1 tablespoon white rum

1 fresh pineapple, peeled,
  cored, and cut into chunks
2 cups strawberries, sliced
  Mint sprigs for garnish

In a medium saucepan, combine the sugar with ½ cup water and bring to a boil. Lower the heat and simmer, stirring, for 5 minutes. Add the pineapple, cinnamon, and allspice and cook, stirring occasionally, for about 25 minutes, or until the pineapple loses its shape.

Stir in the rum and let cool. Chill and serve over pineapple chunks and strawberries. Garnish with mint.

SERVES 6

Grilled Lamb Cubes with Pineapple

1 pound boneless leg of
lamb, cut into 1-inch
cubes
1 medium pineapple, peeled,
cored, and cut into 1-inch
cubes, juice reserved

MARINADE

⅓ cup olive oil
2 tablespoons reserved
pineapple juice
1 clove garlic, minced
½ teaspoon ground cumin
¼ teaspoon cayenne
½ teaspoon salt
½ teaspoon freshly ground
black pepper

MAKES ABOUT 30
APPETIZER PORTIONS OR 6
MAIN-COURSE PORTIONS

Place the lamb in a shallow nonreactive bowl. Combine
the marinade ingredients and pour over the lamb,
stirring to coat well. Let the lamb marinate at room
temperature for 2 hours or in the refrigerator for up to
8 hours.

Preheat the broiler or grill until very hot.

Thread the lamb and pineapple cubes on 6-inch
skewers and brush with the marinade remaining in the
bowl. Place the skewers on the grill or 6 inches from
the broiler source and cook for about 8 minutes,
turning every so often.

Pineapple-Cornmeal Coffee Cake

1 cup (2 sticks) butter, at
  room temperature
1¼ cups sugar
3 eggs
1 teaspoon almond extract
1 tablespoon orange zest
1½ cups flour
1 cup yellow cornmeal
1 teaspoon baking powder
1 fresh medium pineapple,
  peeled, quartered, cored,
  and sliced ½ inch thick
¼ teaspoon ground
  cinnamon

SERVES 10 TO 12

Preheat the oven to 350°F. Grease a 10-inch round or square cake pan and line the bottom with waxed paper or parchment paper.

In a large mixing bowl, beat half the butter with ¾ cup sugar until light and fluffy. Add the eggs gradually, beating well after each addition. Beat in the almond extract and orange zest. Combine ¾ cup flour with ½ cup cornmeal and the baking powder. Stir into the butter mixture and turn the batter into the prepared pan. Arrange the pineapple on top in concentric circles, overlapping slightly and leaving a 1-inch margin at the edge.

Melt the remaining butter and let it cool slightly. Combine the remaining ½ cup sugar, ¾ cup flour, and the cinnamon. Pour the melted butter over the flour mixture and mix with a fork until crumbly. Sprinkle over the pineapple and batter.

Bake for about 1 hour, or until a knife inserted in the center comes out clean. Let cool on a rack for 15 minutes. Unmold on a serving plate, remove the paper, and invert again. Serve warm or at room temperature.

Pineapple-Buttermilk Sherbet

1 quart buttermilk
3 cups cubed pineapple
1½ cups sugar

MAKES ABOUT 1½ QUARTS

Combine the ingredients until the sugar has dissolved. Pour into an ice-cream maker and follow the manufacturer's directions.

Categorically Cooking

QUICK-FIX RECIPES (dishes that can be prepared in about 30 minutes)

Warm Asparagus and Parmesan Salad

Cold Broccoli with Red-Hot Peanut Sauce

Broccoli, Carrots, and Prawns with Oriental Noodles

Green Pasta with Spicy Carrots

Cauliflower, Mushroom, and Red Pepper Sauté

Cucumber and Snap Pea Sauté with Cumin

Jícama, Shiitake, and Scallop Stir-Fry

Three-Pea Sauté

Potatoes Steamed in White Wine

Summer Tomato Soup

Avocado and Chicken Soup

Chicken with Raspberry Vinegar and Fresh Raspberries

Fig and Cheese Crostini

Fresh Figs in Yogurt

Kiwi and Fennel Salad

Persimmon-Ginger Fool

Sautéed Shrimp with Warm Strawberry Vinaigrette

CROWD PLEASERS: These dishes can be expanded to feed a crowd. Not only are they suitable for larger groups because of their universal appeal, they can easily be made ahead of time.

Rigatoni with Broccoli and Hot Sausage

Marinated Kohlrabi and Carrots

Napa Cabbage and Carrot Slaw with Toasted Sesame Seeds

Caraway Cabbage with Potatoes and Sausage

Pickled Carrots with Ginger

Cauliflower Salad with Sweet Sausage and Three-Mustard Dressing

Baked Barley with Red Onions and Celery

Eggplant Salad Agridolce

Rigatoni with Eggplant and Lamb

Green Bean and Barley Soup

Mixed Mushroom and Lentil Chili

Sweet Onion and Zucchini Relish

Baked Peppers Stuffed with Confetti Couscous

Potato and Asparagus Salad with Smoked Salmon

Summer Squash Crumble

Curried Pork and Pumpkin Stew

Apple-Cheddar Whole-Wheat Popovers

Walnut and Gorgonzola–Stuffed Apricots

Berry-Cornmeal Scones

Spicy Olive and Lemon Caponata

Peach Pockets

Peach and Raspberry Cornmeal Cobbler

Low-Lows (dishes that are low in fat and cholesterol)

Artichokes with Honey-Mustard Dipping Sauce

Artichoke Soup with Lemon and Tarragon

Sautéed Chicken with Artichoke Hearts and Black Olives

Beet and Apple Sauté

Broccoli and Tomato Soup with Garbanzos

Broccoli, Carrots, and Prawns with Oriental Noodles

Pickled Carrots with Ginger

Lemon Cucumber and Cantaloupe Soup

Cucumber Pineapple Salsa

Kohlrabi Mushroom Soup

Cauliflower, Mushroom, and Red Pepper Sauté

Baked Barley with Red Onions and Celery

Fish Stew with Fennel

Green Beans with Garlic and Prawns

Enoki Mushrooms in Mushroom Broth

Mixed Mushroom Ratatouille

Radish and Carrot Salad with Honey-Lemon Vinaigrette

Curried Spinach and Apple Bisque

Spaghetti Squash with Turkey Meatballs

Apple, Cabbage, and Leek Soup

Summer Tomato Soup

Smothered Chicken and Winter Roots

Baked Apples in White Zinfandel

Hot-Sweet Banana Relish

Chicken with Raspberry Vinegar and Fresh Raspberries

Chicken with Cherries

Pan-fried Snapper with Tarragon and Lime

Pickled Grapes

Winter Fruit Salad with Kiwi Sauce

Grilled Chicken with Rhubarb Relish

Strawberry-Cinnamon Compote

Turkey Cutlets in Plum-Mustard Sauce

Pineapple Relish with Mustard Seed

Thyme and Lime–Marinated Grilled Eggplant Slices

Grilled Corn with Ginger Butter

Grilled Jícama

Rosemary-Scented Grilled Squash

Grilled Melon Wrapped in Pancetta

Grilled Chicken with Rhubarb Relish

Grilled Lamb Cubes with Pineapple

Grilled Salmon with Asparagus Puree

Grilled Swordfish with Mango-Mustard Sauce

Basic Recipes

Chicken Stock

1 leek, white part and about
   1 inch of green
2 carrots
2 celery stalks
1 onion, cut in half and
   stuck with 6 cloves
1 whole chicken or a mixture
   of necks, backs, and wings
   weighing about 5 pounds
6 peppercorns
½ teaspoon dried thyme
1 bay leaf

MAKES ABOUT 4 QUARTS

Cut the leek, carrots, and celery into 1-inch pieces. Place in a large stockpot with the remaining ingredients and 4 quarts of water and bring to a boil. Skim the foam as it accumulates. Reduce to a simmer and cook, uncovered or partially covered, for about 2 hours. Add more water if more than 1 cup evaporates during cooking time. Strain into a bowl or storage container and refrigerate or freeze.

Fish Stock

2 pounds fish bones from
   nonoily fish (not salmon)
1 carrot, sliced
1 leek (white part only),
   sliced
1 celery stalk, sliced
½ teaspoon dried thyme
1 bay leaf
1 sprig parsley
3 peppercorns
   Pinch salt
1 slice lemon
2 cups dry white wine

MAKES ABOUT 1 QUART

Place all of the ingredients in a large pot with 2 cups water and bring to a boil. Reduce to a simmer and cook, uncovered, for 25 minutes. Strain and store in the refrigerator or freezer.

NOTE: If fish bones are difficult to obtain, a suitable substitute can be made using 2 cups bottled or canned clam juice, 1 cup dry white wine, 1 cup water, and specified herbs and spices, simmered for 5 minutes.

Beef or Veal Stock

8 pounds beef and/or veal
    bones, cut into 3-inch
    pieces
2 onions, sliced
2 carrots, sliced
2 celery stalks, sliced
2 tomatoes, quartered
1 bouquet garni

MAKES ABOUT 3½ QUARTS

Preheat the oven to 450°F.

Arrange the beef bones and onions in a large roasting pan and place in the oven. Brown on all sides, turning as necessary. Transfer the bones and onions to a large stockpot and add the remaining ingredients and 4 quarts water. Discard the fat from the roasting pan and deglaze with 1 cup of water, scraping up all particles sticking to the bottom of the pan. (This will give your stock flavor and color.) Add the pan juices to the stockpot and bring the contents to a boil. Reduce to a simmer and skim foam as it accumulates on the surface. Simmer, partially covered, at least 4 hours, adding more water if more than 1 cup evaporates during cooking. Strain into a bowl or storage container and refrigerate or freeze.

Pâte Brisée

1½ cups all-purpose flour
    Pinch salt
½ cup (1 stick) cold butter,
    cut into 8 pieces
2 tablespoons cold vegetable
    shortening, cut into pieces
    About 5 tablespoons ice
    water

MAKES ENOUGH PASTRY
FOR A 9- OR 10-INCH TART

In a bowl or food processor, mix the flour and salt. Cut in the butter and shortening until the mixture is crumbly. Add half the water and mix or process just until the dough holds together. If the mixture seems too dry, add the remaining water but do not overprocess. Form into a disk, wrap, and refrigerate for at least 1 hour before using.

Pâte Sucrée

1 cup flour
¼ teaspoon salt
3 tablespoons sugar
½ cup (1 stick) cold butter,
    cut into 8 pieces
    About 3 tablespoons ice
    water

MAKES ENOUGH PASTRY
FOR A 9-INCH TART

In a bowl or food processor, mix the flour, salt, and sugar. Cut in the butter with two knives or a pastry blender, or process, until the mixture is crumbly. Sprinkle 1 tablespoon of the ice water and mix or process; add just enough of the remaining water so that the dough forms into a ball. Flatten it into a 5-inch disk, wrap the dough in plastic wrap, and chill for at least 1 hour before using.

Mayonnaise (Food Processor Method)

1 egg at room temperature
1 teaspoon Dijon mustard
1 tablespoon fresh lemon
   juice or vinegar
   Salt and pepper to taste
1 cup oil (vegetable or olive,
   or a mixture)

MAKES 1¼ CUPS

Place all of the ingredients except the oil in a food processor bowl fitted with the steel blade and process well to combine. With the machine running, add the oil very slowly through the feed tube. As the mayonnaise thickens, the oil can be added faster. Taste and correct seasonings.

Mayonnaise (Hand Method)

2 egg yolks
   Pinch salt
1 teaspoon Dijon mustard
1 cup oil (vegetable or olive,
   or a mixture)
1 tablespoon fresh lemon
   juice or vinegar

MAKES 1¼ CUPS

In a small bowl, whisk the yolks, salt, and mustard until thick. Begin adding the oil very slowly, almost drop by drop, beating well after each addition. When the mayonnaise has thickened, add the oil more quickly, making sure it has all been incorporated in the mixture. Stir in the lemon juice or vinegar. May be stored in refrigerator for up to 10 days. Do not freeze.

Herbed Mayonnaise
Using either method described, stir in tablespoons of finely chopped herbs of your choice. We like watercress, chives, dill, and basil in combination or each by itself. Let the mayonnaise rest for about 30 minutes before using to allow the herbs to infuse.

Basic Methods

STORING AND COOKING IN ACIDULATED WATER

When slicing some vegetables and fruits, such as Jerusalem artichokes, jícama, artichokes, apples, and pears, drop the cut pieces into water containing a few tablespoons of vinegar or lemon juice to prevent darkening. Artichokes should always be cooked in acidulated water.

TOASTING NUTS AND SEEDS

NUTS: Spread the desired amount of nuts on a baking sheet and place in a preheated 350°F oven for about 10 minutes, shaking the pan once during that time. The nuts should be no darker than a light golden-brown.

SEEDS: Place the desired amount of seeds in a preheated skillet (preferably nonstick). Cook over low heat, shaking the pan occasionally, just until the seeds turn golden-brown.

COOKING ARTICHOKES

Cut off the stem and the small leaves around the base. With a very sharp knife, slice about ½ inch off the prickly top, leaving a fairly flat surface. With sharp scissors, snip off the prickly tips of the remaining leaves. Boil, uncovered, in a large pot of salted water with half a lemon for 30 to 40 minutes. The artichoke is done when the leaves pull out easily. Drain upside down on paper towels. To remove the inedible choke, spread the leaves open from the center. Pull out the cone of light green leaves, and, with a small spoon, scrape out the fuzzy core, which is the choke.

PEELING TOMATOES

Place the tomatoes in boiling water for 30 seconds. Remove, let cool, and peel with small paring knife.

Roasting Peppers

Place the peppers over a gas burner, under a broiler, or on a barbecue grill. Roast until the skins blister and blacken, turning the peppers often. Place in a plastic bag until cool enough to handle; then scrape the skins away with a small paring knife.

Handling Hot Peppers

Owing to the volatile oils in hot peppers, such as jalapeños or serranos, they require careful handling. Kitchen gloves should be worn when cutting them, especially if there are cuts or wounds on hands. If working without gloves, wash hands well after handling peppers because any remaining oils can cause painful and sometimes dangerous irritations, particularly to eyes.

Deglazing

To capture the flavors and precious pan juices and browned particles after the sautéing or roasting process, first pour off the fat. Add liquid (stock, wine, water, or cream) and cook over medium heat while scraping and stirring.

Blanching

Place the vegetables or fruits briefly into boiling water (not more than a few minutes) to remove raw taste, set color, or facilitate the peeling of fruits and tomatoes.

Cutting Vegetables

Julienne: Cut food into matchstick-size pieces.
Chiffonade: Stack the leaves (sorrel, basil, spinach, chard, etc.), roll them up like a cigarette, and cut shreds crosswise with a sharp knife.

REDUCING LIQUIDS

This technique is used to evaporate and thicken a liquid, such as a stock, soup, or sauce. Boil the liquid rapidly to concentrate its flavor and reduce its volume according to individual recipes.

PROOFING YEAST

To be activated, yeast must be dissolved in warm liquid, about 105 to 115°F. Stir the yeast into the warm liquid and let the mixture stand for 5 to 10 minutes. If the yeast is active and alive, a foam will form on the surface. If the yeast is no longer active, it will sink to the bottom. If the latter happens, discard the mixture and begin again with fresh yeast.

BAIN-MARIE OR WATER BATH

Most frequently used for delicate custard-based dishes, a *bain-marie* is simply a large pan filled with hot water in which the custard molds are placed to be cooked or kept warm.

ZEST

The outer, colored part of the rind (not the pith) of citrus fruits (lemon, orange, lime) contains flavorful oils. It is removed with a tool called a zester, or a grater or peeler, and added to various dishes for flavor.

DRIED BEANS—QUICK-SOAK METHOD

Place the beans in a large pot with enough cold water to cover. Bring to a boil and cook for 2 minutes. Remove from the heat and let beans stand for 1 hour. Drain and proceed with the recipe.

PARCHMENT PAPER

Packaged in rolls like waxed paper, this silicone-treated paper is excellent as a nonstick lining for baking pans. Wiped clean, the paper may be reused. Food can be wrapped and baked in parchment for an effect very much like steaming, since the paper is nonporous and the food thus cooks in its own juices and vapors. This paper can usually be found in specialty cookware shops.

Index

About the Authors

Jeannette Ferrary has done various types of writing since her first post-college jobs in advertising and promotion. After heading her own agency for several years, she began writing about food, wine, and anything even vaguely culinary for several publications, including the *New York Times*, the *Journal of Gastronomy*, and the *San Francisco Chronicle* and *Examiner*. She spent a summer in France studying cooking with Simone Beck at her school in Chateauneuf de Grasse. She is the author of *Between Friends: M. F. K. Fisher and Me*, a memoir biography published by Atlantic Monthly Press. This is her third co-authored book with Louise Fiszer, the first two being *The California-American Cookbook* and *Season to Taste*. She lives in Belmont, California, with historian and author Peter Carroll and their eleven-year-old daughter, Natasha.

Louise Fiszer has been teaching cooking at Louise's Pantry Cooking School and Cookware Shop since she founded it fifteen years ago in Menlo Park, California. This popular school has been featured in many publications, including the *New York Times*. She is the co-author with Jeannette Ferrary of *The California-American Cookbook* and *Season to Taste*. She writes a bimonthly food column on entertaining for the *San Jose Mercury News*. Louise Fiszer lives in Palo Alto, California, with her husband, Max. Sons Mike and Mitch are frequent visitors to the Fiszer kitchen.